Social Responsibilities of the Businessman

*This Book Is One of a Series on Ethics and Economic Life
Produced by a Study Committee of the Federal Council of Churches
Charles P. Taft, Department Chairman
A. Dudley Ward, Director of Studies*

TOWARD AN UNDERSTANDING OF THE ETHICS AND ECONOMICS OF SOCIETY

Social Responsibilities

of the Businessman

by

Howard R. Bowen

Professor of Economics, Williams College

with a Commentary by

F. ERNEST JOHNSON

of the National Council of Churches

HARPER & BROTHERS · PUBLISHERS · NEW YORK

Library of Congress catalog card number: 53-5434

Contents

FOREWORD *by Charles P. Taft*   vii

PREFACE   xi

PART I

1. INTRODUCTION   3

2. ECONOMIC GOALS   8

3. SOCIAL RESPONSIBILITIES AND LAISSEZ FAIRE   14

4. SOCIAL ASPECTS OF BUSINESS DECISIONS IN PRESENT-DAY
   CAPITALISM   22

5. PROTESTANT VIEWS OF THE SOCIAL RESPONSIBILITIES OF
   BUSINESSMEN   31

6. THE BUSINESSMAN'S CONCEPTION OF HIS SOCIAL
   RESPONSIBILITIES   44

7. THE BUSINESSMAN'S VIEW OF HIS SPECIFIC RESPONSIBILITIES   54

8. WHY ARE BUSINESSMEN CONCERNED ABOUT THEIR SOCIAL
   RESPONSIBILITIES?   69

9. WHY ARE BUSINESSMEN CONCERNED ABOUT THEIR SOCIAL
   RESPONSIBILITIES? (CONTINUED)   84

10. THE DOCTRINE OF SOCIAL RESPONSIBILITY: SOME CRITICISMS 107

11. THE LAW AND THE DOCTRINE OF SOCIAL RESPONSIBILITY   125

12. TOWARD INCREASING THE EFFECTIVENESS OF SOCIAL RESPON-
    SIBILITY IN BUSINESS DECISIONS   135

13. PROPOSALS: CHANGES IN BUSINESS ORGANIZATION AND
    PRACTICE   151

14. PROPOSALS: THE INDUSTRY COUNCIL PLAN   164

15. OTHER PROPOSALS   177

v

16. Ethical Issues Relating to the Distribution of Income 193

17. Other Ethical Issues Facing Businessmen 207

PART II

18. Commentary on the Ethical Implications of the Study by F. Ernest Johnson 233

Appendix A Bibliography of Protestant Views on the Social Responsibilities of Businessmen 261

Appendix B Sources on the Businessman's Conception of His Social Responsibilities 265

Index 271

Foreword

by CHARLES P. TAFT
*Chairman of the Department of the Church and Economic
Life and of Its Study Committee*

This volume forms part of a larger study of *Christian Ethics and
Economic Life* which was begun by the Department of the Church
and Economic Life of the Federal Council of the Churches of
Christ in America in 1949. At the beginning of 1951 the Federal
Council was merged with other interdenominational agencies to
form the National Council of the Churches of Christ in the United
States of America, made up of twenty-nine Protestant and Orthodox
church bodies within the United States.

In recent years, religious leaders have recognized that the ethical
problems of economic life are becoming increasingly urgent. The
ethics of everyday decisions and practices in economic life, private
and public, as we earn our livings, are matters also of wide public
concern. We need to go behind the observed individual acts and
group pressures for a deeper understanding of the motives underlying what people do in order to eat, of how the system fits together,
and of how close our preconceived ideas are to reality.

Change is a dominant characteristic of our national life and perhaps nowhere so much so as in its economic aspects. During the
past half century our ways of life and work have undergone a vast
alteration. This change has been accomplished without violence and
without great apparent upset, but the tempo of its pace is truly
revolutionary. Certainly if people whose span of life was in the nineteenth century could see what we see in everyday life, they would
hardly accept any word but revolution for the process that has
brought it about.

This accelerated change, for all thoughtful people, demands an
understanding of the effects of this revolution upon ethics and
human values. How shall we deal with the dynamism in our
economic life as it affects every segment of national existence, in

order to preserve and extend freedom and justice, concern for the dignity of the individual, and respect for the rights of minorities, sensitivity to the public welfare, and free discussion and peaceful persuasion? We cannot rely upon business statistics alone to measure these intangibles. Judgments of even the best-qualified individuals about actual or impending changes, affected as they are by individual temperament, vested interests, or political partisanship, are equally inadequate if considered separately. The fullest use of all our resources for information and discussion is required for sound progress toward solution of our complex problems.

There is no vital threat to our inherited and cherished values either in the status quo or in change as such. We cannot take ethics into the stratosphere and separate it from practical economic concerns. What is needed is a better understanding both of economic facts and also of those ethical values which have special significance in the meaning and direction which they give to economic activity.

Our world finds many who adopt a fanatic cynicism or a false philosophy in opposition to the very foundations upon which Western Society is based. What earlier generations took for granted, such as the value and integrity of the individual, the character of government as a tool only for service of the people, the capacity of human life for essential decency and justice—these are now challenged with emotional zeal in the name of other conflicting assumptions claimed also to be moral. Here lies the real crisis of the second half of the present century. We must meet this challenge of evil, insofar as it is evil, and clarify in relation to our own institutions the basic ethical affirmations which we support.

The Federal Council of Churches conducted for many years an educational program on the ethical issues involved in economic life. Many denominational bodies have likewise been active in this field. It has become clear, however, that we need a more careful and realistic investigation of economic life and its relation to spiritual and moral values. We need to make use of the capacities of social scientists and theologians, in close association with lay persons drawn from many occupations.

Accordingly, as a beginning of such an investigation, a three-year research study was commenced in 1949 under a grant from the Rockefeller Foundation. The Foundation has not exercised any supervisory control over the studies and does not assume responsibility for any of the findings. The results of the study are to be presented in six volumes: *Goals of Economic Life, The American Economy and the Lives of People, Social Responsibilities of the Businessman, The Organizational Revolution, American Income and Its Use,* and *Ethics and Economic Life.*

The author in his Preface has made acknowledgment of the many individuals who have been especially helpful to him in the preparation of the present volume. Sincere gratitude is due to the author for his devotion and creativity in the writing of this volume. He has also served significantly as the economic consultant for the entire study.

There are others who have made valuable contributions to the total study effort of which this volume is an important part. The Reverend Cameron P. Hall, executive director of the Department, has given the project his unfailing and effective administrative support. The Reverend A. Dudley Ward, Director of the Studies, has carried out his responsibilities as organizer and coordinator, and in the process of evaluation, with imagination and efficiency. A Study Committee of the Department, including both lay and clerical members and representing a variety of occupations, has reviewed the program of the study at various stages. Mr. Charles H. Seaver, secretary of the Department and a member of the Study Committee, has been available consistently for counsel.

As in the other volumes of this series, the authors have been free to write as they wished and to accept or reject suggestions or criticisms. In the final analysis the book is the responsibility of the authors.

The National Council of Churches has taken no official position and assumed no responsibility regarding the content of any of the volumes. In no sense, therefore, can or should any statement in this series be regarded as an official declaration of the National Council of Churches or of any of its units.

Preface

This book is concerned with the role of businessmen in an economy of free enterprise. Its purpose is to explore the implications of the much-discussed "concept of social responsibility" as applied to businessmen. It proceeds from the assumption that the several hundred largest business firms are vital centers of power and decision, and actions of these firms touch the lives of the American people at many points. The basic questions considered are: What responsibilities to society may businessmen reasonably be expected to assume? What tangible benefits might result if the concern of many businessmen about the social implications of their work were spread widely throughout the business structure? What steps might be taken, practically, to give greater effect to the broader social aspects of business decisions? What are other basic ethical issues facing American businessmen today?

Such specific suggestions and proposals as are offered in these pages are to be regarded as tentative. They are presented not in the spirit of definite prescriptions but as appropriate subjects for discussion and further exploration. My reluctance to attempt definitive formulations of *the* social responsibilities of businessmen has been based on a belief that the way to greater responsiveness of businessmen toward their social obligations lies in the processes of broadly based discussion and individual soul-searching on the part of actual participants—not in the spelling out of "answers" by outside observers.

Throughout, I have sought to interpret the problems of businessmen realistically, and to consider their social responsibilities in terms of the practical and the attainable. Some of my critics have felt that my interpretations of business motivation and behavior have been too sympathetic; others, that I have not been sufficiently appreciative of businessmen and their policies and practices. I leave it to the reader to judge.

I have consulted widely and have drawn upon the opinions of many business leaders and scholars. I am deeply indebted to the numerous persons who have assisted directly in the project and to the many others who have left their intellectual imprint upon it. The number of these persons is greater than can be adequately acknowledged here.

Officials of the Department of the Church and Economic Life of the National Council of Churches have been consistently helpful and encouraging: Mr. Charles P. Taft, chairman; Dr. William Adams Brown, vice-chairman; Mr. Charles H. Seaver, secretary; the Reverend Cameron P. Hall, executive director; and the Reverend A. Dudley Ward, Director of Studies.

A special debt of gratitude is due Professor George R. Davies of the University of Iowa, who first stimulated my interest in the ethical aspects of economics; Professor C. Addison Hickman of the University of Illinois and Professor William Vickrey of Columbia University, who have been consistently helpful as critics and counselors; Dr. F. Ernest Johnson of the National Council of Churches, whose able critique is found at the conclusion of this volume; Miss Irene Carey of the University of Illinois, whose assistance was invaluable in the preparation of the manuscript; and Lois Schilling Bowen, who has helped in a hundred ways.

I need scarcely add that no one of these persons should be held responsible for errors or shortcomings.

Howard R. Bowen

Williamstown, Massachusetts
February, 1953

PART I

PART I.

1

Introduction

The businessman occupies a strategic role in American life. It is hardly an exaggeration to say that he is the central figure in American society—the symbol of our culture. Decisions and policies of the greatest import for the general welfare are entrusted to him. He is the man whose judgment, initiative, and administrative skill we rely upon to decide what goods and services shall be produced, to direct the production of these goods and services, to make provision for the economic development of the country, to distribute income to workers and owners, and to provide the economic basis for national defense. True, he does not exercise these functions alone. He shares them with consumers, workers, farmers, government officials, and others. Moreover, he often acts under pressures which leave him little opportunity for independent choice. Nevertheless, in the operation of our economic system, the businessman occupies a position of great influence and leadership.

Social Import of Business Decisions

The decisions and actions of the businessman have a direct bearing on the quality of our lives and personalities. His decisions affect not only himself, his stockholders, his immediate workers, or his customers—they affect the lives and fortunes of us all.

The individual businessman often fails to apprehend fully the connection between his private decisions and the public welfare. He knows that his business represents only a small fraction of the total economy, and he is acutely conscious of the constraints on him. He finds difficulty in realizing, therefore, that his actions have any observable relation to the broad sweep of economic affairs. But added together, the decisions of businessmen—in small businesses as well as in big businesses—in large measure determine for the nation such important matters as the amount of employment and prosperity, the rate of economic progress, the distribution of income among various groups, and the organization of industry and trade. And these decisions have a significant influence upon the morale of our labor force, the satisfactions obtained from work, the character of our consumption, our personal security, the rate of utilization of our natural resources, and even our international relations.

When a businessman decides whether or not to produce a new product or service, he is helping to decide the range of products available to consumers. When he decides whether or not to purchase new plant and equipment, he is helping to determine the rate of economic progress and is influencing the level of employment and prices. When he decides to close down a plant or to move it to another location, he may be affecting the economic future. When he decides to build up or reduce inventories, he may be contributing to inflation or accelerating recession. When he changes his wage policy or dividend policy, he may be influencing both the level of employment and the degree of justice achieved in our distribution of income. When he uses the newspaper, radio, and television for advertising or public relations, he may be influencing moral and cultural standards. When he introduces new personnel policies, he may be contributing toward cooperation and understanding between labor and management or he may be reinforcing existing tensions and frictions. When he transacts business in foreign lands, he may be contributing to international tensions or to international understanding. Many more examples could be cited of the relation between the decisions of individual businessmen, taken collectively, and the operation of our total economic system.

When the far-reaching scope and consequences of private business decisions are recognized, some questions naturally arise: Are businessmen, by virtue of their strategic position and their considerable decision-making power, obligated to consider social consequences when making their private decisions? If so, do they have social responsibilities that transcend obligations to owners or stockholders?

The answer to both these questions is clearly yes. Hundreds of leading businessmen have publicly affirmed, in speeches and by the written word, their keen sensibility of their "social responsibilities." And it is becoming increasingly obvious that a freedom of choice and delegation of power such as businessmen exercise would hardly be permitted to continue without some assumption of social responsibility. True, we do not necessarily depend entirely, or even largely, upon a sense of social responsibility to secure socially desirable behavior on the part of businessmen. Businessmen are controlled by competition, by custom, and by law. Nevertheless, we do and must depend also on their assuming a large measure of responsibility if the economic system of free enterprise is to continue and to prosper.

On this proposition there is, I think, wide agreement. But there is much less agreement on the subsequent and more specific question of precisely what are the social responsibilities which businessmen may be expected to assume. The question may be stated in other ways: What constitutes good citizenship for a business enterprise? How does a moral enterprise behave? What kinds of business decisions promote the ends of modern society and what kinds detract? What are the criteria by which the decisions of businessmen should be judged? What kind of institutional or legal arrangements will best promote the assumption by businessmen of their social responsibilities? To what extent do the interests of business in the long run merge with the interests of society?

Admittedly, these questions—like many *important* questions—cannot be answered definitively. The answers depend in part on technical, economic, and social knowledge which is not yet adequate. The answers depend also upon the fundamental values or objectives which we set for our economic, political, and social order.

On one thing we can be definite. The unrivaled freedom of economic decision-making for millions of private businessmen, which characterizes our free enterprise system, can be justified not if it is good merely for the owners and managers of enterprises, but only if it is good for our entire society. We can support freedom and private control of enterprise only if it is conducive to the general welfare by advancing progress, promoting a high standard of living, contributing to economic justice, etc. We judge its success or failure in terms of the public interest. When we consider proposals for its modification, we do so with the public interest in mind. Business, like government, is basically "of the people, by the people, and for the people."

Such power and freedom of choice as is permitted to private businessmen is given because the "people" believe this decentralization to be desirable. When it is felt that the powers exercised and the choices made by businessmen do not contribute to the general welfare, businessmen have either to revise their behavior voluntarily or to be subjected to controls. In the long run, the degree of choice that is permitted depends upon the kinds of decisions and actions made by private businessmen. If their individual actions lead to abuses, damage other individuals, or detract from the attainment of established and valued social objectives, steps will eventually be taken to curb the freedom of businessmen. If those who exercise freedom are unwilling or unable—even with the best of rationalizations—to relate their private decisions and actions to the attainment of valued social objectives, that freedom is in jeopardy.

SOME DEFINITIONS AND ASSUMPTIONS

1. The term *social responsibilities of businessmen* will be used frequently. It refers to the obligations of businessmen to pursue those policies, to make those decisions, or to follow those lines of action which are desirable in terms of the objectives and values of our society. This definition does not imply that businessmen as members of society lack the right to criticize the values accepted in society and to work toward their improvement. Indeed, in view of their great power and influence, they may well have an obligation to do so. It is assumed, however, that as servants of society, they must not disregard socially accepted values or place their own values above those of society. Synonyms for social responsibility are "public responsibility," "social obligations," and "business morality."

2. The term *doctrine of social responsibility* refers to the idea, now widely expressed, that voluntary assumption of social responsibility by businessmen is, or might be, a practicable means toward ameliorating economic problems and attaining more fully the economic goals we seek.

3. This book is primarily concerned with the social responsibilities of large corporations in the United States. The term *business,* when not otherwise qualified, will refer to the several hundred large corporations which we think of collectively as big business. And the term *businessmen* will refer to the managers and directors of these large corporations. This restriction of the field is for clarity

and brevity. A discussion of the social responsibilities of our several million smaller enterprises would be both useful and important, but it would require special treatment beyond the scope of this volume.

4. The discussion refers exclusively to a capitalistic economic system, such as that now existing in the United States, in which there are predominantly large areas of private initiative and enterprise. It is assumed that it is the desire and intention of the American people to retain this type of system. The discussion pertains, therefore, to the role of businessmen in making that system operate more successfully. No attention is given to possible alternative systems.

PLAN OF THIS BOOK

I shall attempt to present a systematic and critical analysis of the doctrine of social responsibility. The following general topics will be considered: goals of economic life, historical background of the doctrine, Protestant thought on the social responsibilities of businessmen, attitudes of businessmen toward their obligations to society, analysis of certain criticisms of the doctrine, analysis and evaluation of proposals for its further implementation, and other leading ethical issues facing businessmen.

On the whole, the treatment of the doctrine of social responsibility will be sympathetic—but with important reservations. The doctrine is no panacea. It would be both unwise and dangerous to assume that most or many of the problems of economic life could be solved if only businessmen, miraculously, would begin to conduct their affairs with primary regard for the social consequences of their actions. Such an assumption would be unwise and dangerous not only for society—which would surely be disappointed—but also for businessmen themselves. They should not be saddled with responsibilities which they cannot hope to discharge effectively. But even though the doctrine of social responsibility is no cure-all, it contains important truth. With proper qualification and limitation, it is not to be brushed aside as mere wishful thinking on the part of idealistic reformers or as business propaganda.

2

Economic Goals

The social responsibilities of businessmen have meaning only in relation to the goals or values which we seek from our economic system. The doctrine of social responsibility rests upon the idea that business should be conducted with concern for the effects of business operations upon the attainment of valued social goals. This suggests that the first step in our analysis is to consider the question: What are the goals toward which businessmen should orient themselves insofar as they are willing or able to consider the social consequences of their actions?

TENTATIVE LIST OF GOALS

This is not the place to undertake a full-scale consideration of values. This has been done in another volume in this series.[1] However, I shall attempt to indicate some of the goals which many thoughtful people would accept, at least in principle. In so doing, I am not attempting to state precisely *the* goals which are accepted by a majority of the American people or by any particular group. I am trying only to illustrate the kinds of goals in terms of which the social responsibilities of business must be defined.

1. *High Standard of Living.* This is the goal which comes to mind immediately and which surely ranks high in the American scale of values. By a "high standard of living"[2] is meant an abundance of goods and services available for consumption by the masses of the people and the substantial amounts of leisure which such abundance makes possible. The provision of a high standard of living requires, of course, a high rate of production. Therefore,

[1] *Goals of Economic Life,* New York, Harper & Brothers, 1953. See also J. M. Clark, *Guideposts in Time of Change,* New York, Harper & Brothers, 1949, pp. 49-78; H. G. Moulton, *Controlling Factors in Economic Development,* Washington, Brookings Institution, 1949, pp. 141 ff.

[2] More precisely, this should have been called "high scale of living." I have chosen, however, to follow popular usage.

this goal is often referred to as "high productivity" or "abundance."

2. *Economic Progress.* Not content with the presently attainable standard of living, we accept as one of our goals the *steady advancement of that standard.* This means that we place a high value upon technological progress leading to new methods of production and to new products. We believe that it is desirable to increase our plant and equipment, and also to increase our nonmaterial capital in the form of education, training, and energy of our workers. And we hold that it is important to utilize our natural resources prudently so that progress will not be slowed down by lack of land and natural materials.

3. *Economic Stability.* Largely as a result of our experiences during the past thirty-five years of alternating inflation and widespread unemployment, we attach great importance to economic stability as a goal. To expect perfect stability in anything so dynamic as our economic system would be unreasonable, but we feel that it is important to temper fluctuations in economic activity.

4. *Personal Security.* Our concern about insecurity due to unemployment, sickness, accident, old age, and death has increased with the growth of these problems during the Great Depression of the 'thirties. In a more individualistic era, personal security was considered important but it was assumed that each person (or his family) is responsible to provide for his contingencies. In recent years, we have moved toward a new concept. It is that some contingencies are beyond the control of the individual, and therefore provision for security against such contingencies is a matter for collective responsibility. What was once regarded as exclusively an individual or family problem has become largely a social problem.

5. *Order.* Order as a social goal is usually associated with the political system. It also has economic connotations. The attainment of order in economic life requires the regular flow of goods to the market, the systematic equalization of demand and supply in all markets, and the absence of violent strife in economic relationships.

6. *Justice.* Our concept of justice in economic affairs pertains to "equity" in the distribution of income and broad diffusion of opportunity for personal development and economic advancement. It includes provision of wide access to education, improvement of neighborhood and family environments, provision of public health services, sanctions against nepotism, and removal of restrictions

based upon color, race, national origin, religion, sex, age, political opinion, physical appearance, or social status.

7. *Freedom.* In the economic sphere, freedom has many facets, just as it has in the political sphere. Moreover, for every freedom there is a corresponding responsibility. The freedom we hear most about is *freedom of enterprise.* This refers to the right of any individual (or group of individuals) to organize such land, labor, and capital as he owns or can command in the market, to manage the use of these resources in the production and distribution of goods and services, and to enjoy the resulting profit or suffer the resulting loss. Another freedom of cardinal importance is *freedom of consumer choice.* This is the right of any individual to buy whatever is for sale when he pleases, with any purchasing power at his command. *Freedom of choice of occupation* implies the right of each individual to decide what vocation to follow, and to change his vocation or place of employment whenever he chooses. *Freedom of organization* refers to the right of individuals to band together for common purposes. We are familiar with such organizations in the form of corporations, labor unions, trade associations, farm organizations, and professional associations.

8. *Development of the Individual Person.* Most human beings spend a large portion of their waking hours in some form of economic activity. They function, during a large part of each day, as workers, as managers, as buyers and sellers, as consumers, and as investors. Moreover, a large part of all human relationships occurs in the workshop, the office, and the market place. This means that the substance and quality of human life are determined in large measure by the physical environment in which economic activity takes place, by the nature of the tasks which people choose or are called upon to undertake, by the quality of human relationships involved, and by the opportunities present for achieving the development and expression of the human personality. As Professor Clark has said: "The individual is so molded in body, mind, and character by his economic activities and relations, stimuli and disabilities, freedoms and servitudes, that industry can truly be said to make the men and women who work in it, no less truly than the commodities it turns out for the market."[3]

[3] J. M. Clark, *Social Control of Business*, 1st ed., Chicago, University of Chicago Press, 1926, p. 47.

Too frequently we have assumed that economic activity relates solely to means rather than ends. The truth of the matter is that economic activity relates at the same time to both means and ends. It is a means to the goods and services we wish to enjoy, but it is also an end in that it comprises so large an element of human time, of human interrelationship, and of personality expression. It is not only a means to human life and human ends but a large part of human life, and an end in itself.

When this is clearly understood, it becomes apparent that one of the important goals of economic life is to provide the kind of physical and social environment which will yield pleasure in work, satisfying human relations, and development of the human personality. This implies the importance of safe, healthful, and pleasant work places; mutual respect and consideration in the relationships of individuals as workers, employers, sellers, customers, competitors, investors, government officials, etc.; and widespread opportunities for creative activity, craftsmanship, artistic and scientific achievement, inventiveness, administrative skill, participation in decisions, assumption of responsibility, cultural advancement, and social and recreational activities.

9. *Community Improvement.* Economic activity has a direct influence on the quality of the local community in which it occurs. A goal of economic life is to arrange the location of factories and shops, the disposal of smoke and waste, the appearance of buildings and grounds, the use of signs, etc., so that the living environment will be healthful and aesthetically satisfying. The possible role of industry in creating aesthetic values is a neglected aspect of political economy.[4] A related goal is to achieve the kind of community organization, services, and facilities which will provide a wholesome and satisfying social environment.

10. *National Security.* In recent years the goal of national security, including the defense of liberal institutions, has become an important—even dominant—preoccupation of the American people. Economic activity is directly related to this goal because military power is based on the diversion of productive resources from civilian to military purposes.

[4] Cf. C. A. Beard, *The Nature of the Social Sciences*, New York, Charles Scribner's Sons, 1934; and C. H. Cooley, "The Progress of Pecuniary Valuation," *Quarterly Journal of Economics*, Nov., 1915, pp. 1-21.

11. *Personal Integrity.* A goal of economic life, which few would deny, is to maintain high standards of honor in all economic activities and transactions. This includes truthfulness in advertising and selling, observance of contract, fairness in relations with competitors, avoidance of questionable financial manipulation, compliance with taxation, and general adherence to the "rules of the game" both in letter and in spirit.

SOCIAL RESPONSIBILITIES AND ECONOMIC GOALS

To make such a list of the goals of economic life is not difficult or controversial. However, when we attempt to translate these goals into action, we find difficulty. Some of the goals are found to be mutually conflicting in the sense that the attempt to achieve one of them may be at the sacrifice of another. For example, security may be achieved at the cost of a lower standard of living or of a reduced rate of progress; justice may interfere with personal security; freedom may conflict with stability; etc. Therefore, in applying these goals we are necessarily faced with compromises. Different individuals value the various goals differently, and different generations look upon them differently in light of their experiences and according to their fundamental views of life. Nevertheless, any appraisal of our economic system, any judgment of proposals for change in that system, and any conception of the responsibilities of businessmen must be formulated in terms of these goals as they are interpreted at any given time and place.

In general, the goals listed above are those by which the social performance of private business is judged today. These are the goals which businessmen are expected to consider, along with their own interests, when they are making decisions on production, prices, personnel, inventories, investment, etc. The questions which a businessman might ask when he faces a decision are: What will this decision mean in terms of the standard of living of the American people? Is it consistent with economic progress? Does it promote economic stability? Is it good for personal security? Does it help to preserve order? Is it just? Does it advance freedom? Does it help people toward personal self-realization? Is it good for the community? Is it helpful toward national security? Is it honorable?

When it is suggested that businessmen should assume responsibility to act in ways that will help in the achievement of economic goals, this is not imposing a new burden. Businessmen have always been expected to act according to sanctioned rules of conduct. This was even true under laissez faire—as will be shown in the next chapter. Indeed, all social organization—of which economic organization is but one aspect—requires that individual members of the group accept common values and goals, and guide their behavior accordingly. If they fail to do so to any significant extent, organized society ceases to exist, and chaos and anarchy prevail.

The economic system is characterized by specialization, division of labor, interdependence, and need for articulation of many diverse parts. Such a system requires the highest standards of conformity to socially sanctioned rules. It cannot function otherwise. In this sense, morality is one of the foundations of all economic life.

The rules necessary for the successful functioning of the economic system may be, and often are, embodied in law and subject to legal enforcement. We all know, however, that enforcement of law itself rests on a moral foundation in that it is not possible (at least in the long run) to impose rules of behavior which are not acceptable to the great majority of people.

We also know that a large part of our conduct is determined by custom and enforced by the sanctions of public opinion; and that another part of our conduct is left to the judgment and discretion of individuals, the only control being the conscience of the individual and the implicit assumption that frequent or prolonged abuse will lead to some form of social control. Morality is unquestionably vital in those branches of conduct which are not controlled by law.

That morality is basic to economic organization has been well understood—at least by philosophers and religious leaders—during most of world history. In modern times, however, with the ascendancy of laissez faire, the moral basis of economic life has tended to become obscured by the idea that self-interest of individuals is an adequate guide to conduct. The prevalence of the laissez-faire doctrine during several generations has created in some quarters the illusion that any revival of social controls is unnecessary and moral principles may have only limited application in economic life. This illusion persists even though we are drifting away from laissez faire in practice. Therefore, it may be worth while to analyze the system of laissez faire from the point of view of its moral requirements.

3

Social Responsibilities and Laissez Faire

One of the leading tenets of eighteenth-century thought was that the pursuit of self-interest by individuals is not always or necessarily antisocial. This is a principle of the first order of importance—one sometimes neglected in ethical thought. Because ethical problems frequently arise when individual and social interests are in conflict, the assumption is often made that ethical conduct invariably requires suppression of self-interest or sacrifice by the individual. This notion is, of course, false. Throughout great areas of life, self-interest (or, at least, intelligent and far-sighted self-interest) is, or can be made to be, consistent with the social interest. This is particularly true in the economic sphere. Indeed, it is one of the great tasks of economic engineering to develop social arrangements under which individual self-interest and the social interest become, so far as possible, mutually compatible.

Many intellectual leaders of the eighteenth and nineteenth centuries, in their struggle against mercantilist and feudal restrictions on economic life, went far beyond the doctrine that individual self-interest and the social interest are not necessarily or always inconsistent. They advanced the idea, especially with reference to economic affairs, that the untrammeled pursuit of self-interest would automatically lead to the best or most economical use of society's productive resources. This was the theory of laissez faire. It has had a profound influence.

It is true that the theory of laissez faire rested on certain conditions which we now believe have never been and could not be fully realized in practice. But the advocates of this doctrine believed that these conditions were realizable, at least to a degree, and that the principal aim of social economic policy was to achieve them. It is a tribute to the optimism of the nineteenth century that so many people seriously thought these conditions might be achieved in sufficient detail to make of laissez faire a workable social system.

LAISSEZ FAIRE IN THEORY

In theory, the system of laissez faire refers to an exchange economy in which the following institutions would be operative: private property, free labor, free enterprise, free consumer choice, and ubiquitous competition. Income would be distributed functionally in the sense that the income of each individual would be received as compensation for the services of whatever land, labor, or capital he owned. And government would be restricted to such activities as protection of property rights; national defense; establishment of weights, measures, and the monetary unit; education; and provision of a few public works such as roads and aids to navigation.[1]

The general mechanics of the theoretical laissez-faire system are these: The use of the factors of production (land, labor, and capital) is determined as a resultant of the separate and independent decisions and actions of individuals who function freely as suppliers of the factors, as consumers, and as managers of firms. The factors of production are hired by the firms which pay the owners for them; the income received in this way by the owners is then used to buy the products of the firms; the money received by the firms for the sale of their products, in turn, is used to pay for the factors of production employed, etc. Thus a constant stream of money passes (1) from firms to owners of the factors (via the market for the factors of production), and (2) from owners of the factors back to firms (via the market for goods).

The influence of each individual upon the prices of goods and of factors is small enough so that each individual neglects whatever influence he may in fact have. Consequently, each individual assumes that the prevailing system of prices, whatever it may be, is a given fact. He attempts to adjust his consumption, the disposal of his factors, and his managerial decisions in the light of these prices so as to maximize his net advantage. In adjusting to any

[1] Cf. H. R. Bowen, *Toward Social Economy*, New York, Rinehart & Company, 1948, pp. 246-49.

given system of prices, however, the combined effect of the separate actions of many individuals is likely to bring about changes in the prices. These price changes will in turn lead individuals to alter their actions, which will bring about still further price changes. This apparently endless succession of changes ceases only when a system of prices is established which induces no further changes in the actions of individuals and which, therefore, tends to be stable. When such a price system has been established and actions of individuals have been adjusted to it, the economic system is said to be in *equilibrium*. Once equilibrium is established, any departure from it is likely to set in motion forces tending to restore it. In short, the laissez-faire system may be characterized as an automatic self-regulating system motivated by the self-interest of individuals and regulated by competition.

Economists have never questioned seriously that there would be tendencies toward a kind of equilibrium in an economy based on laissez-faire principles. Much of so-called classical economics has been an elaboration of the nature of this equilibrium and of the process by which it would be approached. But the important part of the faith of those who advanced the theory of laissez faire was that this equilibrium toward which the system would tend represented the best possible use of the factors of production from the point of view of *society*—society being regarded as a sum total of all the individuals in it. It was thought that if the self-interest of individuals were given free play, restrained only by competition of other individuals but not by government or any form of social control, the best of all possible *social* results would automatically follow.[2]

---

[2] Adam Smith furnished perhaps the most eloquent expression of this idea. See his *An Inquiry into the Nature and Cause of the Wealth of Nations*, Book IV, Chapter III. Another statement of the same idea, written at a time when the philosophy of laissez faire was perhaps at its height, is to be found in the London *Economist* of February 13, 1847: "It may be hurtful to the pride of statesmen to discover how little they can really do ... to eradicate misery, to alleviate suffering, and to improve society. Yet—so it is—the progress of civilization shows more and more how few and simple are the real duties of a Government, and how impossible it is to add to those duties without inflicting permanent mischief on a community. ... The chief aim of all the statesmen who have acquired a high reputation has been to remove regulations and restrictions imposed by others —to remedy the errors of former statesmen by *removing old* regulations, and not by *imposing new* ones. All that can be said of the greatest statesman is, that he discovered error and removed it; that he found a country harassed by restrictions and regulations, and that he freed it."

It was, of course, a serious delusion to believe that in a laissez-faire system no rules for the individual would be required except those of following one's self-interest ardently and competing vigorously. The successful functioning of the system would clearly require reasonable adherence to a moral code. Indeed, the inability of people to live up to the moral requirements of laissez faire partially explains the fact that, historically, the laissez-faire system was never adopted in full and that in recent decades it has been largely abandoned as a principle of economic organization.[3]

Moral Rules for the Businessman in Laissez Faire

Because of his strategic position in a laissez-faire economy, the businessman is particularly subject to important moral requirements. This would be true in a hypothetical system of "pure" laissez faire. It was also true during the historical period when England, the United States, and a few other countries were attempting to put laissez-faire principles into practice (mainly in the nineteenth century). At that time, certain ethical rules for economic conduct were more or less generally accepted—though by no means always followed.

The basic moral rules for the businessman in the nineteenth-century economy were (1) observance of the principles of private property, (2) observance of contract, and (3) avoidance of deception and fraud. These rules were enforced by laws. However, these laws—like any successful laws—were effective because they were rooted in long-established moral principles widely accepted and socially sanctioned. Nevertheless, the enforcement of these laws presented many problems, especially as new forms of property, new types of contractual relationships, and new opportunities for deception and fraud developed with the growth of the market, the increase of specialization, the creation of new types of business organization, and the adoption of new business methods. The workability of the nineteenth-century experiment rested, therefore, on

---

[3] Professor J. J. Spengler has shown that it is easy to underestimate the degree to which the ideal of laissez faire was actually approached in practice. He points out that the records of intervention are accessible to historians, whereas the records of nonintervention do not exist. Even today, we probably assume that the ratio of control to freedom is higher than it is simply because controls are noticed and freedom is taken for granted. See his: "Laissez Faire and Intervention," *Journal of Political Economy*, October, 1949, pp. 438-41.

the evolution of law and of correlative moral principles, at a rate sufficient to keep pace with changing economic conditions and institutions.

If the nineteenth-century system were to achieve its goal of efficiency and progress, it would also be necessary for businessmen to organize the productive factors under their command as efficiently as possible in relation to market demands, and to promote economic progress. This would mean that businessmen should be efficient, they should exhibit keenness in sensing opportunities, they should seek out and be receptive to new products and less costly methods, and they should strive to improve productive factors under their control. The acceptance of this rule was never a serious problem. The social climate of the time favored experimentation in productive methods and the incentives of the system were adequate to identify the self-interest of the individual businessman with the larger interest of society in maximal production and economic progress. One of the strongest arguments for laissez faire, as practiced in the nineteenth century, was that it provided powerful incentives to production.

Another moral rule was that businessmen were responsible to conduct their affairs so that the life, limb, and health of workers and of the general public would be protected. This was a principle which businessmen often failed to accept, as the records of working conditions in the nineteenth century testify. This failure brought about the demands for social control of business which probably started the trend away from laissez faire.

Because the nineteenth-century system relied almost wholly upon competition to hold self-interest in check, it followed that a cardinal moral principle for businessmen was to compete vigorously, both in the sale of their products and in the markets in which they were buyers. The principle of competition also meant that if a businessman found himself, for technical or other reasons, without vigorous competitors, he should voluntarily restrain himself and conduct his affairs *as though* he were being controlled by competition. This, of course, was a troublesome rule. Even Adam Smith was not optimistic about the practicability of the injunction to compete.[4]

⁴ Adam Smith, *op. cit.*, Book I, Chapter X; Book II, Chapter VIII.

One of the underlying and most fundamental principles of the nineteenth-century system was that individuals in their various roles in economic life should exercise wide freedom of choice. Consumers were to be free to choose from among whatever goods were available within the limits of their incomes; workers were to be free to choose their occupations, their employers, and their geographic location; owners of land, capital goods, and liquid assets were to be free to use or dispose of their wealth in any way they wished; and individuals were to be free to organize enterprises of any kind they chose, to operate these enterprises as they wished, and to discontinue these enterprises when they chose. In all of these economic activities, individuals were to be free from restrictions. It followed from these principles that businessmen were obliged to respect these freedoms, and to take no actions which would infringe upon them. The history of the nineteenth century indicates, of course, that these freedoms were sometimes abridged—sometimes in the form of coercion based on economic power, sometimes in the form of influence on governmental policy.

Businessmen, as employers, had obligations to deal with their workers as human beings, to recognize them as human personalities, to assist in their personal development, and to provide the conditions under which work *per se* is rewarding and satisfying. In the nineteenth century, however, the relations between employers and workers were frequently conducted on the theory that employers have no responsibility for workers beyond the payment of wages for work performed, and that workers are properly subject without recourse to the discipline of employers.

To summarize, during the historical period when laissez faire was the guiding theory underlying economic organization, the tacit moral obligations of businessmen were (1) to observe the rules of property; (2) to honor contracts; (3) to refrain from deception and fraud; (4) to be efficient and to promote economic progress; (5) to protect life, limb, and health of workers and of the general public; (6) to compete vigorously, and in case of failure of competition to act with restraint; (7) to accept and respect the economic freedoms of consumers, workers, and owners; and (8) to have regard for the human rights of workers. The willing acceptance of these considerable obligations by businessmen was a fundamental requirement of the system.[5]

PROBLEMS OF LAISSEZ FAIRE

The system of laissez faire—ideally and to the extent that it was practiced—had much to commend it. It provided a simple set of generalized rules regarding property, contract, and honesty in dealings. Under these rules, the widest latitude for individual freedom of choice was permitted, and a minimal amount of conscious governmental direction was required. The incentives to individuals in their various economic roles were powerful enough to produce a dynamic, progressive economy; and competition provided a powerful check on self-interest. The system of laissez faire was remarkable in that it represented an almost unique aberration from the world trend of thought and practice. Whereas most moral systems have tried to curb self-interest by social control or by teaching self-restraint, the laissez-faire system minimized both social control and individual self-restraint. Instead, it attempted to harness self-interest to the social interest, and to make morality virtually painless.

In practice, however, many conflicts arose between individual and social interests. Some of these conflicts developed because of the inability or failure of people to accept the moral responsibilities necessary if the system were to achieve acceptable social results. Examples were tendencies of businessmen toward deceptive behavior—especially of the more sophisticated and manipulative varieties associated with merchandising and high finance; failure of businessmen to provide for the protection of life, limb, and health; the frequent failure of competition and the lack of restraint in imperfectly competitive situations; and frequent failure to recognize the human rights of workers. The earliest tendencies toward social or governmental control of business arose from these failures. Society was forced to insist upon higher standards of honesty, protection of persons, restraint of monopoly, and treatment of workers as human beings. Other groups beside businessmen also had moral obligations under laissez faire, and the failures of these groups to

[5] Cf. Alvin S. Johnson, "The Soul of Capitalism," *Unpopular Review*, April, 1914, pp. 227-44.

meet their obligations also had an influence in the decline of laissez faire. But the businessman as the dominant functionary in this system no doubt carried a considerable onus of moral responsibility for the decline.

But the decline of laissez faire was due not alone to moral failures. It was due also to technical conditions. Among these were (1) growth of large-scale enterprise and concentration of economic power; (2) fluctuating general business activity with recurrent periods of unemployment; (3) technological unemployment; (4) personal insecurity of people with reference to sickness, old age, and death; (5) disparities in the distribution of income; (6) disparities in the distribution of economic opportunity; (7) overly rapid and wasteful exploitation of natural resources; (8) materialistic, competitive, and invidious standards of consumption; and (9) frequent disregard for the social costs of economic activity and the social values that might be derived from economic activity.

Efforts of society and of groups within society to deal with these problems in the past fifty or seventy-five years have led—for better or worse—to the progressive decline of laissez faire both in theory and in practice, and to a rapid increase in social control over economic life. In some countries, this development of social control has culminated in socialism of one form or another. In the United States it has led to our present-day blend of free enterprise and social control, to which the name *welfare capitalism* or *mixed economy* is sometimes applied.

4

Social Aspects of Business Decisions in Present-Day Capitalism

The difficulties encountered under the system of near laissez faire, as practiced in the nineteenth century, led to a long series of *ad hoc* reform measures. Indeed, the earliest of these measures were enacted long before the final vestiges of mercantilistic control had been thrown off. Modern labor legislation, for example, dates from the English Health and Morals of Apprentices Act of 1802, an act in which humanitarian motives were prominent. An act of 1819 restricted employment of children. The right to form labor unions was legally recognized in England in 1824. Drastic reorganization and liberalization of the poor laws occurred in 1834. There were similar early beginnings of social legislation in the United States during the 1830's and 1840's, and the story of subsequent legislation providing varied economic controls is a familiar one.[1]

[1] Karl Polanyi refers to a paradox in the origins of laissez faire and of subsequent governmental intervention. He says: "While *laissez-faire* economy was the product of deliberate state action, subsequent restrictions on *laissez-faire* started in a spontaneous way. *Laissez-faire* was planned; planning was not. . . . If ever there was conscious use of the executive in the service of a deliberate government-controlled policy, it was on the part of the Benthamites in the heroic period of *laissez-faire*." In Dicey's studies, says Polanyi, "no evidence of a 'collectivist trend' in public opinion *prior* to the laws which appeared to represent such a trend could be found . . . there had been complete absence of any deliberate intention to extend the functions of the state, or to restrict the freedom of the individual, on the part of those who were directly responsible for the restrictive enactments of the 1870's and 1880's. The legislative spearhead of the countermovement against a self-regulating market as it developed in the half-century following 1860 turned out to be spontaneous, undirected by opinion, and actuated by a purely pragmatic spirit." *The Great Transformation*, New York, Rinehart & Company, 1944, p. 141.

22

GOVERNMENTAL INTERVENTION

In the United States, in an effort to overcome the more subtle problems of deception, fraud, and financial manipulation, "blue sky" laws were enacted, and the Federal Trade Commission and the Securities and Exchange Commission were established. To combat or control monopoly, collusion, and undue concentration of economic power, regulation of railroads and public utilities was instituted, antitrust and "fair trade" laws were enacted, and special aids to small business were provided. To achieve greater stability of economic activity, monetary control and fiscal policy were invoked. To alleviate the problems of poverty and personal insecurity, relief, social insurance, and farm-price supports were provided on a steadily increasing scale. To protect the life, limb, and health of workers and of the general public, factory laws, safety codes, housing ordinances, pure-food laws, and public-health services were provided. To improve the status of labor and to prevent strife in labor-management relations, trade unions were accorded recognition and their relations with employers subjected to public supervision. To increase equity in the distribution of income and of personal opportunity, provision was made for free public education, graduated income and death taxes, social insurance, minimum-wage laws, farm price supports, and public housing. To prevent the wastage of natural resources, conservation measures were enacted, river-valley projects were undertaken, and the government retained or acquired ownership of vast tracts of land. To promote productivity and economic development, the government subsidized industries, supported research and adult education, and—in a throwback to mercantilism—imposed import duties.

This is by no means an exhaustive catalogue of the measures ployed to overcome the problems, real or fancied, arising under laissez faire. It does serve to illustrate the extensive scope of governmental intervention in economic life—some of it no doubt ill-advised—that has emerged from the century-long effort to solve what were believed to be the problems of laissez faire and to enhance the satisfactions derived from economic life.[2]

[2] Walter Lippmann in his *Preface to Morals* (New York, The Macmillan Company, 1931, pp. 243-44) says: ". . . the social history of the last seventy-five years has in large measure been concerned with the birth pains of an industrial philosophy that will really suit the machine technology and the nature of man.

In the course of effecting these changes, the values and attitudes of people toward their economic system also changed. The past century and a half has been a period of rapid development in humanitarian sentiments and in concern for the welfare of individuals. The socially accepted standards by which the economic system is judged have become more exacting. Hence, as particular reforms have been achieved, the demand for still more reforms has become insistent.

During most of the period of economic reform by *ad hoc* legislation, specific measures were designed to overcome each of the problems by appropriate special controls, while retaining generally the individual initiative and the freedom of action characteristic of laissez faire. The philosophy underlying these measures was that laissez faire was to be retained as the general principle of economic organization, and that each departure from this norm was to be justified as a special exception to solve a particular problem. The intention was to retain the incentives, the efficiency, and the creative satisfactions flowing from individual initiative and from the delegation of economic decisions to private individuals and groups, while overcoming the specific problems of instability, insecurity, and injustice which were found to crop out under the regimen of laissez faire. The purpose was to achieve the advantages of laissez faire without a commitment to comprehensive and coordinated state planning of economic life. Moreover, the purpose was to control the general environment in which economic activity takes place rather than to control the specific decisions of private businessmen, consumers, workers, investors, etc. In the United States of today, it is still true that the great majority of our economic controls are designed to lay down certain general conditions or rules under which economic affairs are to be conducted, rather than to intervene in the decision-making process directly.

For the notion that an intricate and delicately poised industrial mechanism could be operated by uneducated men snatching competitively at profits was soon exposed as a simple-minded delusion. . . . So little has *laissez faire* worked under actual· experience that all the powers of government have actually had to be invoked to preserve a certain amount of compulsory 'free competition.' For the industrial machine, as soon as it passes out of the early phase of rough exploitation in virgin territory, becomes unmanageable by naively competitive and acquisitive men." Professor K. E. Boulding has expressed a similar view (*Economics of the Peace*, New York, Prentice-Hall, 1945, pp. 216-7).

ORGANIZED GROUPS

While these developments in the role of government were occurring, fundamental changes also were taking place in the organization of private individuals for economic purposes. Whereas, in the early nineteenth century, individuals functioned largely as *individuals* or in small groups, today many have become members of enormous and powerful groups which act for them in various ways and which sometimes exercise controls over them.[3] Examples are corporations, labor unions, farm organizations, trade associations, and cooperatives. These groups are supposed to function chiefly in the interests of their members—their interests being not always identical with the interests of the public at large. To gain their ends, these groups often exercise monopoly power in varying degrees; sometimes they use intimidation, force, strikes, boycotts, etc.; and almost always they use political pressure.

PRESENT-DAY CAPITALISM

Each governmental measure, or each step in the development of organized economic groups, taken singly, was intended to solve a particular problem or mitigate a specific evil. It was not intended to modify the basic character of the economy. As a people, we believe overwhelmingly that, despite these changes, our economic system is predominantly one of individual initiative and private enterprise. Even labor leaders and workers will stoutly assert that they are in favor of the "free-enterprise system" and see no incompatibility between these organizations and that system. Nevertheless, the combined effect of governmental action and group organization has resulted in an economic system that departs significantly, in fundamental organization and philosophy, from the laissez faire system.

We now have in the United States what is often referred to as a *mixed economy,* in that it combines important elements of laissez faire and of socialism, and even has some of the qualities of syndi-

[3] For a discussion of the role of organized groups in economic life, see the volume of this series: Kenneth E. Boulding, *The Organizational Revolution: A Study in the Ethics of Economic Organization,* New York, Harper & Brothers, 1953.

calism.[4] It retains a substantial amount of individual initiative and individual freedom of choice in matters of production, consumption, choice of occupation, and geographic mobility of persons. There are substantial elements of socialism, as evidenced by governmental ownership, regulation, control, and planning. And there are elements of syndicalism, as evidenced by the strategic role of labor and other organized groups. This development has occurred as a result of the efforts of men to reconcile the goals of freedom and economic progress, which are paramount in the laissez-faire philosophy, with the goals of stability, security, justice, and personality development, which are emphasized in modern humanitarian philosophy. The resulting mixed economy I have chosen to call *present-day capitalism.*[5]

The evolution toward present-day capitalism represents partly the attempts of society to achieve an appropriate balance between the freedom of the businessmen on the one hand and the freedom of workers and farmers on the other. The net result of this evolution is an economy characterized by substantial elements of governmental and group control over economic life, and strong tendencies toward centralization of economic power. This is in contrast to the wide delegation of decision-making and the diffusion of economic power that were characteristic of laissez faire—at least in theory.

Throughout the history of the transition to present-day capitalism, and today as well, the underlying motivation has been to preserve the essential elements of laissez faire. Deviations from this system have been accepted only when the need for such deviations was thought to be demonstrated by the emergence of serious problems. By now, however, the deviations have become numerous and far-reaching. It is argued by some that the freedom and motivations and delegations of power characteristic of laissez faire are being eroded to a point where they are no longer the basic elements of our economic organization. We have reached a point, it is said, from which the continued burgeoning of controls by government and by organized economic groups could lead us to some form of

[4] Cf. Henry C. Simons, "Some Reflections on Syndicalism," *Journal of Political Economy,* March, 1944, pp. 1-25.

[5] A semantic problem of no small importance is to find a term that aptly describes the present-day economy of the United States. Most of the usual terms carry emotive connotations or are not accurately descriptive. Therefore, I have elected to use the colorless term *present-day capitalism.*

state socialism.[6] The continuation of well-established trends toward greater governmental control might jeopardize our essential freedoms and curtail the spirit of enterprise, of initiative, of productivity, and of freedom that has distinguished American economic life.[7] At this point in our economic history, therefore, we must seriously consider possible alternatives to detailed and comprehensive direction of the economy by the state. This may be difficult, or even irrelevant, at a time when we are embarking upon what promises to be an indefinitely long period of rearmament. But whatever the immediate requirements for war preparation or war itself, America must choose in the long run between retaining the fundamentals of private self-determination in economic affairs or accepting control by the state and organized groups as the basic tenet of our economic life.

There is little doubt that an overwhelming majority of the American people would prefer that private self-determination be retained as the basic principle of our economic organization. It is not entirely evident, however, that they follow this preference consistently when considering the *ad hoc* measures which, when added one to another, steadily reduce the scope of individual self-determination. I shall assume that it is the intent of the American people—certainly of American businessmen—to retain an economy founded upon the principle of individual self-determination, but individual self-determination tempered by consideration for social welfare. I shall assume also that the American people desire that this system shall operate satisfactorily in the sense that it shall afford reasonable stability, security, justice, etc. With these goals in view, it is

[6] Cf. Edwin G. Nourse, *The 1950's Come First*, New York, Henry Holt & Company, 1951. Another more optimistic view is that society must constantly make adjustments and compromises between individualism and governmental control or between freedom and order or between the ideal of John Locke and the ideal of Plato; and that the adjustments required to meet the unique problems of one age will differ from those required in another age. In this view, the "mixed economy" of modern America represents neither a "trend" toward socialism nor a "defeat" for individualism, but merely the adjustment which is required by the particular problems of our time. See Stephen C. Pepper, *Toward an Adjustable Society* (mimeographed), University of Illinois, Urbana, 1950; and his *A Digest of Purposive Values*, Berkeley, University of California Press, 1947.

[7] The effect of economic planning upon freedom is, of course, not necessarily a settled issue. For opposing points of view, see F. A. von Hayek, *The Road to Serfdom*, Chicago, University of Chicago Press, 1944; and Barbara Wootton, *Freedom under Planning*, Chapel Hill, University of North Carolina Press, 1945.

now possible to consider the social role of the businessman in present-day capitalism.

THE BUSINESSMAN IN PRESENT-DAY CAPITALISM

In the first place, all of the moral rules for the laissez-faire economy[8] are applicable to present-day capitalism. The business-man must continue to observe the rules of property, to honor contracts, to refrain from deception and fraud, to be efficient, to promote economic progress, to protect health and safety, to compete vigorously or to act with restraint in case competition is not effective, and to respect the economic freedoms and human rights of consumers, workers, and owners. But the responsibilities of the businessman who functions in present-day capitalism in America far transcend the moral rules for laissez faire, considerable though these are. His additional responsibilities are of two general types: First, in reaching his private business decisions, he is called upon increasingly to consider their broad economic and social effects, and whenever possible to temper his decisions accordingly. Second, since government has become, and will necessarily continue to be, a partner in all economic affairs, he is expected to cooperate with government in the formulation and execution of public policy.

To the extent that businessmen assume these twin responsibilities, they can assist in improving the operation of the total economy so that its results will be more satisfying to the American people. They will also help solve the economic and social problems which might otherwise give rise to demands for further public intervention in economic affairs. Voluntary assumption of these responsibilities by businessmen is at least one possible alternative to further control of the economy by the state. Because of his crucial role in our economic life, the businessman is in a position, by his own decisions, to help protect the economic system of self-determination and to help prevent the coming of comprehensive state control over economic life. His assumption of his responsibilities, therefore, is at least a partial alternative to socialism.[9]

[8] See Chapter 3, pp. 19-21.
[9] President Arthur T. Hadley expressed this idea as early as 1907 in his *Standards of Public Morality*, New York, The Macmillan Company, 1907, pp. 95-6. See also Charles W. Eliot, *The Ethics of Corporate Management*, 1906; and J.

In singling out the businessman as one who bears social responsibilities, it is not to be inferred that he is alone in having obligations toward the economy. Other groups, for example, consumers, farmers and their leaders, and workers and their leaders also have obligations. A similar analysis could be presented regarding each of these other groups. However, the strategic position of the businessman in our economy places upon him, perhaps, a greater onus of responsibility than upon other functionaries in our system. His decisions, more than those of any other private group, are important in determining how the economy functions and the degree to which it is successful in achieving the various values which the American people expect from it. Moreover, decisions made by him in terms of his own narrow interest do not necessarily contribute to the successful operation of the total economy. Therefore, his private interests must be tempered by the social interest; this means that the social interest must be understood by him and actively considered in his decisions. In this country, we look to business to do voluntarily many of the things which foreign countries are looking to government to do.

When the businessman is asked to consider broad social and economic effects in reaching his decisions, what is involved? In general, he is expected to consider his prospective actions from the point of view of himself or his firm (stockholders), and at the same time from the point of view of society. When the private and social interests are in harmony, as would frequently be true in a well-ordered society, there is no problem. But when the two interests are not identical, a moral issue is present, and the problem is to achieve a reasonable balance between the private and the public interest.

The kinds of decisions which a businessman is called upon to make vary according to the nature and scale of his enterprise and according to the latitude for choice which is permitted within the technical, competitive, and social environment. Almost all of his decisions—whether relating to production, sales, finances, personnel, or prices—have implications for the social interest in that each affects the degree to which one or more of the basic goals of economic life are realized. For example, attainment of the goal of *economic stability* is influenced by the combined effect of

M. Clark, "The Changing Basis of Economic Responsibility," *Journal of Political Economy,* March, 1916, pp. 209-29.

private business decisions on production, investment, prices, and wages. Or the attainment of the goal of *justice* is influenced by private decisions regarding wages, salaries, dividends, prices, and relations with competitors.

The moral problem of the businessman is to recognize the social implications of his decisions and to consider the social interest—*so far as is possible and reasonable*—in arriving at these decisions. His duty is to ask himself how the decisions he makes in the ongoing operation of his business relate to these goals and how he might advance the attainment of these goals by appropriate modification of his decisions.

5

Protestant Views of the Social Responsibilities of Businessmen

Suppose a Protestant businessman should ask: "As a Christian what are my social responsibilities?" Would he be able to find a reasonably authoritative and specific answer? In this chapter, I shall try to take the point of view of the inquiring businessman, and to discover the kind of answer he would find.[1]

There would be no single source to which a businessman might go to find out about the Protestant conception of his social responsibilities. Protestant doctrine on economic affairs is presented in a multitude of scattered sources which have been issued over a long period of years. These include statements of denominational bodies, reports of interdenominational and ecumenical conferences, pronouncements of interdenominational organizations such as the National Council of Churches, and writings of theologians and other individual religious leaders. Only by extensive reading would he begin to achieve a comprehension of the Protestant viewpoint. Even then he would be impressed by the difficulty of applying the

[1] This survey of Protestant views on the responsibilities of businessmen should not be regarded as complete or inclusive of all shades of opinion. It is not confined to *distinctively* Protestant views, but includes many ideas that are shared by other religious and secular groups. It is not an official declaration of the National Council of the Churches of Christ in the United States of America, the organization which sponsored this study. It is intended as a summary of the careful thinking of Protestant leaders and scholars as expressed in official statements and other documents. It is based partly upon a reading of much— but by no means all—of the literature in the field, and it has been reviewed by competent theologians and religious leaders who have had long experience in the consideration of economic and social issues. No attempt is made to present the views of the millions of Protestant laymen. That would be virtually a survey of the opinions of the American public—since Protestant laymen constitute so large a segment of that public. Some of the principal sources are presented in Appendix A of this volume.

doctrine to his specific day-to-day problems and decisions. Indeed, many of the pronouncements of religious leaders and groups on economic affairs state frankly that the Church "cannot provide blueprints,"[2] that its duty rather is only to place economic affairs in a Christian perspective. On the other hand, the businessman would be impressed—and perhaps surprised—by the tremendous amount of constructive thought that has been given to economic problems by religious organizations and leaders. And, if he were a perceptive individual, he would appreciate the difficulties of developing concrete definitions of businessmen's responsibilities that would be clearly and directly applicable to every-day affairs.

THE ECONOMIC SYSTEM

Perhaps the businessman would begin his studies by trying to discover the Protestant view of the capitalistic system itself. If he expected to find an unqualified endorsement of the capitalistic system, he would be disappointed. Protestant thinkers emphatically deny that *any* particular form of social organization is ordained by God's will or has any claim to support on religious grounds. They hold that social institutions are relative to time and place and that a form of social organization which is desirable in one environment or in one stage of man's development may be utterly inappropriate in another. They express regret that in times past churches and church leaders have tried to identify a particular social order (usually, the *status quo*) with divine will, and warn against such attempts in the present and future. Similarly, leading Protestant thinkers are specific in denouncing the idea (associated with the laissez-faire doctrine) that economic affairs are dominated by independent or quasi-natural "laws" which are not subject to human choices and human regulation. They contend that such phenomena as business fluctuations, wages, prices, and outputs of commodities are subject to "control or modification by deliberate human choice."[3]

On the other hand, Protestant thinkers are equally definite in their contention that the form of social organization at any given

---

[2] For example, Federal Council of Churches, *Report of the National Study Conference on the Church and Economic Life* (Pittsburgh), New York, 1947, Section II.

[3] Federal Council of the Churches of Christ in America, *Information Service*, Jan. 25, 1947, p. 2.

time and place is a matter of great importance. Christianity can be practiced only if the prevailing institutions are reasonably suitable. The Church, therefore, must not restrict its ministry and its activities to the spiritual life of the individual and disregard the form of the social institutions which are so influential in molding his character and personality.

The Church and individual Christians have a duty to work for a better social order—better in the sense that it facilitates the application of Christian principles to everyday life and contributes to the development of the Christian spirit. The duty to work for a better social order includes specifically the obligation to be informed on social affairs and to participate and work actively in organizations, parties, and movements which are attempting to achieve improvement in social institutions. Often this duty is linked with the concept of the Christian vocation. Yet Protestant thinkers, always deeply conscious of the sinful tendencies of mankind, are suspicious of Utopian thinking. They reject the idea that through changes in social institutions human perfection will be achieved.

PRIVATE PROPERTY

Just as the businessman would not find in Protestant declarations unqualified endorsement of the capitalistic system, he would not find unqualified support for the institution of private property. Protestant thinkers have said a good deal about property, most of it under the heading of "stewardship" or "trusteeship." In their view, property is not an absolute or inherent right, and it can be justified only to the extent that the welfare of the community is served by permitting material things to be owned and administered by private individuals. Those who own property have the duty of using and administering it, not exclusively for their own purposes, but in ways that will serve the needs of the whole society. From the moral point of view, there must be no such thing as unrestricted and irresponsible ownership. The owner is a trustee accountable to God and society.

There is no necessary presumption that all types of property must be held on identical terms of ownership, and experimentation in varying systems of ownership is called for. Some types of property confer great power on owners (e.g., landed estates and business capital) and may reasonably be subjected to special limitations and regulations, to cooperative ownership, or even to public ownership. Property in land and natural resources involves special responsibility for owners or special regulation, because these are gifts of God intended for the use of all mankind including unborn generations.

On the other hand, other types of property (e.g., family farms, small business, family dwellings) which confer freedom and independence upon their owners should be encouraged—possibly by specific social measures. In general, because of the relation of property to power and freedom, a wide distribution of property is greatly to be preferred over a narrow concentration.

Thus, Protestant pronouncements on economic affairs do not specifically defend private property, nor do they attack it. Rather, they take the pragmatic view that property is a conditional right; that the form of ownership should vary according to changes in the needs of society, and according to the degree of stewardship shown by private owners; that different kinds of property may be owned in different ways; that property or some kinds of it may be subjected to public or cooperative control; and that private property always places upon owners the responsibility of administration in the social interest.

POWER

Closely connected with the Protestant view of property is the attitude toward *power*. In general, Protestant thinkers are deeply suspicious of power in whatever guise it appears. They distrust power partly because of its effect on the personalities of those who wield it and those who are subject to it and partly because they regard power as a source of injustice. They recognize that under modern conditions of large-scale production great power over the lives of people is centered in the relatively few men who preside over our great corporations. Though the stock ownership of these corporations may be diffused, effective ownership in terms of control resides in management. Protestant thinkers point out unequivocally that such power entails the responsibility to use it in the social interest. At the same time, they indicate considerable skepticism as to whether the power will in fact be so used. Hence, they tend to suggest the need of public regulation and of competing centers of power, such as cooperative organizations and labor unions. They are suspicious of arguments by businessmen that their power is being used—or will be used—benevolently and point out the frequent proclivity of men in a given social class to hold views consistent with the interests of their class.

In accordance with these ideals, Protestant leaders have for many years championed the cause of organized labor, and that of farmers and the cooperative movement. More recently, however, as labor and agriculture have gained in power, there has been a tendency to view these new concentrations of power as subject to the same dangers, and the same requirement of responsibility, as business. At present, one of the unresolved dilemmas of Protestant thinkers is the question of how to achieve reasonable balance and harmonious relationships among the several centers of organized power in our society. Moral principles, originally developed to apply to relationships among human beings as individuals, do not apply neatly to relationships among groups of men.

Sometimes, Protestant pronouncements suggest the desirability of wider diffusion of property ownership and even look back longingly to the Jeffersonian ideal of a society of independent artisans and farmers. But in general, they accept organized power groups as here to stay and are chiefly concerned to find ways of dealing with them.

MOTIVES AND VALUES

In the Protestant view of the capitalist system, perhaps the most trenchant criticism is directed toward the motivations and values which have been prevalent in that system. Frequent reference is made to the fact that under capitalism, men are dominated by the desire for material acquisition, luxury, power, and self-aggrandizement. Money and material prosperity are the accepted symbols of success and the central aims of human strivings. The material takes precedence over the spiritual, and the motive of selfish gain predominates over the motive of service to the community. In these circumstances the Calvinist idea that material prosperity is a mark of God's favor has lost its hold on Protestant thinking.

Protestant pronouncements are often emphatic in their denunciation of the profit motive. Sometimes a distinction is made between "profits" and the "profit motive." For example, the report of the National Study Conference on the Church and Economic Life held at Pittsburgh (Section II) stated: "Profits are characteristic of a money economy and are thoroughly defensible, subject to proper methods of accumulating and distributing them. The profit motive is a further question, concerned more directly with the motives and aspirations of men. Christians must be activated more largely by a service motive than by a profit motive." Some writings on the subject of profits do not attempt fine distinction between profits and the profit motive, and do not define what is meant by either term.[4] These give the general impression of hostility toward the profit motive and suspicion of profit itself. This attitude has led many churchmen to espouse cooperatives as a form of economic organization in which service motives are claimed to be more fully expressed than in conventional private business.

On the other hand, in some of the more careful and complete writings on profits, it is suggested that the profit system is defensible if the amount of profits and their use are determined with the needs of society in view.[5] This is the familiar doctrine of stewardship. In this connection, some Protestant writers are definite in stating that selfish motives must be relied upon in providing the incentives to work, enterprise, efficiency, risk taking, and innovation which are essential to a productive economy. But, they add, these must be harmonized with concern for the general social welfare.

VOCATION

Another frequent Protestant criticism is that the conditions of employment under capitalism are such as to nullify the workers' sense of Christian vocation. The extent to which this charge is against modern methods of mass production, as distinct from the capitalistic method of economic organization, is not always made clear. However, this criticism is leveled at least partly against the capitalistic system. It is asked: How can a worker feel a sense of serving his fellow man or a sense of the social importance of his work when the proximate objective of his activity is the profit of his employer? And it is suggested that one of the great needs of

---

[4] A notable exception is found in The Federal Council of Churches, *Information Service*, Jan. 25, 1947, pp. 6-7.

[5] *Ibid.*, p. 7.

modern life is to restore the sense of vocation so that one's job in which one spends most of his life is regarded as more than a mere means to a weekly pay check and more than a necessary evil to which one devotes as little of his talent and energy as possible.

Closely related to "vocation" is the problem of the term of employment and the mode of compensating workers for their services. Running through many Protestant pronouncements is the implication that the modern labor market violates the dignity of the worker as a person. The phrase, "Labor must not be treated as a commodity," occurs repeatedly. By this is meant, first, that the employment relationship must be one in which the worker is treated by the employer with dignity and respect, and, second, that wage payments must be related not alone to the market value of the worker's services, but also to average family needs.

DISTRIBUTION OF INCOME

Protestant writers consider that the distribution of income should be determined primarily on the basis of justice. While they do not argue for equality of income and recognize the need for adequate incentives, they are explicit in condemning poverty of the kind that is "crippling to human personality" and they repeatedly advocate a "just" share to labor, a "living wage," an "annual income," minimum-wage laws, and minimum standards of living to which all may have access. More recently, as the idea has gained acceptance that wide distribution of purchasing power to the masses is necessary for the maintenance of full employment, Protestant pronouncements have mentioned the purchasing-power argument with apparent approval. Nowhere have I found any explicit statement of proposed methods of wage determination in accordance with these principles. There is no indication of the content of the phrases "living wage," "minimal standards of living," "poverty," etc., and no formula to guide employers if they should wish to modify market wages according to these precepts.

OTHER CRITICISMS

In addition to these Protestant criticisms of the capitalistic system must be added other more conventional complaints. Protestant thinkers have consistently criticized the conditions of labor with respect to hours, safety, sanitation, employment of women and child labor, and have advocated both legislative reforms and voluntary improvement by individual employers. They have vigorously criticized the insecurity, fear, poverty, and unemployment which they feel has been characteristic of an unregulated capitalistic system, and they have supported social security and other measures designed to mitigate these evils. They are emphatic on the *right*, and the duty, of every able person to work. They have been concerned by the apparent tendency under capitalism for men to divide into classes with opposing interests and points of view and with resulting social conflict. They have viewed this as a serious impediment to realization of the brotherhood of man. In this connection they have been particularly concerned about unsatisfactory relationships between labor and management, and about the loss of intimate personal relations in the work place and the community.

THE AMSTERDAM STATEMENT

To summarize the views of Protestant thinkers on the capitalistic system, they are critical of it—both of its basic premise that the pursuit of self-interest regulated by competition will produce a good society and of many aspects of its detailed operation in practice. On the other hand, they are even more strongly opposed to communism. Their position was eloquently expressed in the Report of Section III of the Amsterdam Conference of the World Council of Churches:

Two chief factors contribute to the crisis of our age. One of these is the vast concentrations of power—which are under capitalism mainly economic and under communism both economic and political. In such conditions, social evil is manifest on the largest scale not only in the greed, pride, and cruelty of persons and groups; but also in the momentum or inertia of huge organizations of men which diminish their ability to act as moral and accountable beings. . . .

The Church cannot resolve the debate between those who feel that the primary solution is to socialize the means of production, and those who fear that such a course will merely lead to new and inordinate combinations of political and economic power, culminating finally in an omnicompetent State. In the light of the Christian understanding of man we must, however, say to the advocates of socialization that the institution of property is not the root of the corruption of human nature. We must equally say to the defenders of existing property relations that ownership is not an unconditional right; it must, therefore, be preserved, curtailed, or distributed in accordance with the requirements of justice.

On the one hand we must vindicate the supremacy of persons over purely technical considerations by subordinating all economic processes and cherished rights to the needs of the community as a whole. On the other hand, we must preserve the possibility of a satisfying life for "little men in big societies." We must prevent abuse of authority and keep open as wide a sphere as possible in which men can have direct and responsible relations with each other as persons.

Conclusions

The essential constructive conclusion one draws from Protestant documents on economic life is that the road to economic and social welfare lies not in dogmatic adherence to some closed system, but rather in evolution toward a mixed system containing elements of private enterprise, cooperative enterprise, and public enterprise; motivated partly by self-interest and partly by social interest with the latter predominating; controlled partly by competition, partly by private concern for the social interest, and partly by public regulation; and distributing income partly on the basis of market prices of the factors and partly on the basis of the needs of persons. This is hardly a neat or symmetrical theoretical structure which would attract the person looking for a simple unidimensional system. Moreover, its detailed operation has not been thought through and is lacking in specific guidance to those who would try to implement it. Yet here, in general outline, is a serious proposal for the ordering of our economic life, a proposal that has behind it the weight of Protestant intellectual leadership.

From this general background of the Protestant viewpoint on economic life and from more specific statements on various subjects, one can distill from Protestant doctrine certain fairly definite principles and recommendations to guide the businessman who wishes to discharge his Christian duty.

1. The businessman should be actuated by the motive of serving society rather than maximizing profit as the sole end of enterprise. His role is that of a steward and he is justified in retaining his social

position only if the interests of society, on balance, are best served thereby.

2. As a corollary to the doctrine of stewardship he is to administer all natural resources that come under his control with special care so that the interests of both present and future generations are safeguarded.

3. The businessman should help to advance the efficiency and productivity of society, because greater production is required to eliminate poverty and drudgery and to meet the "needs" of mankind. In measuring efficiency, human factors and nonpecuniary costs are to be taken into account.

4. The businessman should be imbued with respect for the dignity and essential worth of all men and with a spirit of compassion, shown in his relationships with his workers, customers, suppliers, competitors, and others with whom he has business dealing.

5. As a corollary to the doctrine of human dignity, he must refrain from discrimination among persons on grounds of race, religion, political views, national origin, social status, physical appearance, or sex (except as these characteristics affect actual work performances). The businessman is to work actively to bring about a lessening of such discrimination.

6. As another corollary to the doctrine of human dignity, equal opportunity is to be accorded all persons—particularly young persons—for personal development commensurate with their potentialities.

7. Wholesome, safe, and healthful working conditions are to be provided, with reasonable hours and reasonable provision for the physical and cultural needs of workers.

8. Reasonable security is to be afforded all workers either through social insurance or through voluntary programs such as company retirement plans, sickness benefits, regularization of work, guaranteed annual employment, etc.

9. The integrity and welfare of the family is to be protected, and arrangements relating to terms and conditions of employment must be guided by this objective.

10. The sense of vocation among workers must be strengthened. The nature and terms of employment should be such that the

worker finds meaning in his work and is given a sense of serving his fellow man through his daily tasks.

11. Compensation of labor should take into account human family needs as well as the market value of services performed. Large incomes, on the other hand, should be limited to what is justified by social considerations of need, incentive, and capital formation.

12. The businessman must respect the right of labor to organize and must join with labor in collective bargaining.

13. So far as possible and practicable, the distribution of property and power should be diffused widely, and economic and political organization should be decentralized.

14. Prices, wages, and profits should be determined with considerations of justice paramount.

15. Honesty should be observed in all transactions.

16. Only worthy products designed to meet worthy needs of people should be produced, and advertising and selling methods should not impair the moral and cultural standards of the public.

These principles and recommendations are in many respects similar to those advanced by leading businessmen themselves.[6] It is to be hoped that Christian thought has been influential in convincing businessmen of the validity of these principles. But whatever the direction of influence, there is no doubt of the great similarity between the conception of social responsibility held by businessmen and that implicit in Protestant pronouncements on economic affairs. The outstanding difference lies in the attitude toward the capitalistic system itself. The businessman, accepting it as inherently desirable, may see need only of a more persuasive "selling job," whereas Protestant thinkers are likely to be much more skeptical of capitalism undiluted. The idea of the "mixed economy," with large mixtures of social control and social ownership, seems much more acceptable to Protestant thinkers than to businessmen.

PARTICIPATION

But there is another important idea implicit in much Protestant doctrine which has not yet found complete acceptance in business circles. This is the idea of participation of workers, consumers, and

[6] See Chapters 6 and 7.

possibly of other groups in business decisions. It is true that business-men have by this time accepted the right of labor to organize, the duty of business to join with labor in collective bargaining, the desirability of conveying information to workers on company poli-cies, and even the advantages of limited participation of workers in decisions affecting working conditions. But the idea that workers and others should participate in business decisions generally has surely not been adopted by many American businessmen. Yet this idea is present, explicitly or implicitly, in many Protestant pro-nouncements on economic affairs.

The idea of broad participation in decision-making was an out-growth of the concept that *workers* should have a voice in matters affecting *them*. Once this idea was accepted, however, it was soon realized that almost all business decisions affect workers—whether they be decisions on wages, working conditions, output, methods of production, prices, location of plants, capital expansion, or any other. And so, it was argued that it is reasonable for labor to par-ticipate as a partner of management not only in decisions relating to wages and working conditions, but in all decisions. But then, it was further pointed out, not only workers but also consumers are affected by business decisions and their interests may differ from those both of management and labor. Therefore, consumers should be represented. Next, suppliers—of whom farmers are conspicuous examples—also were found to have a stake in business decisions. And thus justification was found for representation or participation of all interest groups in business decisions.

The businessman's viewpoint is that management should func-tion as a trustee mediating among the several interest groups, but that the power of decision-making should rest exclusively with management. But Protestant thought questions this solution. It is regarded as just another application of the familiar but discredited doctrine of benevolent use of power—a kind of neopaternalism. This doctrine is criticized on three grounds: (1) that the people of any class, regardless of their good intentions and of their sincerity, are inclined to view problems with vision distorted by their one-sided experiences and interests; (2) that genuine participation in decision-making by all interested groups is necessary if all points of view are to be reconciled or balanced; and (3) that participation is the only way to achieve responsibility, social harmony, and social solidarity.

I do not wish to leave the impression that there are many fully developed statements by Protestant writers of the theme of broad participation in business management. True, the idea is occasionally suggested explicitly[7] though without detail. But the idea is surely implicit in much Protestant doctrine on economic affairs. Even the perennial advocacy of the cooperative movement springs partly from the desire to place control of production in the hands of those who are affected by it.

[7] See for example: Evangelical Church, *Report on the Family, Public Morals, Temperance, and Sabbath*, 1934; Congregational and Christian Churches, *Resolutions and Minutes of General Council*, 1931; The Methodist Church, *Social Creed, Uniting Conference*, 1939; Federal Council of Churches, "Christianity and the Economic Order," *Information Service*, June 29, 1946, pp. 3-4; *Report of the National Study Conference on the Church and Economic Life* (Pittsburgh), Section II, Item 11.

6

The Businessman's Conception of His Social Responsibilities

There is no doubt of an increasing awareness on the part of businessmen that they have important obligations to society. The concept of "stewardship" is, of course, an old one, and many businessmen have been thinking in this direction. Only within the past few years, however, have large numbers of business leaders publicly acknowledged and actively preached the doctrine that they are servants of society and that management merely in the interests (narrowly defined) of stockholders is not the sole end of their duties. Indeed, discussion of the "social responsibilities of business" has become not only acceptable in leading business circles, but even fashionable. Many heads of major corporations have made eloquent and apparently sincere expressions of the obligations of business to society at large,[1] introducing a positive and constructive note into the social thinking of businessmen.

Prior to World War II, much of their social thinking had been reflected in attacks on the New Deal and on organized labor, with strong feelings of persecution and bitter resentment against the authors of new restrictions. During the war, however, the success

[1] In 1946, businessmen were polled by *Fortune* magazine regarding their social responsibilities. The following are two of the questions asked and the replies (*Fortune*, March, 1946, pp. 197-98):

"A few years ago it was frequently said that businessmen ought to acquire a 'social consciousness.' What was usually meant was that businessmen were responsible for the consequences of their actions in a sphere somewhat wider than that covered by their profit-and-loss statements. Do you think that businessmen should recognize such responsibilities and do their best to fulfill them?

"Yes, 93.5%; no, 1.6%; depends, 4.7%; don't know, 0.2%.

"About what proportion of the businessmen you know would you rate as having a 'social consciousness' of this sort?

None, 0.4%; less than 10%, 11.8%; about a quarter, 22.2%; about a half, 29.2%; about three-quarters, 26.7%; all, 3.0%; don't know, 6.7%."

of American business in meeting productive requirements was so spectacular that public attitudes toward business notably changed. And with continuing postwar prosperity, businessmen regained, in large measure, the respect of the community and their own self-confidence. No longer have they been so deeply troubled by the persecution complex which had colored their thoughts and actions in the years before the war.

Nevertheless, the experience of the 'thirties, combined with worldwide tendencies toward social control and socialization of business, has led businessmen to think deeply about the conditions which must be met if the private-enterprise system is to continue as the basic economic organization of this country. They have seen clearly that private enterprise would be accepted and could continue only if it demonstrably served society better than any alternative system. Passionately sincere in their belief that the private-enterprise system is superior to alternatives, their problem has been to consider how business should be conducted if it is to serve society well, and how to demonstrate that business does in fact serve society well. From this line of thinking emerged the new emphasis of businessmen upon their social responsibilities.

In this and the following chapter, I shall summarize the verbal statements of top executives in large corporations toward their responsibilities to society. In doing so, frankly, I shall not attempt to present all of the many views held by various businessmen or to indicate the proportion of businessmen who hold any particular view. I am not offering a business opinion poll based upon a scientifically selected sample. My purpose, rather, is to describe the thinking of a large and growing group of businessmen who are actively and articulately concerned about their role in society. The summary is based partly upon speeches, articles, annual reports, official testimony, and many other public pronouncements in which businessmen have professed their social ideals.[2] (The number of such documents runs into hundreds, perhaps thousands.) And it is based partly also upon numerous personal contacts with businessmen.

An analysis of this kind is open to criticism on the ground that it is impossible to distinguish the propaganda, the pious declara-

[2] A list of some of the businessmen whose published statements have been consulted is presented in Appendix B.

tions, and the rationalizations of businessmen from their genuine beliefs as expressed in their policies and actions. This criticism is plausible, but not wholly valid. The expressed views of businessmen are often reasonably consistent with their evolving policies and actions, and there is much evidence of sincere soul-searching and of attempts to think through the difficult problems of how to achieve a satisfying economic life for the masses of the people within the framework of private enterprise. No one would deny, however, that businessmen, like the rest of us, fall short of their professed ideals.

THE BUSINESSMAN'S ECONOMICS

A first step in understanding the businessman's conception of his social responsibilities is to examine his economic ideas. The businessman is an eloquent spokesman in our society for abundant production. In his view, it is axiomatic that the primary aim of economic life is an ever-higher standard of living; and, if we are to achieve this aim, that we must produce more and more and more.

Most of the businessman's economic ideas flow from his concern for production. For example, he almost uniformly opposes any measures or attitudes which conflict with productive efficiency. He believes strongly in research as a way of developing better methods, new products, and ultimately a higher standard of living. He is interested in high labor productivity and is concerned about any tendencies toward reduced output on the part of workers.

The businessman favors strong incentives toward higher productivity. He believes that profits provide the greatest and most dependable incentive to businessmen; that the prospect and possibility of "reasonable" returns on capital are essential as incentives to the maintenance and advancement of production. He believes also that profits are necessary as a source of capital for expansion. He would have workers at all levels paid according to their net productive contributions, not only as incentive to high productivity but also as a matter of simple justice. He believes also that there should be widespread opportunities for people to get ahead on the basis of demonstrated abilities.

The businessman's belief that production is the sole source of our high standard of living and that growing production is a prerequisite to economic progress also leads him to the view that the interests of the various classes of society—particularly those of laborers and capitalists—are fundamentally in harmony and mutual dependence rather than in conflict. Since higher real wages can be obtained, as he sees it, only through greater production, labor has as much interest as capital in promoting higher output. The businessman, therefore, is distressed when he finds that labor sometimes focuses its attention on the division of the output between capital and labor rather than on the total amount of the output to be divided. The businessman feels that his concept of the identity of interest between labor and capital is so important, and the concept of conflicting interest so fallacious, that he makes a great effort to "educate" his workers and the general public in these ideas.

When the objection is raised that the real wages of workers *are* related not only to the size of the pie but also to the manner in which it is divided, the businessman answers that "tools" are indispensable to production and that the effectiveness of labor is related to the kind and quantity of tools it has to work with. In order to provide the tools, capitalists must have an adequate incentive in the form of a good return. Moreover, a large part of the necessary capital derives directly from profits as they are plowed back into the business or reinvested by stockholders. Therefore, any attempt to raise wages at the expense of profits is likely to slow up the growth of production and, in the long run, to hurt labor both in terms of real wages and in terms of employment opportunities.

As part of his interest in growing production, the businessman believes that business must aggressively create the demands for an expanding output by means of advertising and other sales-promotion techniques. Business is not to wait supinely for demand to keep up with the possible rate of production progress, but is to prod it continuously. At the same time, business must sell its products at the lowest possible prices consistent with "reasonable" returns on capital. Only in this way will the fruits of technological advance be passed on to consumers and a growing market be assured.

The businessman believes in free enterprise on the ground that it provides the motivation, permits the flexibility, and mobilizes the imaginative energies required for a dynamic and progressive economy. By the same token, he believes in the efficacy of competition as a control on the individual enterprise. He also believes in free consumer choice. It is the job of business to produce products that will have consumer acceptance. He does not concern himself much with the kind of choices made by consumers, except in the market for his own product. He is content to let the consumer exercise his sovereignty and to adjust production accordingly. Consumer acceptance, therefore, becomes one of the tests of business success. The existence of a profit is an indication *prima facie* that the business has succeeded in producing something which consumers want and value. Free enterprise and free consumer choice are not only economically sound but absolutely indispensable to political freedom.

GENERAL VIEWS ON SOCIAL RESPONSIBILITY

In keeping with the businessman's production-oriented economics, he regards his primary responsibility to be the achievement of ever-expanding production. This calls for operating efficiency, research, incentives to worker productivity, growth of capital, aggressive sales promotion, and low prices. In achieving the goal of increasing production, the businessman regards the making of a profit as his first and foremost duty. To him, a business that fails to make an adequate profit is a house of cards. It cannot grow or provide more jobs or pay higher wages. In the long run, it cannot even survive. It offers no stability or security or opportunity for its workers and investors. It cannot meet its broader obligations to society. It is a failure from all points of view. If a business is to make a profit, and thus to avoid failure, it must produce goods that are attractive in quality and price, and it must produce them efficiently and at low cost. These are the primary responsibilities of businessmen, and, indeed, the primary conditions of being in business at all. Only then is a business in a position to consider its other responsibilities to society.

Having laid down this general principle, a considerable number of businessmen express the view that the directors of a corporation are trustees, not alone for stockholders or owners, but also for workers, suppliers, consumers, the immediate community, and the general public. According to this view, the board of directors should serve as a mediator, equitably balancing the legitimate interests of the several principal beneficiaries of corporate activity. The duty of the directors is to see that the interests of each group are fully recognized and protected. As early as 1929, Owen D. Young, then chairman of General Electric Company, expressed this view.[3]

Similar statements of this general idea have multiplied in recent years to the extent that this has become a widely prevalent theme in the thinking of American business leaders. One of the more thoughtful and complete statements of this idea was made by the late Lewis Brown, chairman of Johns-Manville Corporation, who said:

In the evolution of a complex industrial society the social responsibility of management has broadened correspondingly. Management no longer represents, as it once did, merely the *single interest* of ownership; increasingly it functions on the basis of a *trusteeship* which endeavors to maintain, between four basic interlocking groups, a proper balance of equity. Today the executive head of every business is accountable not only to his stockholders, but to the members of his working organization, to his customers, and to the public.[4]

In a similar vein, Clarence Francis, chairman of General Foods Corporation, has said:

Today, most managements, in fact, operate as trustees in recognition of the claims of employees, investors, consumers, and government. The task is to keep these forces in balance and to see that each gets a fair share of industry's rewards.[5]

The same note has recently been sounded by Beardsley Ruml, who also has interesting suggestions for its further implementation. Mr. Ruml referred to business as a system of private government of stockholders, suppliers, customers, and employees.[6]

These statements of leading businessmen—and many more such statements could be exhibited—clearly suggest the emergence of

[3] Quoted in John H. Sears, *The New Place of the Stockholder*, New York, Harper & Brothers, 1929, pp. 209-10.

[4] Quoted by Bronson Batchelor in *The New Outlook in Business*, New York, Harper & Brothers, 1940.

[5] Address at Annual Conference of Harvard Business School Alumni Association, June 12, 1948.

[6] "Corporate Management as a Locus of Power," Address to Conference on the Social Meaning of Legal Concepts, New York University School of Law, April 3, 1951.

a kind of managerial thinking in which social responsibility is a fundamental ingredient. Once the *sine qua non* of a reasonable profit has been attained, then, according to these views, it becomes the duty of corporate directors and mangers to conduct their enterprises with concern for all the interests affected. The function of management is one of mediation among these interests—to ensure that each gets a square deal and that the interests of no one party are unduly sacrificed to those of others.

This theory of managerial responsibility assumes (1) that businessmen have considerable latitude in determining their prices, costs, and operating decisions; and (2) that within the limits of this latitude, product prices, wages, salaries, prices paid to suppliers, dividends, reinvested earnings, and operating decisions should be set so that the interests of all parties may be equitably balanced. In this context, the businessman's vocabulary contains many phrases such as "low price for a product of good quality," "fair wages," "reasonable return to investors," and "sound growth of the company." So far as can be determined, the businessman seldom considers the precise meaning of these phrases. It is doubtful that many businessmen could supply criteria for determining when prices are or are not low; when wages are or are not fair; when the return to investors is or is not reasonable; etc. Nevertheless, the businessman thinks of these magnitudes as being determinable in part through business decisions rather than through the impersonal forces of the market, and he thinks of them as having ethical connotations which extend far beyond the narrow principle of profit maximization.

In line with this thinking, an increasing number of businessmen are beginning to regard management as a profession having underlying ethical principles and social responsibilities similar to the learned professions of medicine or law.[7]

[7] These ideas are thoughtfully expressed by Frank W. Abrams, chairman of the Standard Oil Company (New Jersey): "I would like especially to impress upon you my own feeling that business management in the United States is well on its way toward achieving many of the characteristics of a profession. It is recognizing the kind of responsibility to the community as a whole which all professions must see and acknowledge. The profession of medicine, without its observance of the Hippocratic Oath, would not have the integrity and standing which it enjoys. The profession of teaching, without the magnificent roster of great teachers and devoted men and women who have set an example to the world by their devotion to the idea of education, would not today have so fully

ALTRUISM VERSUS SELF-INTEREST

The protestations of businessmen regarding their responsibilities as trustees for the several interests affected by business operations do not necessarily derive from altruism. This is not to suggest that these ideas are advanced thoughtlessly or insincerely. They are advanced primarily because of a conviction that if business fails demonstrably to serve the interests of consumers, workers, and the general public it will be inviting repudiation in the form of deteriorated public relations, increased public control, and even socialization.[8]

---

won the confidence and respect of the world. The legal profession, without a history of public service, would not in any true sense be a profession today. It is my belief that technical education and training are not enough, if business managers are to have true professional competence. A clear sense of responsibility to and integration with the public welfare is a prerequisite to successful business management in today's complex world."—"What Top Management Expects of Collegiate Education," *Proceedings of the Golden Anniversary Convocation of the School of Commerce, Accounts and Finance*, New York University, 1950.

[8] This thought has been ably expressed by Mr. Frank W. Pierce, director of the Standard Oil Company (New Jersey): "It is becoming clear that in our modern society top management has the opportunity—in fact, I should say the duty—to act as a balance wheel in relation to three groups of interests—the interests of owners, of employees, and of the public, all of whom have a stake in the output of industry. Management can best represent the interests of ownership by acting fairly and wisely with respect to the claims of employees and public as well. It is a difficult but vital role. It seems to me only too obvious that the very survival of private enterprise requires that private enterprise act to maintain a productive and equitable relation among these three elements: the individual's right to, and the social necessity for, profits; the economic and human aspirations of all workers; and the public's demand for an abundance of goods at low cost. The alternative is plainly intensified industrial conflict followed by increased government regulation forced by an impatient public."— "Developing Tomorrow's Business Leaders," an address before the Cincinnati Chapter of the Society for the Advancement of Management, December 6, 1945.

Also Senator Ralph E. Flanders, who was for years a leading businessman, has also expressed this idea: "In this age of management, in which the manager enjoys power, material reward, and a feeling of satisfaction in exercising his experience and abilities, the preservation of his position must be to him and to his class a matter of serious consideration. That preservation can only come as a result of the sensitiveness of the members of the management class to their responsibilities as trustees for stockholders, for suppliers, for employees, and for their customers. Fortunately, the tradition on which this class has been developed is on the whole favorable to this sensitiveness. . . . As for myself, I do not believe that this recognition of the general interest involves the neglect of the private interest. I hold the opposite view and have a very simple reason. The private interest is involved in the public interest. If the public interest is not served, the

Some businessmen have frankly suggested that the unfriendly public attitudes toward business and the resulting vulnerability of the free-enterprise system are due to abuses on the part of businessmen in the past, or to an excessively narrow preoccupation with the interests of stockholders.[9]

The important point which more and more businessmen are seeing is that the climate of public opinion and of political forces within which business is operating today is drastically different from that of fifty or even twenty-five years ago. The experience at home of depression, war, and inflation, and the observation abroad of socialism and communism, have changed the criteria by which the operations of private business are judged. In Holmes' words, "Man's mind once stretched to a new idea never returns to its former dimensions."

The day of plunder, human exploitation, and financial chicanery by private businessmen has largely passed. And the day when profit maximization was the sole criterion of business success is rapidly fading. We are entering an era when private business will be judged solely in terms of its demonstrable contribution to the general welfare. Leading thinkers among businessmen understand this clearly. For them, therefore, the acceptance of obligations to workers, consumers, and the general public is a condition for survival of the free-enterprise system. Hence, even if the interests of stockholders

---

private interest ends in disaster. What we are faced with here is the distinction between short-range private interests and long-range private interests. As we grow in experience and intelligence, we see farther and farther into our long-range interests, and, except as we do this, our short-range interests will lead us into disaster."—*The Function of Management in American Life*, Graduate School of Business, Stanford University, 1948, pp. 8, 9, 51.

[9] Mr. Morris Sayre, president of the Corn Products Refining Company, has said:

"Let's be frank about it. If our predecessors in management, two or three generations ago, had devoted a mere modicum of their time to some individual soul-searching about their motives, about their good faith, about the responsibilities they owe to the people—we wouldn't be facing some of the tough problems we face today. . . . An active social conscience . . . and individual recognition of social responsibilities will compel us, as individuals, to test *every* managerial practice, measure *every* policy by a simple yardstick. Not 'What does it mean for me,' but rather 'What will this mean to my *workers* as *people*, to my *customers*, to my *suppliers*, to my *stockholders*, to the *community* in which my plant is located, to my *government*, to the *industry* of which I am a part, to the *economy* as a whole?' These tests, honestly made, of *every* individual managerial action, policy, and practice, will be evidence of true social consciousness."—"We Owe It to America," an address before the Congress of American Industry, December 3, 1948.

be taken as the sole aim of business, concern for broader social objectives becomes obligatory for management.

That the businessman's concern for his social responsibilities is rooted in self-interest does not in any sense detract from the credit that should be his for recognizing and acting upon his obligations. As history has shown repeatedly, it is all too easy for a social class to ignore changes in the world about it and to fail to adjust its outlook and its social functions accordingly.[10] If American businessmen prove to be adaptable to changing conditions and changing concepts of their social role, they should receive the highest commendation, even though such adaptation is entirely consistent with their own long-run interests. Moreover, the fact that socially constructive business behavior often is, or can be made to be, consistent with self-interest means that such behavior is more dependable than it would be if it were based upon altruism or even upon legal controls. Also, it is not necessarily a valid criticism of these new concepts of social responsibility that businessmen do not always in practice live up to their professed concern for the social interest. Businessmen are human. Like any of us, they sometimes engage in behavior that does not conform to their highest ideals. And not all of them are in agreement on ideals. But the fact that their ideals and their conception of their social role are changing is of the greatest significance, even though performance does not measure up in every case.

The changing viewpoint of businessmen is a vivid example of the power of public values and attitudes over economic life. The changing values and attitudes of the public have persuaded businessmen, in a decisive way, to reconsider their social role and the aims of their activity. This illustrates the strength of moral sanctions and suggests the method by which religious and other ethically motivated groups may exert a powerful impact upon economic life.

[10] In an address before a business group, Walter Lippmann has said that if any businessman "imagines that consideration of public policy can be treated lightly, improvised without prolonged study and consultation and self-examination, or settled by saying the hell with the New Deal, the hell with the labor unions, the hell with the Russians, the hell with the British, the hell with all foreigners, politicians, professors, theorists who do not have to meet a payroll, they are talking and acting exactly like all other governing classes who throughout history were on their way down and on their way out."—"Why an Inferiority Complex in Business Leaders?" *Commercial and Financial Chronicle*, November 29, 1945, p. 2606.

7

The Businessman's View of His Specific Responsibilities

We turn now to a discussion of the specific responsibilities which businessmen believe flow from this general concept of trusteeship.

EDUCATING THE AMERICAN PUBLIC

Almost all leading businessmen agree that one of their first responsibilities is to "sell" the American system of free enterprise and the ideology on which it is based. They believe that too few people understand how business functions or appreciate its contributions. As the former president of the Chamber of Commerce of the United States has said, on a plaintive note:

Why is it today, for example, that many people in this country are willing to admit that we make wonderful products, that the engineering and research departments of our various industrial concerns cannot be equalled anywhere in the world, that our finance men are giants in their own field, and that our sales organizations are superb—and yet they reject what we represent in toto?[1]

Moreover, businessmen believe that the public has been indoctrinated with mistaken economic ideas which underrate the importance of production and incentives to production. They feel that "business" has been under unfair and unsound attack by demagogues and that it has had a bad "press." They feel that people lack a passionate belief in our system. They believe that we are living in a world of ideologies in which enticing but deceptive theories of communism, socialism, and state planning of economic

[1] Herman W. Steinkraus, "The Job of Selling America to the Americans," an address before the National Sales Executives Club, February 28, 1950.

life are rampant, and that an unwary public may be led astray unless the ideology of free enterprise is attractively and convincingly presented.[2]

Businessmen themselves are deeply imbued with this ideology. They have unswerving confidence in the efficacy and superiority of the free-enterprise system. They believe, perhaps naïvely, that if only other people knew what they know and could have full access to the facts they are aware of, all sections of the public would stand shoulder-to-shoulder with them in defense of free enterprise. They believe that people lack this understanding because of the complexity of the economic system, which makes it difficult for them to understand it or their own personal places in it. They believe that the problem is further accentuated by the lack of face-to-face relationships between businessmen and workers or between businessmen and the general public. So they feel that if only people generally could gain some understanding of the businessman as a human being and some comprehension of his problems and his aspirations, their attitudes toward the business system would become more favorable.

Many businessmen recognize that they have not in the past been as assiduous as they might have been in cultivating good public attitudes toward the free-enterprise system. They feel that they have been too preoccupied with production, sales, finance, and other details of business and have neglected their functions in public relations. Moreover, they feel that businessmen as a group are too exclusive. They associate together socially and in trade associations, and their speeches are made to each other. They do not mingle or communicate effectively with other groups. As Frank W. Abrams, chairman of the Standard Oil Company (New Jersey) has said:

But self discipline and restraint by business management, essential though it is, is not enough if we are to succeed in reestablishing genuine public acceptance of our economic leadership. We must reestablish the common touch with our fellowmen. We must reappear in the role of warm-hearted human beings—which is what we are.[3]

[2] Cf. Alfred S. Cleveland, "N.A.M., Spokesman for Industry," *Harvard Business Review*, May, 1948, pp. 353-71.

[3] "The Businessman's View," in *How Can a Better Understanding of Our Economic System Be Fostered?* Committee for Economic Development, 1950.

The businessman's appraisal of the climate of opinion and attitudes within which he functions leads him to the conclusion that one of his foremost responsibilities (he often thinks of it as a responsibility to society) is to carry out a persistent and large-scale educational program to help create the kind of public understanding he seeks. Many businessmen think of their educational function as the teaching of sound economic principles to the masses of the people. As Paul G. Hoffman expressed it, businessmen should be "torchbearers of economic literacy." Businessmen feel that the education must be directed toward stockholders, workers, citizens of the communities in which business operates, consumers, government officials, and the general public. Only a small minority of businessmen express the thought that they themselves need some "education" toward appreciating more fully their social responsibilities and understanding the points of view of other groups in society.

The specific purposes of the educational efforts the businessman proposes are (1) to quicken the interest of stockholders in the companies they own and in the enterprise system generally; (2) to achieve better labor relations and greater labor productivity; (3) to achieve better public relations in the communities in which individual businesses operate; (4) to develop more favorable attitudes toward the individual companies and the enterprise system among consumers, government officials, and the general public; and even (5) to persuade foreign peoples of the advantages of capitalism. On the defensive side, these programs are intended to prevent governmental controls, to oppose the spread of socialism, to combat unfavorable publicity, and to counter political and other attacks on business.

On the question of how the educational job should be done, businessmen are not in agreement or they place emphasis on different techniques which are not mutually exclusive. A large group of businessmen apparently believe that the methods used in selling soap or television sets will be equally effective in selling the free-enterprise system and in purveying economic education. One finds frequent references such as the following: "It is a continuous selling job," "We must merchandise certain simple facts," "We should take people by their mental hands," "A down-to-earth simple approach will get results." In line with this conception of the problem, many conventional methods of selling and public relations are employed or proposed: for example, institutional advertising, glamorous company reports, speeches and forums, publicity, pamphlets, posters, plant tours, special programs for clergymen, teachers, and professors, etc.[4]

In this connection, the advertising industry has formed an interesting cooperative organization known as the Advertising Council. This Council, originally formed for the purpose of serving in the war effort during World War II, has since utilized advertising in support of many public and philanthropic activities. One of its functions is to interpret the American economic system to the public.[5]

Many business leaders feel that the "educational" or "communications" or "public relations" job is an inescapable responsibility of top management—one which cannot easily be delegated. A recent survey of a sample of large companies revealed that "54% of chief executives now play a part in communications to the plant community or the public as a whole, 40% take part in community affairs—local government, fund drives, and civic groups; 35% work at employee communications; 35% work within trade and business groups."[6] The same survey also shows that expenditures and activity in the field of public relations are on a rising trend.

On the other hand, a survey by Elmo Roper reveals a remarkable lack of interest on the part of stockholders, workers, and the general public in obtaining more information on the affairs of corporations. For example, only 11 per cent of stockholder respondents indicated that they would like additional information beyond what they are now getting, and less than half of the employee respondents indicated interest in obtaining more information.[7]

Some businessmen are less confident that the traditional methods of public relations are sufficient to do the job of winning the public

[4] Cf. Opinion Research Corporation, "Industry's Communications System—1950," *Public Opinion Index for Industry*, Vol. VIII, No. 10, October, 1950.

[5] Samuel C. Gale, "The Fourth Dimension of Advertising," *Proceedings of the Business Leadership Conference*, University of Washington, Seattle, 1950. See also "How Business Helps Solve Public Problems," *A Report of the Eighth Year of the Advertising Council*, March, 1949, to March, 1950.

[6] Opinion Research Corporation, *op. cit.*

[7] Elmo Roper, *A Report on What Information People Want About Policies and Financial Conditions of Corporations*, prepared for Controllership Foundation, Inc., 1948, Vol. I, pp. 19, 68-96.

over to the businessman's economic ideas.[8] Many businessmen feel that the persuasion must be based upon deed and example, that public relations are of no value unless they are founded upon high ethical standards and conduct in the social interest. Some feel that business must become less secretive about their activities and disclose full information to workers and to the public. Others feel that public relations begin at home in the sense that each company must pursue sound and ethical policies and must concentrate on communicating its own activities to the public rather than harping on abstractions like the "free-enterprise system" and the "American way." Some feel that a useful approach is to "make every man a capitalist" by promoting a widely diffused ownership of corporate securities. Others feel that economic education must be based upon sound research and facts. A notable effort along this line has been carried on by the Committee for Economic Development, an organization of businessmen and educators founded in 1942.[9] In practice,

[8] Frank W. Abrams has expressed this view: "It always seems rather sad to me that we of the industrial and business world deceive ourselves that we can 'make friends and influence people' through such things as paid newspaper advertising, pamphlets, and billboards. Some of that may help under certain conditions. But when it becomes the main channel of our effort, I think it is almost an insult to the intelligence of the average reader. We live our relatively sheltered and exclusive lives, away from the home folks, and expect that a paid notice in the paper will hold their loyalty and admiration for us and what we represent. 'Free enterprise, it's wonderful,' we say, and then we congratulate each other on what a swell 'ad' we have written. What I am trying to say is that I don't think that business has a chance to do the kind of job it honestly wants to do, and the kind of job for which it is trained and equipped—it does not have a chance to make its full contribution to the welfare of all, unless businessmen get out and sell themselves personally to the other major groups that make up the people of good faith in America. Part of that selling is the exercise of conscientious care and restraint in our businesses, and part is the simple matter of re-meeting the folks. I am sure that too few people really know those responsible in business organizations. We have gone too far down the road of setting up what might be called a business aristocracy, simply by mingling and talking only with ourselves."—"The Businessman's View," in How Can a Better Understanding of Our Economic System be Fostered? Committee for Economic Development, 1950.

[9] The C.E.D. gives as its basic objectives: (1) To develop, through objective research and discussion, findings and recommendations for business and public policy which will contribute to the preservation and strengthening of our free society, and to the maintenance of high employment, increasing productivity and living standards, greater economic stability, and greater opportunity for all our people. (2) To bring about increasing public understanding of the importance of these objectives and the ways in which they can be achieved.

the C.E.D. has devoted much of its energies to research and investigation which have provided the basis for its educational efforts.

Despite the great interest of businessmen generally in winning public approval, a few decry such efforts, declaring that what the public wants from business is goods and services of high quality at low prices, and that business is not engaged in a popularity contest. According to this view, business should follow "sound" practices—whether these practices are popular is a secondary consideration.

Most businessmen, even those who are not particularly concerned about general public relations, are interested in the attitudes of workers. They feel that one base for building better labor relations and enhancing productivity is worker education. In this connection, many companies are using various communication devices, among them formal courses in economics.[10] Great importance is attached to the functions of foremen and supervisors, who are the representatives of management having direct, face-to-face relationship with employees.

To summarize, there is little doubt that the great majority of leading businessmen are deeply concerned about public attitudes toward them and toward the free-enterprise system. They regard educational efforts toward modifying these attitudes as one of their primary obligations. Usually, they have conducted their educational efforts with dignity and without recriminations against opposing persons and dogmas. Their public-relations activities have on occasion served the useful purpose of informing the public about private enterprise and in correcting many half-truths or distortions which have been advanced by the opponents of private enterprise. Like all propaganda in the interests of a particular group, however, these efforts have fallen far short of telling an objective or unbiased story.[11]

[10] Other businessmen, however, are wary of obvious attempts to "educate workers"—not that they are opposed to the objectives, but that they question the means. They feel that such methods are likely to create antagonism and suspicion in the minds of workers.

[11] An interesting and critical analysis of the public-relations efforts of modern business is contained in the book *Is Anybody Listening?* by William H. Whyte, Jr., and the editors of *Fortune*, New York, Simon & Schuster, 1952. This book is based on a series of articles in *Fortune*.

HUMAN RELATIONS

Spokesmen for business are almost unanimous in recognizing that they have obligations toward workers. They conceive of these obligations not merely in terms of fair wages or "harmony" in labor relations. They are thinking also of the need for creating a sense of vocation among employees and for enhancing the degree of personal satisfaction derived by workers from their jobs.[12]

Businessmen, by the nature of their work, are faced with peculiarly difficult and trying problems of human relations. They are especially sensitive, therefore, to the idea that the great challenge of our age is no longer to achieve mastery over the physical environment, but rather to achieve humane and satisfying interpersonal and intergroup relations. In terms of business management, this means that human relations take precedence over the traditional problems of physical production, finance, and sales. As some businessmen put it, the problems of the future pertain to human values, not to costs and prices; it is the ability to make work rewarding that will count, not the ability to produce in the physical sense; we must overcome the "psychological curse of the assembly line" and the human costs of work simplification and minute division of labor.

But businessmen do not establish a dichotomy between good human relations and technical efficiency. They recognize that efficiency itself is dependent on the attitudes of workers as well as on the technical methods of production. Therefore, good human relations become not only an end that is desirable in the general social interest, but also a condition of efficient business operation that is in the interests of business from the narrow profit-seeking point of view. Wise human-relations policies are considered good social policy and good business.

Businessmen often express the view that the presently unsatisfactory nature of human relations in business is a result of several factors, among them, the complexity of our economic system, the large size of business operations, and our extreme division of labor. Under these conditions, the individual worker is unable to comprehend the social significance of his work, his job is often monotonous, and he lacks personal and face-to-face relationships with employers, customers, and others concerned with his work.

[12] Cf. Robert W. Johnson and others, *Human Relations in Modern Business,* New York, Prentice-Hall, 1949.

In analyzing the conditions necessary to good human relations, many businessmen have cited such needs of workers as the following: reasonable standard of comfort for worker and his dependents; reasonable security; justice, in the sense of fair play and square dealing; sense of self-respect, individual importance, personal worth, dignity; sense of accomplishment or perspective on the importance of the job in the totality of economic life; sense of belonging to an organization, playing an important part in its success, and participation; enjoyment—pleasure, satisfaction, fun—from work itself; opportunity to get ahead; opportunity for personal and cultural development.

Almost all businessmen are agreed that the wants and needs of workers extend far beyond wages, and that it is a responsibility of management to take the initiative in giving workers the things essential to make of work a satisfying and rewarding human experience.[13] Many businessmen recognize the obvious—but often neglected—fact that work is a large part of life, and that if life is to be good, the job which takes up so much of a lifetime must also be good. Some businessmen suggest that research should be devoted to the problem of human relations in exactly the same way and on the same scale as to engineering methods, product development, and marketing.

Many businessmen think of their enterprises as "a group of people working together." They want the group to function as a team and to be imbued with the kind of institutional morale that is associated with team spirit. They want this both because they think it is good for their workers and because it is good for efficiency.

Businessmen frequently turn then to the question of how these things are to be provided. Pleasant, healthful, and safe working conditions are taken for granted as necessary. For some business-

[13] Cf. Bill of Rights for workers as stated by James C. Worthy of Sears-Roebuck & Co. (reported in *Chicago Tribune*, September 22, 1949):

"1. The right of every man to be treated as an individual and respected as a person

"2. The right of every man to a voice in his own affairs, which includes his right to contribute to the best of his ability in the solution of common problems

"3. The right of every man to recognition for his contribution to the common good

"4. The right of every man to develop and make use of his highest capacities

"5. The right of every man to fairness and justice in all his relations with his fellows and superiors"

men, this involves locating as much of the production as possible in smaller cities and towns in order to provide more healthful and wholesome community life for workers. Measures to increase worker security, such as reduced seasonal fluctuations, guaranteed annual wage, career employment, retirement plans, life and sickness insurance, etc., are also spreading. Beyond these, businessmen are increasingly emphasizing two objectives: to "personalize" business, and to provide abundant opportunity for individual self-development and advancement.

The personalizing of business requires, in the opinion of many business leaders, an all-out effort to establish face-to-face relationships and a friendly atmosphere within the company. Businessmen feel that they should present themselves in the role of "warmhearted human beings." Managers, supervisors, and foremen should be friendly people who impart qualities of kindliness, understanding, consideration, respect, and fairness. Workers should be accepted as associates. Personnel policies should be backed up by attitudes toward workers that are "right," and known by workers to be "right."

Businessmen attach great importance to the provision of opportunity for the individual worker to develop his own powers and abilities and to get ahead. One may suspect that the businessman reflects his own background and personality in his emphasis on *opportunity*. It may be that, typically, he is the kind of person who values opportunity and "getting ahead" more highly than the average worker. At any rate, he feels strongly "the obligation to keep the door of opportunity open to all," or "the right of every worker to a chance to get ahead," or "the right of every worker to develop the best that is in him." He feels that he has a moral duty to recognize and encourage talent and to see that it has an opportunity for expression. This is to be done by careful job selection, promotion, incentives, decentralization of decision-making, and education. Some businessmen, but by no means a majority, see the problem of opportunity as partly one of eliminating discrimination based on sex, race, religion, national origin, social position, connections, physical appearance, etc. They point out that talent is not restricted to any particular group or class and that the business enterprise must be an example of democracy in action in the sense of providing equal opportunity for all.

In their concern with human relations, businessmen sometimes express one caution, namely, that business must not become too closely involved in the private lives of people. Workers should have the right of privacy in their personal lives and should be free from meddling in their personal affairs. In this connection, businessmen are alert to the pitfalls in old-fashioned paternalism.

Local Community Relations

Closely associated with the businessman's interest in educating the American public and his concern for human relations is his interest in community relations. The corporation is regarded as a citizen and neighbor in the local community (or communities) in which its establishments are located; hence, it has the obligations and duties of a good citizen and a good neighbor. This involves participation by officials and employees in community activities pertaining to government, education, religion, recreation, etc., and financial support of these activities. There is a growing tendency for businessmen to advocate the giving of company time for community activities and to support them from company funds.

But community activities are thought of not only in purely altruistic terms. Businessmen feel that a good reputation in the community is good business. It enhances employee morale and general public relations. It helps to create a favorable labor supply in the community and to enlist the cooperation of community leaders and public officials.

Relations with Government

The relation of business to government (federal, state, and local) is a subject of deep concern to businessmen. However, there is among them a wide diversity of opinion on the question of how good relations should be cultivated. On the one hand, there are those who feel that it is the businessman's duty to influence public policy toward the interests of business and toward the preservation of the free-enterprise system. This includes the duty of opposing policies of control or restriction on business and of supporting policies of freedom and aid to business. For many businessmen it also includes trying to get specific advantages for particular businesses and particular industries. Others decry the tendency of businessmen to go to Washington "hat in hand" trying to get special benefits at public expense. A small group of businessmen are recognizing their obligation to use their influence in seeking public policies which will make the economic system work better from the point of view of all classes—not merely from the point of view of business. The Committee for Economic Development has been in the vanguard of this type of thinking.

Most businessmen feel that individually they have an obligation to become more informed and more active in public affairs, and that they should give time and thought to government according to their talents and abilities. They feel that businessmen have something unique to offer in public life and that their voices should be heard. In this connection, they feel that the trade association and the paid lobbyist are not adequate substitutes for the direct participation of businessmen themselves, who, they feel, have the ability and the obligation to offer leadership to the American people.

As part of their relations with government, businessmen universally acknowledge an obligation to engage in production for national defense. They are, in fact, proud of their achievements and abilities in this field, and often express the view that America's world leadership is dependent on the enormous productivity of American business.

PRODUCTIVITY, EFFICIENCY, AND EXPANSION

In accordance with the businessman's production-oriented economic thinking, he tends to feel that rising productivity, efficiency, and expansion of output are high on the list of his social responsibilities. He believes that business has an urgent obligation "to be a productive and creative force in society"; that it must "build, expand, and pour forth goods in abundance." He feels this way because he knows that rising standards of living must be based ultimately upon greater production, and also because he knows that in a growing society more and more jobs must be created if there is to be full employment.

To achieve the desired expansion, businessmen look to research, reinvestment of profits in new tools and equipment, aggressive sales promotion, provision of incentives for workers, and initiative and imagination on the part of managers. Some of them also express the desirability of continually lowering prices so that the increased output can be readily marketed.[14]

ECONOMIC STABILITY

Businessmen know that the vulnerability of the private-enterprise system is due primarily to the fact that it is subject to violent fluctuations in employment and production. Consequently they are alert to the need for finding ways of mitigating this instability while at the same time preserving the essentials of free enterprise. No businessman, so far as I know, supposes that economic stability can be achieved fully or satisfactorily through the voluntary efforts of private companies. However, many businessmen feel that the individual enterprise should contribute to general economic stability by stabilizing its own operations as fully as possible.

They believe especially that individual businesses should try to level out seasonal peaks and valleys. They recommend for this purpose accurate sales forecasting and production scheduling, seasonal variations in inventories, diversifying products, stimulating sales in off-seasons, appropriate timing of introduction of new models, etc. Some businessmen favor the guaranteed annual wage or guaranteed annual amount of work in order to transmute seasonal stability of the firm into psychological security for the worker.

On the question of the contribution of private companies to greater cyclical stability, businessmen are less definite. Many of them express the idea that business (or business and labor) should do something about it, but few come up with concrete suggestions. Those who do propose the following ideas: that sales and advertis-

[14] "People in this country want better things, better-made things and better-looking things, and they want to pay less for them, so they may enjoy more of them. That, reduced to simple terms, is the American way of life. We must remember the significance in this country of a Ford automobile selling for around five hundred dollars. We must remember the significance of F. W. Woolworth's five-and-ten-cent store concept. More things for more people, selling in vast quantities at relatively low prices, providing millions of jobs to people who make and sell them. But do we understand that the key to the whole equation is low prices and greater aggregate profit produced by lesser unit profit spread over more articles made and sold? Sometimes I wonder whether either business or labor understands the nature of the American goose and its golden eggs." Jack I. Straus, "The Responsibilities of the Businessman to the Consumer," in *Responsibilities of Business Leadership*, H. F. Merrell, editor, Cambridge, Harvard University Press, 1948, pp. 53-54.

ing expenditures be increased in time of depression and reduced in time of prosperity; that restraint be exercised in price and wage policies during periods of inflationary boom; that deferrable expenditures (e.g., for plant maintenance) be made during periods of slack business; that investments in new plant and equipment be made, so far as possible, in times of slack business, etc. As businessmen well know, these are counsels of perfection and it is not always possible for individual businesses—which have their own survival to consider—to behave in ways that are good from the standpoint of general economic stability. Nevertheless, there are possibilities of some accomplishment in these areas, and many businessmen are earnestly considering how their own policies might be adapted to the social requirements of economic stability.

COMPETITION

Businessmen express a wholehearted belief in competition. They are incredulous when they are told by economists and public officials that there is a widespread lack or "imperfection" or "impurity" of competition. Businessmen almost uniformly regard themselves as engaged in keen and unrelenting rivalry with other existing firms, and as being in potential rivalry with incipient new firms which are always ready to spring up when there is opportunity to turn an honest dollar. With this attitude, it is not surprising that businessmen believe in the efficacy of competition as a control over their activities and therefore often make statements in defense of competition as a principle. They regard competition not only as a regulator but also as a driving force, and they are opposed—in principle at least—to restrictions on competition. On the other hand, they often express approval of "orderly markets," "fair competition," and "live and let live," and they sometimes regard antitrust enforcement as persecution.

CONSERVATION OF NATURAL RESOURCES

Businessmen in the extractive industries are faced directly with the conservation problem. They are inclined to admit that the past record of business in the use of natural resources has been less than illustrious, but they prefer to emphasize the improvement which they feel has been achieved during the past generation and to suggest that more progress is in sight. They are agreed that wise and careful use of natural resources is a social obligation. They differ as to what constitutes wisdom in this regard, and they often oppose governmental measures for conservation; but at least the obligation is acknowledged.

CONCLUSIONS

Our survey of the opinions of leading businessmen regarding their social responsibilities leads to certain conclusions.

First, there is widespread and sincere interest in the subject.

Second, the pronouncements of businessmen regarding their general responsibilities (e.g., the concept of trusteeship for several interests) are frequent and eloquent. But businessmen are noticeably less articulate about the specific duties which flow from these general responsibilities. The new theories of the role of business in modern society are in a relatively primitive or formative state. Because of their newness and because of the intricacy of their implications, these theories have by no means developed into full-blown plans of action. This suggests that businessmen have much hard thinking and soul-searching ahead of them. It also suggests that they will need professional guidance in translating their general aims into concrete policies and actions. Such translation, since it would point up the practical implications of the general aims, might of course have the effect of modifying the aims themselves.

Third, the fact that businessmen are so unanimous in their belief in the need for public education implies that, in their opinions, the required adjustments are two-directional. On the one hand, businessmen must adjust their operations to the needs of society at large; on the other hand, society must develop attitudes and policies more favorable to business.

Fourth, the great concern of businessmen for better public relations, which they hope to achieve both by "education" of the public and by adoption of socially oriented policies, indicates the power of public opinion over business and suggests the efficacy of control or influence over business by means of moral sanctions exerted by an alert and articulate public. A change in the climate of opinion—

without any change in formal controls—can doubtless exert great influence over businessmen.

Fifth, in spelling out their specific responsibilities, businessmen give noticeably more attention to those obligations which are clearly in their own long-run interest than to those which are not so clearly advantageous to them.[15] For example, they give great emphasis to developing better public relations, and to increasing productivity and efficiency. Doubtless, these are all desirable from the social point of view, but they are preeminently desirable from the point of view of business. When businessmen are concerned with general economic stability, they think of it in terms of the stability of their own operations—which has a strong flavor of self-interest. Those who advocate a low-price policy do so not only because it is good social policy but also because it is good business in the long run. The number who express concern about things which are not so clearly in the business interest are relatively few.

The fact that businessmen are interested in those responsibilities which are affected with the long-run private interest as well as the public interest should be cause for neither surprise nor regret. Rather, it should be a source of profound satisfaction that the private and the social interest are found to be coincident over significant areas, because action in the social interest is doubtless more reliable when it is reinforced by the private interest. The fact that businessmen consider certain actions which are in the social interest to be also in the long-run self-interest is due not to a sudden conversion of businessmen, but rather to a change in the climate of public opinion within which they are operating. It is self-interest in a new setting. The things that are expected of businessmen today—and which they, therefore, regard as their responsibilities—are based upon a shift in public attitudes regarding business and its role in our society. This implies that, under the pressure of public opinion, businessmen can be persuaded to accept new duties and obligations which today they do not accept simply because the public does not expect them to be accepted. The means of achieving higher morality in business behavior is to create public attitudes which enlarge the moral responsibilities of business. Once this is done, business, with its new and broadened concern for public approval, will respond.

[15] Cf. Alfred S. Cleveland, *op. cit.*

8

Why Are Businessmen Concerned About Their Social Responsibilities?

Many businessmen are concerned about their social responsibilities and are giving serious thought to the question of how their social obligations—as they see them—may be fulfilled. Not everyone will agree that businessmen on the whole see their obligations clearly or fully, but many of them are sincerely interested and are seeking to relate their activities to social ends.

The interest of businessmen in their social responsibilities is also expressed in policies and actions. Business today is more humane and more fully attuned to social needs than it was twenty-five or fifty years ago. The following are some recent examples of American business policies carrying distinct overtones of social interest. I would not suggest that these policies are devoid of private interest, or that they have been adopted without strong social pressures, or even that all of them have been successful or have served the social end implied. I would submit, however, that these policies represent earnest attempts of private business to discharge its social obligations.

American business as a whole has a magnificent record of cooperation with the government in war and defense production.

Many companies have deliberately held prices below the market level during the postwar inflation, and some have even reduced prices in the face of inflationary demands.[1]

Many businesses have worked out effective codes of ethics designed to improve their business practices and have developed and strengthened these codes over the years.

Great progress has occurred in overcoming misrepresentation and adulteration of products, short weights, and other similar sharp

[1] There may be some question whether this was genuinely in the social interest.

practices. Better Business Bureaus, Chambers of Commerce, and other voluntary agencies have carried on effective work in this field.

Individual companies have made great efforts to improve working conditions, to reduce hours, to give vacations, and to provide greater security to workers against old age, sickness, and unemployment.

Unions have been recognized and the right of workers to organize and bargain collectively has been widely accepted.

Individual companies have shown increasing concern for the human problems of workers, to regard them as persons, to treat them with dignity and respect, and to consult with them on the affairs of the enterprise.

In some companies, discrimination among workers on the basis of sex, race, and religion has been reduced.

The atmosphere of secrecy in business has given way to fuller reporting and accounting to workers and the public.

Businesses have actively supported community activities such as education, welfare programs, and recreation.

Businesses have become more actively interested in the conservation of natural resources and have improved methods in the use of these resources.

Some companies have considered social factors in the location of new plants and the abandonment of old plants.

Definite and constructive efforts have been made to smooth out seasonal and other variations in the rate of production and employment, and some compromises have provided guaranteed annual employment or wages.

Many companies have tried to avoid speculative accumulation of inventories.

Important efforts have been made to smooth out variations in the rate of investment in new plant and equipment and in the maintenance of existing plant and equipment.

Business practices in the field of consumer credit, insurance, and mortgage lending have been greatly improved.

Business practices relating to the flotation of securities and reorganization and promotion of companies have improved.

Commercial bankers have cooperated in voluntary credit control.

Business leaders have organized the Committee for Economic Development for the objective study of public policy.

These are solid accomplishments. To appreciate their significance, it is necessary only to read the literature about the attitudes and practices of business during the "muckraking" period at the beginning of the century and to read some of the more discerning writings of the 1920's.[2] It can be said with some justice that many reforms were achieved only with great reluctance on the part of businessmen and only under extreme pressure exerted by public opinion and by government reflecting that opinion. It can also be pointed out that many companies have been laggard in these developments, and that in many aspects of business operations improvement is still urgent. It is even possible that any relaxation of pressure on business will bring a reversion to former acquisitive and antisocial tendencies. Yet the fact remains that remarkable progress has been made, and that most of the new developments have become assimilated into the beliefs and behavior patterns of businessmen. The businessmen's attitude toward labor unions provides a good example of the change. Originally, they opposed—vigorously and indignantly—the rise of unions. By now many of them have reached the conclusion that unions are here to stay and that the job ahead is to learn to live with them.

To say that businessmen have shown, both by word and by deed, that they are more concerned about their social responsibilities and more responsive to the public interest does not imply that the millennium has arrived. It means only that progress has been made and that it is perhaps not unreasonable to expect more advancement along the same lines. But to understand the change in business attitudes, it is necessary to consider the factors that have been responsible for the change. As one would suspect, there have been many complex and interrelated forces at work. The changed outlook does not represent a sudden, and therefore temporary, conversion to a new faith, but is the product of hard experience over a long period of years.

EVOLUTION OF AMERICAN SOCIAL IDEALS

Perhaps the most basic explanation of the new business ethos has been the marked evolution in the underlying social ideals of the

[2] Cf. Edward N. Saveth, "What Historians Teach About Business," *Fortune*, April, 1952, pp. 118-9, 165-74. This article suggests that the "muckrakers" may have overstressed the undesirable features of earlier big business in America. The current interest of economic historians in "business history" may provide a new point of view on the "robber barons." See also "The Moral History of U. S. Business," *Fortune*, December, 1949, pp. 143ff.

American people. In the last fifty or seventy-five years, humanitarian concern for the individual human being has become widespread. There has been increasing interest in the ideals of opportunity, justice, freedom, security, plenty, dignity, and personal development—all these for the common man. After centuries of struggle against the age-old curses of social inferiority, injustice, tyranny, poverty, insecurity, and squalor, the masses of people have come to hope and believe that through the powers of science, technology, education, and democracy a new and better life for them is possible. They have come to believe that a high standard of living, including comforts and luxuries, need not be the exclusive right of the privileged few. Moreover, they have become conscious of their power to bring these things about through political and collective group action. Accordingly, reforms—hopefully designed to make the American dream come true—have been insistently demanded.

These ideas were reinforced by the advancement of the scientific knowledge of society. Facts were gathered and disseminated on the distribution of income, the extent of poverty, the degree of malnutrition, the incidence of tuberculosis, the state of housing and sanitation, the conditions of labor, discrimination among persons, illiteracy, crime, mental disorder, and other social problems. As a result of developments in transportation and mass communication, thinking about social problems was extending beyond the neighborhood and community to the whole country and the whole world. The concept of the good neighbor and responsibility for individual welfare was extending from the immediate family or the local area of man-to-man contact to the nation and even the world. It was recognized that the fate of individuals was determined not alone by their own initiative, hard work, and "goodness," as suggested by Calvinist doctrine, but also by powerful social forces beyond their personal control. At the same time students of society and public investigating bodies were advancing proposals pointing toward reform. As measures to deal with these problems became more systematic, a new professional group, the social workers, came to a position of influence. Various special-interest groups, each attempting to promote the welfare of its members, became powerful elements in society, chief among them the labor unions and the farm organizations. Novelists and other literary figures gave powerful support to the movement.[3] Politicians, sensing the drift of public opinion, attacked the "old order" and advocated reforms. And, throughout, the aspirations of the American people were undoubtedly raised as a result of universal public education.

Since many of the evils under criticism were associated with the economic system, and since the economic system was dominated by business, the business system and the businessmen were subjected to systematic and relentless attack. "Wall Street," which was regarded as the general headquarters and nerve center of the business system, became a symbol of predatory power.

During the period of national expansion, personal frustration and social pressures had been greatly alleviated by the continuous presence of new lands in the West. The closing of the frontier removed an important safety valve in American life and turned people's attention toward social reform as a way of securing the good life. The economic maturity of the country also led to the rather sudden realization that rich natural resources had been exploited with careless extravagance and that much of the remaining resources (other than farm land) had fallen into the hands of business firms and wealthy individuals who were using them to make large incomes. The resultant of these factors was increased antipathy toward business and widespread interest in the "conservation" of natural resources through various measures involving public control or ownership.

During a few short years in the 1920's, when the country was both prosperous and hopeful that the war to end wars had been fought, the agitation for social reform subsided, and businessmen found themselves again in a position of apparent security and power. This happy state was destined, however, to an abrupt and undignified end in 1929, and dissatisfaction with the existing order reached its climax in the great depression of 1929-40. The events of that unhappy period were clear evidence to everyone that all was not right with the economic system and that reforms were in order.

Reform in a Hurry. At this time, the combination of obvious problems requiring solution and the effective popular leadership of the Roosevelt administration combined to quicken the impulses

[3] John Chamberlain, "The Businessman in Fiction," *Fortune*, November, 1948, pp. 134-48. See also Max Lerner, "The Historian, the Novelist, and the Faith," *New Republic*, December 6, 1948, pp. 16-20.

of the American people toward social idealism and social reform. Economic problems became a primary concern and a major topic of discussion. It was at this time that long-advocated measures were enacted with bold successive strokes in the fields of social insurance, relief, banking, finance, conservation, public works, fiscal policy, taxation, housing, child labor, collective bargaining, etc. The misery and insecurity of the time were largely ascribed to the inefficiency of a business system operated without appropriate governmental controls. The idea of laissez faire, already suspect, lost much of its popular appeal. Businessmen became objects of public abuse, and there was talk of "driving the moneychangers from the temple."[4]

Yet the march of the common man in the United States was generally directed toward demands for relatively mild reforms, and the temper of the country remained generally favorable to modified free enterprise. Only a few discontented groups on the fringe of society seriously advocated more drastic measures such as Marxian socialism. But in other parts of the world, the socialist movement, in its various forms and guises, was a growing threat to the free-enterprise system, and in at least one great country thoroughgoing socialism was an established fact. American businessmen began to comprehend the forces leading toward socialism in various parts of the world and to recognize that they might one day be threatened in the same way unless the trend of social thought were somehow redirected and unless the operation of the free-enterprise system could be modified so as to meet the aspirations of the American people more fully. Indeed, many businessmen interpreted the New Deal as the entering wedge of socialism.

Revival of Respect. But with the onset of World War II, the political fortunes of business changed perceptibly. Just as the Great Depression demonstrated for all to see certain crucial and almost

---

[4] "The fickle public, terrified by unemployment and resentful of depression, drove out its old idols from the temples. Like savages who must blame even the breaking of a fishline on some evil spirit, the American people began a great witch hunt for the crooked businessmen who had caused the Great Depression. As if honest concerns had not failed with the dishonest, and as if ignorance and stupidity were not infinitely more important than fraud! The businessman never fully returned to his position of prestige. Shaken of self-confidence by a decade of considerable losses, lampooned by novelists, harassed by government and labor, pounced upon by the courts for violation of anti-trust laws he had forgotten existed, it is little wonder that he was dyspeptic before the war."—P. A. Samuelson, *Economics*, 2nd ed., New York, McGraw-Hill Book Co., 1951, p. 95.

fatal weakness in the business system, World War II demonstrated with equal clarity that the business system, if given adequate demand, could perform miracles in producing goods and services. The magnificent wartime record of American business restored much of its former prestige. With the continued prosperity following the war, businessmen have again been able to hold their heads high and to proclaim that the system of private enterprise is neither moribund nor antisocial. It cannot be said, however, that past suspicions and past antagonisms toward the business system are dead or even dormant. The lessons of the Great Depression have been engraved indelibly upon the memories of the American public. There is much apprehension that the present prosperity, based upon government spending for defense, is artificial and ephemeral, and that one day the old problems of depression, unemployment, poverty, and insecurity will return to haunt us.[5]

The evolution of American attitudes—so briefly sketched here—has had a double effect upon the businessman. On the one hand, it has created a social environment and a set of public attitudes which constantly threaten to produce more governmental and social controls over business. In this atmosphere, it has behooved the businessman to consider his actions carefully from the point of view of their objective social effects and from the point of view of public reactions to them. On the other hand, the businessman is a person sharing with all other members of the society a common social environment and common influences. Therefore, he has come to assent in his own way to the newer social ideals and has participated in the struggle to realize them. His acceptance of these ideals has caused him to formulate his policies and to appraise his actions in terms of new and more humanitarian standards than his predecessors would have applied fifty or seventy-five years ago. In short, the businessman has been subjected to pressures originating from the new social climate in which he operates, and at the same time he himself has assimilated many of the values and attitudes that are characteristic of this new social climate.

The critic may hold that the new social concern of businessmen

[5] For recent surveys of public attitudes toward American business, see Elmo Roper, "The Public Looks at Business," *Harvard Business Review*, March, 1949, pp. 165-74; and Survey Research Center, University of Michigan, *Big Business from the Viewpoint of the Public*, Ann Arbor, 1951.

is long overdue and derives solely from the pressures and threats and insecurity to which he has been subjected in past decades. There has been no change of heart but only a belated recognition of the realities of the modern situation. This view, in my opinion, overlooks the fact that the businessman is not wholly isolated from our society but is a part of it. He is subjected to many of the same influences—education, religion, radio, the press, literature, personal contacts, etc.—as are other members of society, and he cannot escape the impact of these forces upon his own character. To say that businessmen, as a class, are not interested in freedom or security or stability or meaningful work or comfort for the masses of the people just is not so. True, there are individual businessmen without much social perspective or idealism, but so are there workers, farmers, teachers, and even clergymen without adequate perception of or concern for these things.

To conclude, the evolution of American social ideals has been a basic force leading businessmen toward increasing concern for their social responsibilities. But other related forces have also been at work.

The Labor Movement

The rise of organized labor in membership and power has constituted a direct challenge to businessmen. At first the tendency of many of them was to resist. Some of the more sordid examples of stupid and ruthless behavior on the part of businessmen have occurred in their dealings with organized labor. But eventually, businessmen were taught the futility of belligerent antagonism. And from their experiences in labor relations, businessmen were able to learn much about the needs and aspirations of workers and about their own consequent responsibilities toward workers. This is not to say that all businessmen have turned over a new leaf or that businessmen generally are delighted at the prospect of sharing some of their power, more or less permanently, with unions. It does mean that realistic businessmen—and most of them are realistic—have come to the conclusion that unions are here to stay, that control over wages and working conditions must be shared with unions, and, more important, that the needs and aspirations that have given rise to unions are on the whole legitimate and worthy of consideration. This represents a dramatic change.[6]

BUSINESS AND GOVERNMENT

An influence of great importance upon business thinking in the past twenty years has been the growing number of first-hand contacts of businessmen with government. The NRA did have at least one effect of outstanding and lasting significance. It inaugurated a practice of widespread participation of businessmen in government—a practice which has developed along many lines. As we have moved through the various "emergencies" growing out of depression, war, and inflation, businessmen have been organized into scores of advisory committees, individual businessmen have been asked to testify or to consult on problems of particular industries, and thousands of businessmen have served the government either as civilian employees or members of the armed forces—some of them in important jobs. The high point of this participation was reached during World War II, in OPA, WPB, and the armed forces; but the practice has been continued following the war and is growing rapidly today under the administration of President Eisenhower.

Working with government provided a broadening experience for many businessmen. Although usually called into government because of their knowledge of particular industries, businessmen were frequently forced to think—sometimes for the first time—about the relations of their particular firms and industries to the needs and problems of the whole country. This was a new and vital experience, and it inevitably influenced their thinking in relation to their own business decisions. It is true that many businessmen scoffed at Washington with its "confusion," "waste," and "bureaucracy"; and that some businessmen used their entree to government with cynical disregard of all but their own interests. Yet the great majority were sincere in their desire to help, and they were visibly moved by the broader perspective they obtained when

[6] Correspondingly, the attitudes of labor and of labor leaders have changed over the years, especially as unions have won recognition and security and as the methods of collective bargaining have become more fully institutionalized. Cf. T. W. Kheel, "Defense Asset—Labor Stability," *The New York Times Magazine*, July 1, 1951, p. 27.

they were able to view their own businesses and their own interests from the vantage point of a government of all the people.

BUSINESS EDUCATION

Professional education for business is a relatively new phenomenon in American colleges and universities. The first school of business was founded at the University of Pennsylvania in 1881 and the second at the University of Chicago in 1898. By 1910, there were fourteen such schools and by 1925, there were 183. Today, approximately 600 colleges and universities grant degrees in business,[7] and the number of business executives who have been trained in business schools runs into the thousands.

As collegiate business education has been finding its place in American life and adjusting to changing conditions, educational objectives have been modified, and there has been continuous experimentation in content and method of instruction. Today, the philosophy of business education is still somewhat ambiguous and there are important differences in point of view and practice among various institutions. In particular, there are differences as to the relative emphasis placed upon technical subjects, such as accounting, salesmanship, advertising, and secretarial skills, as compared with the "liberal" subjects, such as economics, government, psychology, history, natural sciences, and the humanities.[8] And there are differences in relative emphasis on the "case" or "problem" approach and on the systematic "textbook" approach. A great majority of business educators, however, agree that a relatively broad education is desirable for business leaders in modern society, and that an indispensable task of the business school is to prepare future business leaders to comprehend their social role and to accept their social responsibilities.

Business schools have unquestionably contributed both directly and indirectly to the recognition among businessmen that their decisions and policies are of deep social concern and that they have

[7] J. Hugh Jackson, "Business Education and Business," *Proceedings of Business Leadership Conference*, University of Washington, 1950, p. 25.

[8] The American Association of Collegiate Schools of Business requires of its members that "At least forty percent of 120 credit hours or its equivalent required for the bachelor's degree must be taken in subjects other than economics and commerce."

important obligations to society. And they have been pioneers in this respect—as the earlier literature on the philosophy of business education clearly shows.[9]

The writings of business educators, in which they express their educational philosophies, almost uniformly refer to the need for helping students to obtain an understanding of the economy and of the society within which business functions, and an appreciation of the position of businessmen in the social order. This is desirable, it is held, for two reasons.

First, such knowledge is helpful in making practical business decisions that are actuated by the profit motive. Many of the difficult problems facing business today arise out of the relations of the enterprise to the total economy, to labor organizations, to government, and to the public at large. They are by no means always problems of exclusively internal management. In guiding the destiny of companies, therefore, businessmen must understand and be alert to the manifold social forces which increasingly influence or control their activities. Broad knowledge and perspective are essential even to the pursuit of self-interest.

Second, an understanding of the economy and of the society is required if the businessman is to comprehend the economic repercussions and the social significance of his decisions. Only through such understanding is it possible for him to act intelligently in his efforts to meet his social responsibilities. For example, an understanding of the problem of economic instabilty is necessary if he is to adjust his own operations to promote economic stability; or an understanding of the needs, aspirations, and motivations of labor is necessary if he is to help in creating more satisfactory human relations and working conditions. Many business educators feel that the businessmen of tomorrow should be informed particularly on human relations, business fluctuations, government, public finance, international relations, and general economic theory.

Many business educators believe that management is becoming, or should become, a *profession*. They maintain, therefore, that a basic function of the business school is to provide a professional training that imparts a knowledge of the social functions of business

[9] For one of the fullest discussions of the subject, see James H. Bossard and J. Frederick Dewhurst, *University Education for Business*, Philadelphia, Press of the University of Pennsylvania, 1931.

enterprise and a code of ethics in which the social interest occupies a prominent place.[10] The more advanced views of business educators have been summarized by President Conant of Harvard: "As never before, business needs men who appreciate the responsibilities of business to itself and to that unique society of free men which has been developed on this continent. Such men must understand not only the practical workings of business organizations, but also the economic and social climate in which business operates; they must be as well trained as our professional men in law and medicine."

MATURITY OF OUR LARGE CORPORATIONS

Another factor explaining the businessmen's growing sense of responsibility is the increasing maturity of our large corporations. In modern America, large corporate enterprises, each employing thousands of workers and millions of dollars worth of capital, together constitute a substantial fraction of the total economy.

Most of these enterprises have come into existence and attained prominence and large size within the past seventy-five years. Often they were started as relatively modest enterprises and developed into giants through the processes of expansion and merger. Most of them went through an earlier period of striving for leadership, a period when they were "on the make." Today most of these companies are firmly established, well known in the market, adequately financed, led by talented men, and in possession of assured sources of supply.

[10] The following are some of the statements of business educators on the philosophy of business education: Robert D. Calkins, "Objectives of Business Education," *Harvard Business Review*, October, 1946, pp. 46-57; Robert D. Calkins, "Aims of Business Education," in *Education for Professional Responsibility*, Carnegie Institute of Technology, Pittsburgh, 1949, pp. 47-60; Donald K. David, "Business Responsibilities in an Uncertain World," *Harvard Business Review* (supplement), May, 1949; E. E. Day, *Social Responsibilities of Business Education*, Ann Arbor, University of Michigan Press, 1949; *The Challenge of Business Education* (papers published in celebration of the fiftieth anniversary of the founding of the School of Business of the University of Chicago), Chicago, University of Chicago Press, 1949; "The Study of Economics in Schools of Business," *American Economic Review* (supplement), December, 1950, pp. 107-24; H. S. Bossard and J. F. Dewhurst, *University Education for Business*, Philadelphia, Press of the University of Pennsylvania, 1931; L. C. Marshall (ed.), *The Collegiate School of Business*, Chicago, University of Chicago Press, 1928. See also the Proceedings of the Annual Meetings of the American Association of Collegiate Schools of Business.

They are, in short, *mature* companies. They have achieved a certain control of their destinies, a kind of security in the competitive struggle—a security which they did not enjoy in earlier times and which many smaller or newer companies do not have today. This is not to say that these large companies no longer feel competitive pressures or that they are immune from risks and uncertainty. It implies only that they have a degree of security for the future which is denied to newer and smaller companies struggling for places in the business firmament.

The established position and security of large companies is sometimes characterized, less charitably, as "monopoly power." It is held that these companies have elements of monopolistic (or more accurately oligopolistic) control over their outputs and prices even though they may be confronted by actual or potential rivals in the same fields, may face the competition of substitute products, and may be subject to the risks of technological change. Doubtless there is some validity in this view. It is my impression, however, that the security and stability of these companies rests not so much on their monopoly power as upon the excellence of their leadership, personnel, and plant; upon their assured access to natural resources, to capital, and to technology; and upon their ability to adapt to changing conditions through research and long-range planning. All of these things are cumulative in the sense that once an enterprise has become large and successful, it is easier for it to command the talent, resources, and capital necessary to maintain that position. If monopoly exists, it consists more in the monopoly of talent, organization, and resources than in monopoly of a market.

The important point, for our present purpose, is that in the United States there are several hundred large corporations which have achieved a relative degree of security. These corporations together make up a large section of the total economy. Their influence is felt through an even wider sphere in the business world because of their contacts with suppliers, customers, and competitors and because of their preeminent leadership in business practice.

These companies, because of their relative security, are in a position to take a long-range view of things—to plan their operations not for immediate or temporary gain but for the long run. For some purposes, the long run may be very long since these corporations are expected by their managers to exist indefinitely in the future and thus to have a kind of immortality. This is not to say that managers of large companies ordinarily plan for objectives that are centuries away. It does mean that they tend to think in terms of periods much longer than those which seem pertinent to smaller and newer companies whose overriding objective may be to meet next month's payroll or to stay in business until after the next Christmas rush.

Obviously, there will be many exceptions to any generalizations about the planning horizons of large, mature companies as compared with those of small or new companies. There are doubtless many small or new companies that have the security and stability necessary for the long view; and there are old mature companies that sometimes must live from hand to mouth. But, in general, a relatively long-range view is more characteristic of our corporate giants than of smaller or newer companies.[11]

Another feature of the large well-established companies is that their top managements can afford the luxury of philosophizing about their social role. Moreover, because of their large size, they can think in terms of the effects of their decisions upon the total economy and on society, and can overcome the quite understandable tendency of lesser companies to think only of the effects of the total economy on them and to regard their decisions as inconsequential so far as the public welfare is concerned. Economic philosophies have been constructed chiefly by the successful. Improvements in business practices have appeared where some security in the competitive struggle has been attained. Peter Drucker has declared that big corporations are able to have "a policy and to have a special policy-making body which is sufficiently far removed from the actual day-to-day problems to take the long view, and to take into account the relationship between the organization and society."[12]

[11] An excellent illustration of this is to be found in the debate over logging practices in the Pacific Northwest. The larger lumber companies are willing to manage their operations in cooperation with the U. S. Forest Service, on the basis of continuous yield. They are in a position to take the long view and are financially able to wait for returns. The smaller operators, on the other hand, needing an immediate return and lacking the incentive or the capital to plan into the indefinite future, are often opposed to the continuous-yield plan. Cf. E. S. Mason, *Review of Economics and Statistics*, 1949, p. 105.

[12] *Concept of the Corporation*, New York, John Day Company, 1946, pp. 226-7. Cf. Clare E. Griffin, *Enterprise in a Free Society*, Homewood (Ill.), Richard D. Irwin, 1949, pp. 91-92.

Another feature of the large, well-established, and well-known company is that it tends to be constantly in the public eye. Its activities are news. When a new labor contract is negotiated by General Motors, when United States Steel raises its prices, when Weyerhauser Lumber acquires a new tract of timber land, when the New York Central Railroad abandons some trackage, when the du Pont Company markets a new synthetic material, when the Standard Oil Company (New Jersey) develops a new foreign source of petroleum, these things are reported in the newspapers and discussed everywhere. They often become objects of Congressional inquiry and editorial comment. The decisions of such companies are scarcely less private than the Acts of Congress or the proclamations of the President.[13] Obviously, companies operating under such a consistent glare of publicity are bound to think about public reactions to their decisions, which is tantamount to considering how these decisions affect the public interest.

The above comments on the effect of maturity are not in any sense to be construed as necessarily a defense of either business or monopoly. A big company with monopoly power may be, on balance, a threat to the social interest even though its management does think about the broader implications of its decisions and even though it considers long-term interests more fully than do smaller companies. Nevertheless, bigness and maturity and security do tend to shape business thinking toward broader and longer-range implications.[14]

---

[13] Cf. J. M. Clark, *Social Control of Business*, 2nd ed. New York, McGraw-Hill Book Co., 1939, pp. 32-51; and W. H. Hutt, "The Sanctions for Privacy under Private Enterprise," *Economica*, August, 1942, pp. 237-44. See also E. M. Voorhees, *Address Before the Controllers Institute of America*, September 21, 1943.

[14] Cf. George Katona, *Psychological Analysis of Economic Behavior*, New York, McGraw-Hill Book Company, 1951, pp. 206-9.

9

Why Are Businessmen Concerned About Their Social Responsibilities? (Continued)

In this chapter we shall consider several more factors responsible for the greater interest in social responsibilities. These factors derive primarily from changes in the organization and control of corporate enterprise during the past fifty to seventy-five years. So we shall begin with a brief discussion of the much-publicized "separation of ownership and control" in the large corporation.

SEPARATION OF OWNERSHIP AND CONTROL IN THE LARGE CORPORATION

A phenomenon frequently noted by students of industrial organization has been the widespread separation of the functions of ownership (in the sense of legal title to equity capital) and control (in the sense of direction or management) within the large corporation.[1]

This development was the result of the great diffusion of ownership of corporate securities as our corporations grew to many times the size that could be financed by single individuals or small groups of individuals. Indeed, one of the classic advantages of the corporate form of organization is that it provides a method for pooling the capital of many individuals into a single enterprise. With this diffusion of ownership, sometimes among hundreds of thousands of persons, the stockholders increasingly confined their concern with "their" corporations to the price of shares on the stock market and to actual or prospective earnings. They were in no position to

[1] The classic analysis of this tendency is found in A. A. Berle, Jr., and G. C. Means, *The Modern Corporation and Private Property*, Chicago, Commerce Clearing House, 1932. Earlier writers referred to a somewhat different aspect of the same phenomenon by the term "absentee ownership." Cf. Thorstein Veblen, *Absentee Ownership*, New York, Viking Press, 1923.

gain access to the facts necessary for judging the conduct of the business and they were not interested in taking an active part in management even if they were able to do so. As a result, and with the aid of proxy voting, effective control of our large corporations passed largely into the hands of professional salaried managers.[2]

If most large corporations have come under the control of professional salaried managers, as most authorities agree, does a corporation under this type of control respond to different motives, or react to given events, in a different way from a corporation under the control of owner-managers? On this question, the authorities are not in clear agreement. There are those who hold that the professional managers align themselves, on the whole, with wealthy and conservative people, and that their social philosophies and their conception of the proper role of business (especially regarding profits) are very similar to that of the wealthy classes. Indeed, many of these professional managers are themselves wealthy men. Therefore, it is contended that whatever other importance may be ascribed to the separation of ownership and control, one should not leap to the conclusion that it has an important effect upon the overt behavior of the corporation.[3] In discussions of the motivation of managers, it is pointed out, moreover, that they have a strong sense of identification with the corporation and its welfare. They regard the corporation as "their" company or as an extension of their own personalities.[4] Their motives are in many ways similar to those of owner-managers.

The opposing view is that the assumption of corporate control by salaried managers does have a significant influence upon the behavior of the corporation and may be expected to have an even greater influence in the future.[5] Few writers, however, with the possible exception of Burnham, have ascribed overwhelming im-

[2] Mr. James Burnham in *The Managerial Revolution*, New York, John Day Company, 1941, expanded this idea into a whole theory of future social organization. See Walter Lippmann, *Preface to Morals*, New York, The Macmillan Company, 1929, pp. 254-59, for an excellent early account of this process; also, John H. Sears, *The New Place of the Stockholder*, New York, Harper & Brothers, 1929.

[3] Cf. N. S. Buchanan, *The Economics of Corporate Enterprise*, New York, Henry Holt & Company, 1940, pp. 443-49.

[4] Cf. George Katona, *Psychological Analysis of Economic Behavior*, New York, McGraw-Hill Book Company, 1951, p. 197.

[5] The most complete discussion of this subject is to be found in the able study by Professor R. A. Gordon, *Business Leadership in the Large Corporation*, Washington, Brookings Institution, 1945. Cf. also, Berle and Means, *op. cit.*, p. 355.

portance to this change. Let us now examine the basis for the view that the rise of a new salaried managerial class has (or will have) an important influence on the behavior of the corporation. This may be conveniently discussed under four headings: (1) selection of managers, (2) motives of managers, (3) professionalization of management, and (4) broadened participation in decision-making.

SELECTION OF MANAGERS

In an earlier day, managers were self-appointed by virtue of their having obtained enough capital to set up in business, or by virtue of having inherited this capital or even the business itself. (This is, of course, still true of smaller companies.) Today, the salaried managers of the large corporations are usually selected on the basis of their training, experience, and demonstrated competence to administer business affairs regardless of the amount of capital they have amassed or inherited. This process of selection is sometimes said to produce on the whole more humane, more intelligent, and more far-seeing managers than were obtained under earlier methods of selection based upon wealth and inheritance—although definite evidence on this subject is difficult to obtain.

Neither the ability to get rich nor the accident of inheritance is necessarily correlated with the qualities required for able and far-seeing management or for management with one eye on social responsibilities. On the other hand, it is not evident that salaried managers would necessarily have more concern for the social interest than owner-managers. They might conceivably be simply more efficient than owner-managers in pursuing narrow profit motives—particularly in view of the fact that they tend to identify themselves closely with their corporations.

But there is more to the story than this. The modern manager is a symbol of his corporation. His appearance, personality, beliefs, and methods express to the employees, customers, stockholders, and the public at large the character or spirit of the corporation. Therefore, his selection tends to be influenced by the kind of character which the "corporation" wishes to present or feels it must present to the public. There is a tendency for those men to be selected as managers whose backgrounds and whose thinking make them acceptable to the various groups who are affected by the corporation, among them customers, stockholders, suppliers, workers, government officials, and the general public. In a sense, these various interest groups have a kind of indirect voice in selecting the manager. The particular type of executive appointed will tend to be determined by the nature of the various interests and pressures impinging upon the corporation at a given time. At present, with the existing climate of opinions and pressures to which business is subjected, the executive is likely to be a man who is more concerned about the broader aspects of management and who is more attuned to the social implications of his job than was the manager or owner of an earlier day.

MOTIVES OF MANAGERS

Little is known, systematically, about the motivation of the salaried managers who lead most of our large corporations. Almost everything written on the subject tends to be in the form of interesting hypotheses or casual observations rather than scientifically demonstrated fact. Nevertheless, the subject deserves consideration.

The manager, and indeed most other people, tend to regard the corporation as an entity distinct from the persons and things of which it is composed. The legal fiction that a corporation is a "person" has become a psychological reality. Just as a sea captain often thinks in terms of the personality of his ship, which he designates as "she," the manager views the corporation as an entity endowed with personality of its own. It is an object which has needs and aspirations, which experiences many of the vicissitudes of life, and to which one can give selfless devotion and unswerving loyalty. Moreover, the manager thinks of the corporation as having a kind of immortality in that it goes on—or should go on—indefinitely into the future. He thinks of his own leadership of it as temporary. One of his deepest concerns is to see that it prospers under his care. It is as though the corporation were engaged in a perpetual relay race, and that he, the manager, is running with the baton for one lap.

This description of the manager's attitude suggests an almost mystical relationship between him and the corporation. Indeed, there is an element of mysticism present when an institution is endowed with the attributes of life, personality, and even immortality. And it is only this mysticism that explains the intense devotion, loyalty, and personal identification that men bestow on this most mundane of institutions, the business corporation.

The manager feels that the concept of "welfare" can be applied to the corporation itself—as distinct from the people who supply its capital and labor or who consume its products (though, of course, he recognizes that the welfare of the corporation is bound up with the welfare of these people). He considers it his primary duty to advance the welfare of the company.

At first thought, the manager's interest in the corporate welfare may seem inconsistent with the frequently expressed idea that he is (or should be) a trustee mediating among the interests of stockholders, workers, consumers, suppliers, the general public, etc.[6] One suspects that the trusteeship is enunciated by managers in their more philosophic moments and that their real focus of interest is the corporation as such rather than the people affected by it. Yet, paradoxically, the concept of the corporation as an independent entity has probably been a necessary step in the transition to the new idea of trusteeship. The corporation, as originally conceived, was a creature of the stockholders and was presumed to exist solely to serve stockholder interests. When managers and others began to think of the corporation as an entity with interests and a life of its own, this was in effect a break with the traditional view that only the stockholder counted. It then became possible, as a next stage of development, to think not only of the welfare of the corporation but also of the impact of the corporation upon the various groups affected by it, of which the stockholders are only one.[7]

Managers do not frequently use the word "welfare" in describing their goals for the corporation, but they do often use the word "success," which means to them about the same thing. In general, they think of a successful corporation as one that (a) initiates new ideas, new methods, and new products; (b) produces efficiently; (c) has a smoothly running organization; (d) improves and enlarges its facilities, increases its employment, and expands its output; (e) achieves stability, security, and survival; (f) advances

[6] Cf. Chapter 6, pp. 48-9.
[7] Cf. "Communication, Problem for the Front Office," *Fortune*, May, 1951, p. 156.

the welfare of its workers and the public welfare; (g) enjoys a good reputation; and (h) makes a satisfactory profit.

Profit is mentioned last in this list of the criteria of success, not to show that it is least important, but rather to emphasize that the goals of managers for the corporations they control are multiple goals. To be sure, managers are interested in profit.[8] They are interested in it partly for itself, partly for its symbolic significance, and partly because it is a necessary condition to the attainment of the other goals. But they are interested in more than profit. When a businessman says that "Company X is doing a good job," he means much more than that the company is making a large profit. He means that the company is successful according to many of the above criteria. To describe a company which has merely made a large profit, he will say, "Company X made a lot of money last year." This statement carries quite different, and distinctly less laudatory, connotations.[9]

As has been ably shown by Professor Katona,[10] the profit motive is highly complex. A simple statement that managers try to maximize corporate profits, as is frequently assumed in economic theory, is almost meaningless. The concept of profit is a highly tenuous one in that it involves the valuation of assets, the allocation of joint costs, the treatment of developmental expenses, and a host of similar problems for which there are no easy or definite solutions.[11] The idea of profit maximization raises the troublesome question of the time period over which profits are to be maximized, and it is difficult for either managers or observers to calculate the effect on profits of given actions which may affect the business indefinitely in the future. Obviously, businessmen are often deterred by custom and by ethical principle from exacting the highest possible profit. The businessman may forgo profits to avoid the demands of organized labor, or public regulation, or entry of new firms. Busi-

[8] Cf. Perrin Stryker, "P and C for Profit," *Fortune*, April, 1952, pp. 128-29, 156-62; and Keith Powlison, "The Profit Motive Compromised," *Harvard Business Review*, March, 1950, pp. 102-8.

[9] Cf. "Communication, Problem for the Front Office," *Fortune*, May, 1951, pp. 154-56.

[10] *Psychological Analysis of Economic Behavior*, New York, McGraw-Hill Book Company, 1951, pp. 193-210.

[11] For a more complete discussion of profits, see Chapter 16, below. Cf. Joel Dean, "Measurement of Profits for Executive Decisions," *The Accounting Review*, April, 1951, pp. 185-96.

nessmen often show greater interest in business volume and business expansion than they do in profits. Interest in profit probably varies among firms. It is greater in the struggling, unprofitable company than in the solid, successful one—for the obvious reason that at least a minimal profit is a first condition for survival and for the attainment of the multiple goals of the company.[12] Similarly, the interest in profits varies from time to time: "There are some indications, but hardly any reliable data, that in the nineteenth century in the United States the appreciation of higher profits was more pronounced than now. . . ."[13] Also attitudes toward profit may vary with phases of the business cycle.[14] In short, the concept of maximum profit, or any single-valued motivational pattern, is probably unrealistic as applied to businessmen's goals for their companies. They are interested in profit and strive for it, but they want the company to be successful also in other respects, as noted above (pp. 88-89). Many of these goals are contributory to profit but they are also valued for themselves.

It may be more realistic to describe the quest for profit as a seeking for "satisfactory profits" rather than maximum profits ("satisfactory" defined in relation to the profit experience of other firms), the goal of maximum profits paradoxically being more characteristic of the struggling or unprofitable company than of the strong and powerful company.[15] Let us now turn to the motives of the manager as a person.

In view of the manager's close identification with the corporation, his motives are dominated by the desire to achieve success for the company—success being defined in terms of the criteria mentioned above. If his company is successful, then he becomes known among his peers and associates—and perhaps among the general public—as a successful businessman. Much of his ego-satisfaction and his prestige derive from this identification with a successful company.

---

[12] An indication that maximum profit is not necessarily the primary goal of business firms is that when firms experience losses, they almost universally find ways of cutting costs. Cf. A. R. Oxenfeldt, *Industrial Pricing and Market Practices*, New York, Prentice-Hall, 1951.

[13] Katona, *op. cit.*, p. 209.

[14] Cf. Moses Abramovitz, "Monopolistic Selling in a Changing Economy," *Quarterly Journal of Economics*, 1938, p. 201.

[15] Katona, *op. cit.*, pp. 201-2. See also, R. A. Gordon, "Short-Period Price Determination in Theory and Practice," *American Economic Review*, June, 1948, pp. 265-88.

He takes pride in its achievements. Also, there is no doubt that his work provides the satisfactions of self-expression, of creative workmanship in his chosen profession, and of power.

Personal financial reward (in the form of salary and other executive compensation) is important to him as something desirable in itself and as a symbol of his station in life. However, it does not necessarily dominate his desire for the success of his company or transcend his other motives.[16] The earnings of managers are not necessarily correlated closely with the success of their companies. But there is unquestionably a marked relationship between executive compensation and company success. Therefore, on the whole, the manager's interest in financial return is reasonably consistent with his interest in the success of the company. There is surely little basis for the view that managers operate companies primarily for their own financial gain. As Professor Katona says:

> If all motives were ego-centered, one might argue that the managers strive to maximize their own salaries or remuneration. The objective of getting the highest possible profit for oneself from the corporation's activities, that is, the objective of "milking" the company one directs, may prevail in one or the other exceptional instance, but it is contrary to the institutional pattern prevailing in our economy.
>
> Furthermore, this objective is contrary to psychological principles of group belonging.[17]

Financial return is probably less important to the modern manager as a means to public recognition than it was to the tycoon

[16] In 1907, Alfred Marshall gave a most discerning paper on the motivation of businessmen: "The Social Possibilities of Economic Chivalry" (*Economic Journal*, March, 1907, pp. 7-29). He said that businessmen care more for wealth as an indication of successful achievement than as something desired for its own sake, and that the ablest and best businessmen value success rather than money. The problem, as he saw it, is to find devices, other than money, for rewarding and honoring business achievement. "The discriminating favour of the multitude at Athens and Florence gave the strongest stimulus to imaginative art. And if coming generations can search out and honour that which is truly creative and chivalric in modern business work, the world will grow rapidly in material wealth and in wealth of character. Noble efforts could be evoked; and even dull men would gradually cease to pay homage to wealth *per se* without inquiring how it had been acquired. . . . Sordid practices would then prevent wealth from yielding that social *éclat* for which sordid men chiefly prize it, and would go out of favour with men of ability and common sense, however devoid of high principle" (p. 26). Compare also, William Smart, *Second Thoughts of an Economist*, London, The Macmillan Company, 1924, pp. 172-81.

[17] Katona, *op. cit.*, p. 196.

of another era. New devices have been created to give him the honorific distinction which the tycoon achieved through being rich and displaying his wealth. The manager's status is today well displayed regardless of his personal wealth. This is accomplished partly through the elaborate symbolism of richly paneled offices, lush office furnishings, private elevators, private dining rooms, and corps of assistants and secretaries. It is accomplished in part through the services of the expert public-relations man who helps to advertise his accomplishments and to "build him up" into a public figure. His participation in public affairs, his appearances before Congressonal committees, his conspicuous role in trade associations, his work on boards and committees of philanthropic organizations—all serve to give him the recognition that the tycoon of 1890 could get only by building a castle on upper Fifth Avenue or endowing a hospital. Moreover, and perhaps most important, the business leader has attained enormous prestige in American life. The older idea that a commercial career is in some way inferior to a career in one of the learned professions has all but disappeared. There is scarcely a more glamorous role in modern society than that of business leader in a large corporation.

All of this suggests that personal financial remuneration is not necessarily a dominating motive of managers and that it surely is not their sole motive. If further evidence of this is needed, it can be provided by examining the effect of income taxes levied at steeply graduated rates. There has been, of course, much discussion of the effect of these relatively new taxes on the incentives of businessmen. Those who have opposed these taxes or advocated their lowering have consistently predicted that levies such as those now in effect would seriously weaken, if not destroy, the zeal of our business executives.[18] Obviously no such thing has happened.[19] The

[18] This argument assumes, of course, that the newer taxes are borne at least in part by the businessmen on whom they are levied. The increases of salaries to executives may, of course, have offset the taxes in part. Cf. Thomas H. Sanders, *Effects of Taxation on Executives*, Harvard University, Division of Research, Boston, 1951.

[19] "Within recent years, present income tax rates have been frequently and somewhat irresponsibly attacked on grounds that they stifle incentive, initiative, and productive effort. Although a few isolated instances are cited, the deterrent effect of these rates is by no means self-evident. During the very period in which the allegedly excessive rates have been in effect, the number of new businesses established has been at an all-time high; the rate of new capital formation has been beyond anything in our history; the competition among business executives

effect upon businessmen of steeply graduated income taxes has been not to stifle incentive but merely to direct it away from money reward toward other types of reward. With the present tax system it is not always easy to demonstrate success by the amount of money one can keep after taxes or the wealth one owns; so men find other ways, ways that are quite as satisfying and quite as effective, to achieve recognition. The basic motives have not changed. They are still dominantly the desire for recognition of successful achievement. But success is being displayed in ways that do not require great wealth, and so the motivational importance of large financial return has diminished.[20]

One may conclude that the personal financial incentive for managers has been weakened and that other incentives have been strengthened. Increasingly, managers rate themselves and are rated by others on the basis of achievement rather than on the basis of dollars accumulated. In this sense, management is gradually acquiring some of the attributes of the professions. This is not to say that managers are no longer interested in money. No doubt money is still and will continue to be a first-rate motive, but it is not and need not be the *sole* motive.[21]

PROFESSIONALIZATION OF MANAGEMENT

The art of management has increasingly become a subject for study and research by disciplined and disinterested investigators and scholars. The early work in this field is associated with the name of Frederick W. Taylor, who made path-breaking studies of efficiency, especially in the art of cutting metals. Taylor's most im-

---

for promotion to top positions is fully as great as it has ever been; the appearance of new products and the adoption of new methods of production have been rapid; the rate of over-all economic activity has never been greater, and there is little observable tendency for businessmen to retire in advance of the normal retirement age. As a matter of fact, it is more common for leaders of industry to suffer coronary attacks—presumably produced by an excess of incentive—than it is for them to let down because taxes are too high."—H. R. Bowen, *Annals of the American Academy of Political and Social Science*, November, 1949, pp. 119-20. See also "Why Executives Drop Dead," *Fortune*, June, 1950, pp. 88-91, 149-56.

[20] Salary before taxes retains, of course, considerable prestige value and important symbolic significance.

[21] Cf. J. A. Hobson, *Poverty in Plenty*, London, George Allen & Unwin, 1931, p. 90; also, F. W. Taussig, *Inventors and Money Makers*, New York, The Macmillan Company, 1915.

portant contribution, however, was not the particular results of his studies but his approach. He showed that the problems of business might be studied with an effort for the same objectivity, with the same rigor, and with many of the same methods as are common in the laboratories of physical sciences.

In time, many more investigators applied themselves to the problems of business, and their interests were eventually broadened to include not only productive techniques in the factory and offices but also problems of sales, advertising, finance, records, accounting, inventory control, quality control, employee selection and training, job analysis, worker morale, incentives, collective bargaining, public relations, and administrative organization. The effect of these studies, as they have accumulated from the modest beginnings of a half-century ago, is to persuade businessmen (1) that there are efficient and inefficient ways not only of cutting metals but also of meeting problems of business relations; (2) that efficient methods are less costly and therefore more profitable than bad methods; and (3) that the efficient ways may be more easily and surely discovered through the proven methods of painstaking experiment and disinterested observation than through following rules of thumb or uninformed prejudice.

It may be argued of course that the study of management is just another way of prostituting science, and that its contribution is only to teach businessmen to become more skilled in the manipulation of things and persons to their own ends. There would be truth in this if it were not for the fact that the scientific studies have shown that good human relations in industry and good performance require, among other things, that workers be accorded the sense of dignity, vocation, justice, participation, etc., which every humanitarian wants them to have. A businessman when told on Sunday by his clergyman that these things are moral imperatives may retort: "What does he know about business?" But when told these same things by his own efficiency expert or a leading professor from the Harvard School of Business, with facts and figures to back them up, he tends to be impressed.[22]

As a result of the development of an intellectually based technique, the practice of management is becoming an art for which

[22] Cf. Edwin G. Nourse, *The 1950's Come First*, *New York*, Henry Holt & Company, 1951, pp. 65-67.

one must prepare himself through education and experience. The education need not be formal education; yet increasing numbers of younger men are preparing themselves for managerial roles by study in schools of business, and more and more junior executives are studying for positions of greater responsibility by attendance at the many institutes, night classes, and company training programs now being provided. In short, there is a more or less systematic body of knowledge which one must acquire before one is qualified to fill a managerial position in a large corporation. This is not to say that one may learn to become a successful manager by reading books any more than one can become a great physician by reading books. In both cases, certain personal qualities and long years of experience are required. Nevertheless, formal knowledge, though not the whole story, is a practical necessity.[23]

An intellectually based technique is only one of the characteristics of a *profession*. By this criterion, business management is rapidly assuming the form of a profession. However, there are other characteristics of full-fledged professions: (1) the members of a profession tend to be organized into responsible associations which set standards for admission to practice; (2) these associations exert social control over the practices of their members through codes of ethics; and (3) the practitioners assume a relationship of responsibility with their clients.[24]

On the basis of these three latter criteria, it is obvious that business management hardly qualifies as a profession on the same plane with medicine or law. Certain specialized aspects of business management, notably accounting and engineering, have achieved full professional status, but management itself falls short. However, there are clear tendencies in the direction of professionalization.

[23] Cf. F. W. Taussig and C. J. Joslyn, *American Business Leaders*, New York, The Macmillan Company, 1932, Chapter 17; *Fortune*, February, 1940, p. 61; R. A. Gordon, *op. cit.*, p. 324; William Miller, "The Requirement of the American Business Elite," *Quarterly Journal of Economics*, May, 1950, pp. 242-53; E. C. Bursk and D. T. Clark, "Reading Habits of Business Executives," *Harvard Business Review*, May, 1949, pp. 330-45; "The Tycoon is Dead," *Fortune*, September, 1951, p. 184.

[24] Paul Meadows, "Professional Behavior and Industrial Society," *Journal of Business of the University of Chicago*, July, 1946, p. 150. See also A. H. Carr-Saunders and F. A. Wilson, *The Professions*, London, Oxford University Press, 1933; R. H. Tawney, *The Acquisitive Society*, New York, Harcourt, Brace & Howe, 1920, pp. 91-122; and Talcott Parsons, "The Professions and Social Structure," *Social Forces*, May, 1939, pp. 457-67.

The luxuriant growth of trade associations, Better Business Bureaus, Chambers of Commerce, and service clubs has resulted in important efforts to influence business practices, though these organizations do not yet presume to enforce standards of competence for entry into the practice of business management.[25] And the relationship of business to its clients (customers) has surely moved some distance from the old principle of *caveat emptor* to responsibility for an honest product at an honest price.

Carr-Saunders and Wilson, in their study, *The Professions*, have shown that historically the professionalization of various occupations came "with growing intellectual technique and with the need for regulation of the activity."[26] Not more than a century or two ago, the art of healing, now the classic example of a professionalized occupation, was more primitive, more anarchic, more unorganized, and more uncontrolled than modern business management. With the development of an intellectual technique and the need for regulation, medicine gradually acquired its present advanced state of professionalism. And so business may well be on its way toward professional status. Today the difference between business and the recognized professions is one of degree rather than kind.[27]

The eminent jurist, Louis D. Brandeis, as long ago as 1912, was advocating that business should eventually become a profession:

. . . success in business must mean something very different from mere money-making. In business the able man ordinarily earns a larger income than one less able. So does the able man in the recognized professions—in law, medicine, or engineering; and even in those professions more remote from money-making, like the ministry, teaching, or

[25] The Society for the Advancement of Management has recently appointed a Committee on Business Codes. This committee is planning a survey of existing business codes and hopes to develop a "basic management code." See also, Ralph H. Heilman, "Ethical Standards in Business and Business Education," in *The Ethical Problems of Modern Finance*, New York, Ronald Press Company, 1930, pp. 6-15.

[26] *Op. cit.*, p. 289.

[27] Meadows, *op. cit.*, pp. 145-50. See also Henry S. Dennison, *Ethics and Modern Business*, Boston, Houghton Mifflin Company, 1932, pp. 53-68; Commission on Freedom of the Press, *A Free and Responsible Press*, Chicago, University of Chicago Press, 1947, pp. 76-78; J. M. Clark, *Social Control of Business*, New York, McGraw-Hill Book Company, 1939, pp. 201-21; Chester I. Barnard, *Functions of the Executive*, Cambridge, Harvard University Press, 1938, pp. 258-84; F. M. Feiker, "The Profession of Commerce in the Making," *Annals of the American Academy of Political and Social Science*, May, 1922, pp. 203-7.

social work. The world's demand for efficiency is so great and the supply so small, that the price of efficiency is high in every field of human activity.

The recognized professions, however, definitely reject the size of the financial return as the measure of success. They select as their test excellence of performance in the broadest sense—and include, among other things, advance in the particular occupation and service to the community. These are the basis of all worthy reputations in the recognized professions. In them a large income is the ordinary incident of success; but he who exaggerates the value of the incident is apt to fail of real success.

To the business of today a similar test must be applied. True, in business the earning of profit is something more than an incident of success. It is an essential condition of success; because the continued absence of profit itself spells failure. But while loss spells failure, large profits do not connote success. Success must be sought in business also in excellence of performance; and in business, excellence of performance manifests itself, among other things, in the advancing of methods and processes; in the improvement of products; in more perfect organization, eliminating friction as well as waste; in bettering the condition of the workingmen, developing their faculties and promoting their happiness; and in the establishment of right relations with customers and with the community.[28]

Tendencies toward professionalism in business management may be expected in the future to have three important consequences.

First, the spirit of professionalism may strengthen the motive of pride in the progress of a profession and accelerate its advancement.

Second, the increasing intellectual requirement for professional management means that managers must be men of considerable educational background. Such men are likely to be more sensitive to changing aspects of employment relations than were many of the tycoons of an earlier era. Moreover, they are likely to be more conversant with the complex relationships between the behavior of an enterprise and the successful operation of the total economic and social life of the nation. It requires broadly educated and perceptive businessmen to develop a full understanding and appreciation of the social implications of their work.

[28] Louis D. Brandeis, *Business—A Profession*, Boston, Hale, Cushman & Flint, 1933, pp. 3-5.

Third, professional or trade organizations—resulting from professionalism in business management—may exert increasing influence upon the activities of their members through codes of ethics and through interchange of problems and ideas. In the past, the orientation of these associations has often been toward the narrow interests of members, and association officials have often surpassed their membership in reactionary point of view. Nevertheless, such associations can broaden the vision of members by focusing attention on problems of the industry, of the community, or of business at large rather than upon the single enterprise.[29] Professional and trade associations can also be useful in providing the sense of group solidarity which is so essential as a basis for ethical behavior.[30] The individual businessman needs guidance *from sources he respects* to help him distinguish ethical from unethical modes of conduct. The individual businessman is more inclined to respect and follow ethical rules which are formulated and supported by groups consisting of his own peers than he is to follow rules laid down by moralists, economists, or politicians. The trade or professional association, therefore, is a highly useful institution for formulating, sanctioning, and applying group pressure toward ethical conduct on the part of its members. It is one thing for a clergyman to exhort or a politician to orate about what businessmen should do. It is quite another thing for a professional or trade association of which the businessman is a member to formulate a code and to give that code group sanction. The desire to stand well with one's peers is as powerful a motive for businessmen as for anyone else. It is true that many trade and professional associations have been thinking too much about the interests of their members and too little about the duties of these members to society. The history of professionalism suggests, however, that the idea of

[29] There is need for research on the place and significance of the trade associations, conventions, business meetings, and conferences in the *thinking* of the businessman. The study might include an analysis of programs and procedures at business meetings, it might attempt to measure the impact of such meetings on the thinking of businessmen, and it might possibly throw some light on the development of a common point of view among businessmen on political and social affairs.

[30] Wallace B. Donham, "Business Ethics as a Solution to the Conflict between Business and the Community," in *Ethical Problems of Modern Finance*, New York, Ronald Press, 1930, pp. 35-38.

responsibility may occupy a more prominent place as the professional point of view develops more fully.

On the whole, the tendency toward professionalism in management tends to provide more competent and more broadly trained business administrators who can perceive the social implications of their calling. It places greater emphasis upon social responsibility and provides machinery for exerting group pressure on individual conduct. Professionalism is, of course, not without dangers. Professional codes may become rigid and nonadaptive to changing needs of the community or to new developments; professional associations may attempt to apply restrictive practices—tantamount to monopoly—under the guise of protecting professional standards; professional associations may engage in collusive activities or may attempt to exert selfish pressure on government. But regardless of how one weighs the relative advantages and disadvantages of professionalism, it has been a contributing factor to the increasing interest of businessmen in their social responsibilities.

BROADENED PARTICIPATION IN DECISION-MAKING

Another factor may be the broader participation in decision-making that has become characteristic of the modern corporation. There is a clear tendency in present business practice toward a more elaborate and more ramified corporate organization for decision-making.[31]

Provision is now made for the expression of a greater diversity of

[31] "It is the necessity of stabilizing their own business, of directing technical processes which are beyond the understanding of stockholders, of adjusting the supply and demand of the multitudinous elements they deal in, which is the compelling force behind that divorce between management and ownership, that growing use of experts and of statistical measurements, and that development of trade associations, of conferences, committees, and councils, with which modern industry is honeycombed. The captain of industry in the romantic sense tends to disappear in highly evolved industrial organizations. His thundering commands are replaced by the decisions of executives who consult with representatives of the interests involved and check their opinions by the findings of experts. The greater the corporation the more the shareholders and the directors lose the actual direction of the institution. They cannot direct the corporation because they do not really know what it is and what it is doing. That knowledge is subdivided among the executives and bureau chiefs and consultants, all of them on salary; each of them is so relatively small a factor in the whole that his personal success is in very large degree bound up with the success of the institution."—Walter Lippmann, *Preface to Morals*, New York, The Macmillan Company, 1929, p. 256.

interests and a wider range of points of view than was customary in an earlier day. Businesses are seldom today completely dominated by one man. That tyrannical individualist, "the big boss," is rapidly disappearing as an important figure in the American scene. In his place we have the "business leader," who functions as the co-ordinator of a complex network of boards, committees, conferences, reviewing agencies, and subordinate line officials, and who carries out his task with the advice of a host of specialized staff officers and outside "consultants." As a result of these developments, de-cision-making has become a group activity even though the ultimate responsibility must be borne by the top executives. The head of a corporation has in a sense become the responsible coordinator of a decision-making organization rather than the man who "makes" the decisions.

The broadened base of the decision-making process has had two chief results. First, it has provided the machinery for the careful weighing of alternatives, the study of facts, the consideration of all points of view, and the careful and dispassionate derivation of conclusions from all the evidence. This has undoubtedly strength-ened tendencies toward steadiness, patience, and caution in busi-ness management and has reduced tendencies toward arbitrariness, off-the-cuff judgments, playing hunches, plunging, etc.[32] It has provided the vehicle by which the scientific spirit can function in a business setting. By the same token, it may have reduced the imagination and flexibility of a company where decisions were formerly made by one man or a few closely associated men. In short, strong bureaucratic tendencies have been introduced into modern business.[33]

[32] I do not mean to suggest that rationality is universal in large enterprises, or that caution is always a virtue.

[33] J. M. Keynes was an early observer of the trends toward bureaucracy which were perhaps more evident in England than in the United States. He said (*Essays in Persuasion*, New York, Harcourt, Brace & Company, 1932, p. 314-15): "One of the most interesting and unnoticed developments of recent decades has been the tendency of big enterprise to socialize itself. A point arrives in the growth of a big institution . . . at which the owners of the capital, *i.e.*, the shareholders, are almost entirely dissociated from management, with the result that the direct personal interest of the latter in the making of great profit be-comes quite secondary. When this stage is reached, the general stability and reputation of the institution are more considered by the management than the maximum of profit for the shareholders. The shareholders must be satisfied by conventionally adequate dividends; but once this is secured, the direct

Second, the broadened base of decision-making has increased the variety of interests that are considered in formulating business plans. Merely by the participation of more people having differing backgrounds, differing points of view, and differing corporate responsibilities, the number of values or interests that can be considered is greatly increased. For example, if a labor dispute threatens, the "big boss," if he were to act alone, might have a tendency to "crack down" and try to prevent the organization of his workers. His vice-president for labor relations, a man who has had long experience in these matters, may counsel that it is best to be reasonable, accept a union if necessary, and try to get a responsible union that can be worked with. The production manager may feel, as a result of his contacts with the workers, that some wage concessions will satisfy the men and stop the drive for organization. The lawyer may warn against violating certain provisions of the labor law. The vice-president for public relations may point out that a strike in the near future would have unfortunate consequences for the public reputation of the company. The company economist may suggest that an increase in wages will be socially undesirable because it will contribute to inflation. The sales manager may point out that a stoppage of production would be disastrous because of the large number of unfilled orders on hand and the mounting dissatisfaction of customers because of slow deliveries. When all these points of view have been considered in the give and take of conferences, the probabilities are strong that the final decision about the labor policy of this company will differ materially from the decision the boss and a few of his close associates would have reached by themselves. The number of variables and the number of values brought to bear on the problem will have multiplied. And the probability of ariving at a decision more or less in keeping with the generally accepted values of society at large will have increased.

But widespread participation *within* the managerial ranks of the company is not the whole story. Today, an indirect and some-

interest of the management often consists in avoiding criticism from the public and from the customers of the concern. This is particularly the case if their great size or semi-monopolistic position renders them conspicuous in the public eye and vulnerable to public attack." Keynes added that this responsiveness to public opinion is not an unmixed blessing; that it leads to business conservatism and the waning of enterprise.

times powerful role in the decision-making process is played by groups which are nominally not even a part of management. I refer, of course, to labor unions, trade associations, government officials, and even the public. While these groups do not often physically participate in management, their presence is distinctly felt at corporate council tables. Frequent questions at management conferences are: What will the labor unions do about this? Does this conform to the policy of our trade association? Will the Anti-trust Division crack down? What will be public reaction? Thus voices unheard at the corporate council table sometimes speak with authority, and in this way the decision-making process is still further broadened to take into account a still greater variety of interests and still more diverse points of view.

But one further comment must be made. The bringing of many values and many points of view into the decision-making process may be ever so democratic and suggestive of important social responsibilities, but it also introduces confusion as to the goals businessmen are expected to seek. A single goal, such as maximum profit, is simple and reasonably concrete. But when several goals are introduced and businessmen must sometimes choose from among them (e.g., greater immediate profit vs. greater company security, or good labor relations vs. low-cost production, or higher dividends vs. higher wages), then confusion and divided counsel are sometimes inevitable.[34]

[34] Professor R. A. Gordon has ably summed up this point:

"While the development of the large corporation and the diffusion of corporate ownership have centered the leadership function in a group of professional business leaders, the objectives toward which these men should point their leadership are tending to become increasingly confused rather than clarified. . . .

"The business leader in the large corporation today finds himself in a somewhat anomalous position. Our legal institutions still impose upon him the primary obligation of seeking maximum profits for the firm and the stockholders. But he is also under strong pressure from various groups—bankers, minority stockholders, large competitors, labor, and so on—to further their particular sets of interests. Cutting across these pressures is the growing demand, from the government and the public at large, that the business leader adopt broad social criteria, aimed at benefiting some of the weaker interest groups and the economy as a whole, in exercising his leadership. To these various sets of goals we must add the personal aims of the business leader himself. These personal aims are in no insignificant degree nonpecuniary in character, while the receipt of profits from stock held in his own firm tends to form but a small part of the business leader's total money income.

"Governmental regulation has, if anything, added to this confusion. Broad

Conclusions

It is now time to draw together the threads of our argument in answer to the question: Why are today's businessmen concerned about their social responsibilities?

In asking the question, it was assumed that today's businessmen are, in fact, more concerned than were their predecessors; this assumption was supported by citing many illustrations of business policies and actions growing out of this concern, and by analyzing many statements of businessmen.

We can divide our answer to the question into three parts: (1) because they have been *forced* to be more concerned, (2) because they have been *persuaded* to be more concerned, and (3) because, owing largely to the separation of ownership and control in the large corporation, *conditions* have been *favorable* to the development of this concern. Let us consider each of these three parts of the answer separately.

First, businessmen have been forced to consider their responsibilities because they have been operating in a climate of opinion in which increased public regulation, or even public ownership, has been considered an ever-present threat. Moreover, they have been confronted with the relentless pressure of a determined labor movement. Businessmen as a group, therefore, well understood that a condition of business survival, or at least of continued relative business independence, would be the operation of their businesses in conformity with the new standards and new aspirations of the public. The shaping of business policies in accordance with publicly accepted standards had become imperative from the point of view of the businessmen's own long-run self-interest.[35]

---

objectives have not been clarified, nor has responsibility been fixed for their attainment. . . .

"Hence, though the last decade has increased the emphasis on the broader social criteria of business leadership, and though our business leaders have gradually accepted some responsibility for the protection of the interests of labor, consumers, and the community at large, it still remains true that a unified and self-consistent set of objectives for the large corporation has not been clearly formulated. The modern business leader is without a clear-cut set of goals in which he himself believes."—*Business Leadership in the Large Corporation*, Washington, Brookings Institution, 1945, pp. 340-42.

[35] An influential businessman, who has made helpful, though severe, criticisms of this book, feels that I have not given sufficient attention to the spiritual side of industry. He writes: "The fact that businessmen have to do with human

Second, businessmen have been persuaded to consider their social responsibilities. As members of the society they have acquired many of its attitudes and values; hence, they have come to share—in substantial degree but perhaps not completely—the standards of the society as to what a business ought to be like and how it ought to be operated. They have been influenced by business educators, by their direct contacts with the government and its problems, and by the necessity of grappling with new and different problems. Through the rise of a new scientific study of management, they have come to realize that many of the things expected of them (e.g., good working conditions and good human relations) are actually good business in that they promote efficiency and lower costs.

Third, as a result of the separation of ownership and control in the large corporation, the managerial function has been vested in professional salaried managers whose motivation and point of view tend to differ in important respects from that of owner-managers. These new managers are selected because of their qualifications as administrators and their acceptability to various groups affected by the corporation; they are on the whole highly educated and experienced; they are interested in professional achievement (which they define broadly) as well as in personal remuneration; they identify themselves closely with the corporation and view it as having indefinitely long life; they think in terms of the long-range welfare and interests of the corporation as such; they regard the corporation as something more than a mere creature of the stockholders. Also, as a result of the growth of the corporation in complexity and size, the management function has been subdivided so that decision-making has become a social process in which many persons participate and in which various points of view and diverse interests are expressed. In addition, many of our large corporations have attained a kind of maturity and stability which permits them to consider the long view and to take a philosophical approach to their role in

---

beings as a part of their day-to-day activities both in dealing with employees and dealing with customers seems to be ignored, and that raises the whole question of the loyalties which come in as a part of the business picture. Unless management can by its actions and sincerity develop loyalty on the part of those associated with it, it is going to be a very difficult matter to make it successful. Loyalty ties back into the spiritual qualities of idealism, gratitude, and emotion. These are major factors in human welfare and in many ways are far more important than the purely materialistic items."

society. The large size of these corporations makes obvious to their managers the relation between their decisions and the general welfare.

Adding these factors together, one can conclude that there are abundant explanations for the increasing concern of businessmen toward their social responsibilities—that this trend of business thought and action is firmly based upon fundamental features of the modern social environment and on fundamental motives of businessmen. In a sense, a kind of socialization or social responsiveness of business has been achieved spontaneously without resort to formal governmental apparatus—although the tacit threat of further control by government or labor has consistently been in the background.

One must not, of course, exaggerate the extent to which businessmen and their corporations have disavowed their selfish motives and turned their thoughts to the social welfare. One would have difficulty in sharing even today the enthusiasm of a leading businessman, who said, on the very eve of the Great Depression: "The tendency in the banking business toward cooperation for the protection of the public and the establishment of the highest ethical standards has come to its most perfect flowering in the last decade. . . ." Yet a reading of the literature about capitalism and its civilization covering the period of Dickens, of the Granger movement, of the "muckrakers," of the disenchanted 'twenties, of the Great Depression, and of the recent war and postwar years would provide heartening evidence that great progress has occurred both in thinking and in action.

This progress has been achieved primarily as a result of the changes in the social climate of opinion, attitudes, and values. It has been based, in the last analysis, on public opinion—and on what the public has expected of business. In general, business is sensitive to changes in the market for its goods and it is equally sensitive to changes in the market for the business system itself. In both markets, it will rise to what is expected of it—but it will not rise much higher than that. And if public opinion relaxes and expects less of business, some of the gains of a century could easily be lost.

It would be idle to debate whether, or to what extent, this growing social responsiveness of business rests on altruistic or selfish motives. There are elements of both. The fact that self-interest (interpreted broadly and for the long run) is so important gives one confidence in the persistence and further development of these trends.[36]

[36] Cf. C. E. Griffin, *Enterprise in a Free Society*, Homewood (Ill.), Richard D. Irwin, 1949, pp. 90-91.

The situation has been epitomized, with a touch of satire, by Senator Ralph E. Flanders:

"What is required is an evolution of our system, instead of its destruction. Our system is based on the faith announced by Adam Smith that, in the sum total, selfish interests work together for the general good. The time has come when that doctrine is no longer tenable in its historic form.

"If, however, we learn to distinguish between short-sighted selfish interests and long-range selfish interests, then the whole formula still applies and still will work with this simple readjustment of one of its elements. We may still be selfish, but let us be selfish in the long-range view. What harm will there be if the disinterested observer finds it difficult to distinguish our selfishness from old-fashioned virtue?"—"Businessmen's Responsibilities to Government," in *Responsibilities of Business Leadership*, H. F. Merrell, editor, Cambridge, Harvard University Press, 1948, pp. 38-39.

10

The Doctrine of Social Responsibility: Some Criticisms

The increasing interest in social responsibilities on the part of businessmen, while not a cure-all for the ills of society, is an important and welcome development from which much can be expected in terms of the general welfare. This optimistic *doctrine of social responsibility* is subject to several important criticisms and qualifications, a consideration of which will be helpful in placing the doctrine in correct perspective.

COMPETITION

It has been frequently asserted that businessmen—regardless of their good intentions—will be unable to assume obligations beyond those involved in producing a marketable product at minimal cost. It is held that efforts of individual businessmen to "do good" will increase their costs of production and cause them to lose in the competitive race unless all of their rivals are equally concerned about the social welfare. Since it is unlikely that all of them will be so concerned, the efforts of the socially conscientious to do the "right thing" will in the long run be defeated. As in Gresham's law of money, the bad will drive out the good. The argument concludes that only those businessmen who enjoy a degree of monopoly power can afford the cost of engaging in socially oriented activities. These businessmen, we are reminded, will be able to do magnanimous things, supposedly in the social interest, but only with funds which they have extracted from the public in the form of monopoly profits. How much better it would be, so the argument runs, to cut monopolists' prices, by regulation or by enforcing competition, and forget henceforth about social responsibilities of businessmen.

This line of argument has force. The failure of some competitors to accept their social responsibilities may prevent others from doing what they believe is "right" with respect to wages, working conditions, quality of product, economic stability, etc. Surely, it makes no sense to ask businessmen to assume social obligations which can end only in bankruptcy. Even when standards are prescribed by law, businessmen who follow the law are sometimes hampered by the competition of their less scrupulous rivals. Nevertheless, this Gresham's law of business does not wholly dispose of the doctrine of social responsibility.

As all students of business know, perfect competition is a rarity; there are elements of monopoly (or at least defenses against the rigors of perfect competition) throughout much of modern business. All enterprises are, to be sure, constrained by competitive forces in varying degrees. Even when competition seems to be in abeyance, it is always lurking in the background in the form of potential new enterprises, new methods of production, or new products. But an overwhelming proportion of business is done in firms which have some independence of action in matters of production, prices, sales, income distribution, finance, personnnel, etc. This applies not only to the several hundred great corporations which account for a major fraction of American business activity but also to many thousands of small and local businesses. The typical condition in American business is a significant degree of control and an appreciable freedom of action in these matters.[1]

So would it be better to give our attention to the strengthening of competition than to converting monopolists of various shades to a social viewpoint? The problems and difficulties, both technical and practical, of creating perfectly competitive markets are great. Moreover, the two objectives are not necessarily incompatible. Society would be well advised to try both to strengthen competition and to infuse businessmen with a quickened social conscience.

But the argument that competition prevents businessmen from showing their better natures is not wholly true even when business

[1] Cf. J. A. Schumpeter, *Capitalism, Socialism, and Democracy*, 3rd ed., New York, Harper & Brothers, 1950, pp. 72-106.

is conducted in competitive markets. This can be shown by some elementary economic analysis.

The inframarginal or lower-cost firms in a competitive industry will ordinarily have access to relatively superior factors of production. Insofar as the markets for these factors are not completely competitive and not completely fluid, return on these factors need not be entirely commensurate with their productivity. This will be especially so if the factors are "owned" by the firm. The rents[2] of superior factors may therefore be a source of income from which the competitive firm may pay the costs of its socially oriented actions. This may be illustrated by agriculture, which is our outstanding—perhaps unique—example of a competitive industry.

The marginal farmer operating marginal land with marginal equipment is not in a good position to do anything about his social obligations. He, quite rightly, will be preoccupied with the problem of meeting his debts and feeding his family. If, for example, he needs to hire a worker, he will drive the hardest bargain he can and will surely not consider the security or welfare of the worker or any broader social objectives. But suppose a skilled farmer, with rich land and fine equipment, hires a worker. He may easily consider the broader social implications of his role as employer, and provide for the worker's comfort and security beyond the minimum that is absolutely required in order to secure the worker's services. True, this action results in increased costs, but he is able to pay these out of the economic rent from his land, equipment, or labor. But he will not be driven out of business because of his concern for his worker and the resulting extra costs, nor will he lose out in competition. He will merely have chosen to reduce his rents in order to discharge his social obligations as he sees them.

It is probable, moreover, that the high labor standards of the prosperous farmer may in the long run affect the survival, or at least the costs, of the marginal farmer. If farmers generally become interested in the welfare of their workers and accept the principle that it is "right" to provide workers with certain minimal standards of comfort and security, workers will prefer employment where conditions are good and try to reject it elsewhere. In the labor market, therefore, the marginal farmer will find greater difficulty in attracting

---

[2] Rent in this sense refers to incomes received for the services of a factor in excess of what is required to attract that factor into production.

efficient workers and he will be under pressure to improve the working conditions he offers. Since his is a "marginal firm," presumably he cannot do this without financial ruin. For the time being, then, we would find the standards of wages and working conditions lower at the margin than in agriculture generally. This corresponds approximately to the facts of real life.

But the workers of the marginal farmer, if he is lucky enough to find any, are going to be unhappy at their lot; their morale and efficiency will be low, and their turnover high. As a result, the marginal farmer will find his costs increased both by the difficulty of getting labor and by the inefficiency of the labor he does get. Eventually, then, he will be forced out of business. The resulting reduction in the output of farm products will cause a rise in the prices received by the remaining farmers; the costs of their new labor standards will then be absorbed in these higher prices of products, and the full rents of their superior factors will be restored. To end the story, the displaced marginal farmer and his labor will presumably bid themselves into employment in other industries.

But suppose the new labor standards are also being introduced into other industries throughout the economy, and marginal firms and marginal labor are being displaced everywhere. Will this mean that the new labor standards will create a pool of unemployed entrepreneurs and workers? At first, yes. But as these displaced persons bid themselves into employment, wages will tend to fall, marginal firms will be attracted back into business, former rates of production will be restored, and prices will return to their original level. The net result will be a reduction in wages by an amount equal to the costs of the new labor standards. (If labor were organized and resisted such a wage cut, and if the monetary authorities were willing, the adjustment might alternatively be made by holding wages constant and raising prices.)

The general conclusion is that a new labor standard involving an increase in cost can be adopted in competitive industries, but that the cost in the long run will be shifted to workers or consumers. This analysis, however, was based upon the assumption of a stationary economy where the adjustments would be slow and painful. Obviously, the adjustments could be made much more easily and quickly in an expanding progressive economy. In this case, there would be no need to displace marginal firms, and the reduction in wages might be more than offset by increases in wages due to the higher productivity of labor.

In a rapidly growing society, even if industry is predominantly competitive, there is nothing to prevent the society from receiving part of its increasing product in the form of better working conditions, shorter hours, greater security, greater freedom, better products, etc. Gains need not be realized solely in the form of a greater flow of final goods and services. The rising standard of living may consist not alone in an increasing physical quantity of goods and services, but also in improved conditions under which these goods and services are produced.

This conclusion is reinforced by the fact that some of the many socially desirable improvements in business practice have been found to "pay" in the sense of cutting costs or increasing revenues of the individual firm. There has never been any doubt, of course, that if a given change in business practice reduces cost or increases revenues, self-interest will lead to adoption of the practice. Thus, when it was discovered that shorter hours or better light or cleaner washrooms increased the efficiency of workers and reduced unit labor cost, there was little hesitation in adopting these measures which were good from both commercial and social viewpoints. But it has not been fully recognized that the effects of these measures are in part *relative to the accepted standards of the society*.

For example, in a society in which the twelve-hour day is considered to be a reasonable and proper working period, shortening the work day may reduce production. But in a society which is conditioned to the belief that a twelve-hour day is too long, a cut in hours may dramatically increase production. True, the effect of changing the length of the working day may be partly physiological; but it is also partly cultural. Thus in one cultural milieu businessmen may find no gain in cutting hours from twelve to ten, whereas in another climate of opinions, attitudes, and values they may find it clearly in their pecuniary self-interest to cut hours. In this sense, socially accepted standards partially determine what business policies will "pay."[3]

[3] In the past, businessmen have sometimes been slow to recognize that improved working conditions would be in their own long-run interest. This was particularly true regarding the reduction of working hours, as in the case, for example, of the elimination of the twelve-hour day in the steel mills.

Similarly, if filthy washrooms in factories are commonly accepted and meet the standards of the time and place, employers will have little incentive to provide clean and pleasant washrooms. But if socially accepted standards dictate better facilities, then employers will be induced by their own self-interest to comply.

The same reasoning can be applied to policies relating to speed of work, stability of employment, old-age security, recreation, contributions to community betterment, etc. The self-interest of the businessman is always relative to socially accepted standards which are constantly changing. These standards are imposing new costs on business by a kind of tacit threat that if business does not comply worker efficiency or public relations will suffer. We have a standard of living for business as well as for ourselves as consumers, and in the United States of recent decades both standards of living have been rising rapidly.

The improvement of business practices has, of course, been facilitated by laws, actual or threatened, pertaining to health, safety, security, hours, child labor, adulteration of products, etc. But it has been influenced also by attitudes regarding the right and wrong of business practices and by the pressures growing out of these attitudes as expressed by labor unions, trade associations, consumer organizations, civic groups, individuals, and public officials.

INCREASED COSTS

A second argument concerning the doctrine of social responsibility is that businessmen, when they take on numerous social obligations, are subjected to increased costs which in turn must be passed on to consumers in the form of higher prices or lower wages. When businessmen are asked to provide high wages, pensions, recreation, steady employment, charitable contributions, luxurious working conditions, worker participation, conservation of natural resources, stabilization of investment, etc., these things cost money and cannot be provided unless consumers or workers pay for them. The question, then, is whether the public would prefer elegant conditions of production or would rather have lower prices for their products.

There can be no disputing the fact that the execution of socially oriented policies is costly, and it is probable that these costs are passed on in the form of higher prices or lower wages. In other words, because we have such a high standard of living in business it takes more land, labor, and capital to produce a given output than would be required if our standards were lower. Or, to express the same thing in another way, with our high standards we are limited to a smaller quantity of final products. And if in the future we continue to raise our standards still higher, this will further raise prices or lower wages, and restrict the output of final goods (relative to our capacity with lower standards).

To impose upon business the duty of providing old-age pensions or of buying expensive safety equipment or furnishing brightly tiled washrooms or installing air conditioning, when these things are cost-increasing, is much like levying a tax on business. And just as a tax on production may be shifted, at least in the long run, so the costs of bearing social responsibilities may be shifted.

Of course, it may be argued that it is one of the social responsibilities of businessmen to reduce their profits, and that they ought to meet the costs of their socially oriented actions out of profits. It may seem less than magnanimous for businessmen to prate about their social responsibilities and then to levy the costs of their benefactions upon their unsuspecting customers or workers. Certainly in many cases—especially where profits are unusually high due to monopolistic power—businessmen clearly should meet these costs out of profits and perhaps should cut prices as well. But it does not necessarily follow that businessmen should neglect or ignore social objectives merely because the attainment of these objectives might add to consumer prices and subtract from the total of final goods and services produced. The welfare of society is related not only to the quantity of final goods and services but also to the conditions under which these goods and services are produced. For example, a suit of clothes produced in a sweatshop may cost the consumer $35. The same suit produced under modern, sanitary, agreeable working conditions by workers having status and security and receiving a decent living wage may cost the consumer $50. From the point of view of the aggregate of human welfare, the loss to consumers may be far less than the gain to the clothing workers. To take another example, the stabilization of production schedules and employment may sometimes add to the costs of companies, and hence to the prices of their products. But the loss to consumers may well be more than offset by the gain in security and self-respect of the workers employed, and the gain to the community at large through stabilization of employment.

Our standard of living, in other words, consists of two parts: that which derives from the conditions under which production is carried on and that which derives from the goods and services resulting from that production. An improvement in the conditions of production—resulting in a better working environment or better functioning of the economy—may frequently be entirely justified even if achieved at a sacrifice in output of final goods and services.

The improvement in the conditions of production may, of course, be carried too far. To provide workers with a four-hour working day, wages of $10 per hour, guaranteed employment, pensions at the age of forty-five, luxurious club rooms, etc., may be wonderful for the workers and no one would begrudge them these amenities if society could afford them. But the effect on costs would be so drastic that we could no longer believe that the gain would compensate the loss to consumers in the form of final products.

The problem, like all other economic problems, is to achieve a balance between the standard of living in the form of final goods and services and the standard of living in the form of conditions under which production is carried on. We want the marginal expenditure in one direction to yield no more and no less satisfactions than the marginal expenditure in the other direction.

There is sometimes a danger that particular groups of workers who are in a strategic position may demand working conditions for themselves beyond what the community generally can afford (on the principle of balancing the margins). The gains of such workers must be regarded as ill-gotten in the sense that they have attained conditions of work so favorable that the loss to consumers in the form of higher prices exceeds the value of the gains to the particular group of workers. In such cases, it may be the responsibility of businessmen concerned to oppose these benefits for particular groups at the expense of the community as a whole. The same argument would apply to demands of particular groups for exceptional wages far beyond those prevailing for similar kinds of work in the community generally.

One final comment. The fact that costs connected with the social obligations of businessmen can frequently be shifted greatly strengthens the case for the doctrine of social responsibility. If businessmen were to be expected to finance out of profits or rents the costs of providing socially acceptable conditions of production, we might well be highly skeptical as to the outcome. This might be too great a strain on altruism. But if these costs can be shifted, we then can see that social pressures on businessmen can produce the socially desired kind of behavior. Society is not asking for charitable contributions from businessmen but for a good job of management for which they can be compensated.

This is not to suggest that many businessmen are motivated only by selfish impulses or that they must be compensated for their every good deed. It is suggested only that the possibility of shifting the costs gives the doctrine of social responsibility a firm economic base.

MOTIVES OF BUSINESSMEN

Another argument sometimes advanced in opposition to the doctrine of social responsibility is that businessmen are so strongly oriented toward the profit motive and toward the narrow interest of their companies that it is unrealistic to expect them to assume important social obligations. Businessmen, so the argument runs, are so fully imbued with a spirit of profit-making and with pecuniary standards of value that they are unable to see the social implications of their tasks—much less to follow policies directed toward the social interest.[4]

Accordingly, the frequent verbalizations of businessmen about their social responsibilities can be written off as merely hypocritical and deceptive propaganda intended to persuade a gullible public of the virtues of capitalism.

This argument has, of course, a degree of validity. Businessmen are primarily concerned about profits, they do think in pecuniary terms, and they find it all too easy to identify the welfare of business with the welfare of society. They are people and therefore subject to the frailties, the stupidity, and the selfishness of mankind. Doubtless much of the profession of a sense of social responsibility is pure propaganda, and many businessmen show much more concern about "setting straight" the thinking of the American public than they do about adapting the business system to the evolving

[4] In large part, this is the thesis of Veblen in his *Theory of Business Enterprise*, New York, Charles Scribner's Sons, 1904.

values, attitudes, and needs of that public. This can all be taken for granted.

Yet, as has been shown in Chapter 9, we cannot interpret the motives of businessmen solely in terms of profit maximization. The businessman is a person. He lives in society and shares the values and attitudes of that society. He wants to be liked. He wants to do what is expected of him—to be a success in terms of the currently accepted standards of success. He is keenly aware of the pressures on him, especially those emanating from labor, public opinion, and government. He has become deeply concerned about the human problems of business, as distinct from the purely pecuniary problems. He recognizes increasingly that his own long-run self-interest calls for the adjustment of his policies and actions with a regard for their social effects. The very fact that he is so concerned about public opinion and wants so much to change it is a clear indication of the power of that public opinion over his conduct. And finally, the fact that the costs of assuming social responsibilities may be shifted suggests that his concern for social responsibilities need not always run counter to this profit motive.

A variant of the argument that businessmen are motivated exclusively by profits is that the sense of social obligation is too weak and undependable a motive to be seriously relied upon to guide behavior along socially constructive lines. We had best rely on competition or law. The following statement of Professor Henry Simons illustrates this position:

I repeat, the common interest may be implemented only by competition or by authoritarian dictation. There is little hope that mass organizations with monopoly power will submit to competitive prices for their services while they retain their organization and power. No one and no group can be trusted with much power; and it is merely silly to complain because groups exercise power selfishly. The mistake lies in permitting them to have it . . . it is romantic and unreasonable to expect organizations to exercise power only within limits consistent with the common interest. All bargaining power is monopoly power. Such power, once attained, will be used as fully as its conservation permits and also used continuously for its own accretion and consolidation.[5]

[5] "Some Reflections on Syndicalism," *Journal of Political Economy*, March, 1944, pp. 6-7. Cf. also, J. A. Hobson, "The Ethics of Industrialism," in *Ethical Democracy*, edited by Stanton Coit, London, G. Richards, 1900, pp. 81-107;

This argument, I think, ignores the fact that the great bulk of human behavior in any society is regulated by informal social controls. These controls take the form (1) of indoctrinating individuals with the socially accepted values and attitudes and behavior patterns, and (2) of exerting continual informal social pressure on the individual toward conformity. No one, except the anarchist, advocates relying completely on informal social controls. Law and competition have important roles in any society, but even law—as America discovered through the prohibition experiment—must be founded on widespread social acceptance. As professor J. M. Clark has said:

But one cannot look at legislative control intelligently unless one starts with at least a fair understanding of the character and tendencies, virtues and limitations, of the stable substratum of law which furnishes the point of departure for legislation. Indeed it does far more than this, for it pervades legislation itself, via the process of interpretation, and shows a considerable capacity to resist attempts to change it by the legislative route.[6]

The point is that to guide human conduct we do not have to rely solely on one method. All methods—competition, law, and voluntary action—are available and all can be used when appropriate or effective. It is a good rule, however, to "economize coercion."[7] This suggests reliance on competition and informal control so far as possible.

G. W. Stocking and M. W. Watkins, *Monopoly and Free Enterprise*, New York, Twentieth Century Fund, 1951, pp. 518-20; Edward S. Mason, "Controlling Industry," in *The Economics of the Recovery Program*, by D. V. Brown and others, McGraw-Hill Book Co., New York, 1934, pp. 38-63; A. T. Mason, "Welfare Capitalism: Opportunity or Delusion," *Virginia Quarterly Review*, Autumn, 1950, pp, 530-43.

[6] J. M. Clark, *Social Control of Business*, 1st ed., Chicago, University of Chicago Press, 1926, p. 13.

[7] *Op. cit.*, p. 17. See also Professor Clarks' *Alternative to Serfdom*, New York, Alfred A. Knopf, 1948, especially pp. 57-59. Professor P. Sorokin has suggested that altruism, as well as self-interest, can be institutionalized. *The Reconstruction of Humanity*, Boston, The Beacon Press, 1948, pp. 165-71. Talcott Parsons suggests that "the acquisitiveness of modern business is institutional rather than motivational," "The Professions and the Social Structure," *Social Forces*, May, 1939, p. 459.

POWER

A much more telling argument against the doctrine of social responsibility is that businessmen try to use this doctrine as a device for retaining power and as a justification for that power.

According to this argument, the basic struggle in modern society, as in any society, is the struggle for power. In capitalism, power is centered largely in businessmen who make the basic economic decisions as to what goods shall be produced, how production shall be organized, who shall be hired and fired, what shall be the working conditions, how income shall be distributed, how rapidly natural resources shall be exploited, what shall be the rate of capital accumulation, etc. Through their control over the media of mass communications, businessmen also strongly influence consumer choices and the formation of public opinion; and through their financial power, they exercise great influence, directly or indirectly, over government. Businessmen try to justify and to protect their favored position by creating the myth that they are the natural "leaders" or "guardians" of society, who have received their power because of their exceptional qualifications and who exercise this power as benevolent trustees in the interests of society at large.

When businessmen enunciate the doctrine of social responsibility, or the "gospel of wealth" as it used to be called, it is *they* who are supposed to define the public interest and *they* who designate the responsibilities of business. In this respect, their philosophy and their actions are similar to those of ruling classes of other times and places. Historically, most groups who have achieved power have tried to justify it in two ways: (1) by showing that those who exercise the power have been selected in such a way as to insure their qualification for leadership, and (2) by claiming that the power is exercised for the benefit not of the ruling class but of the people. The theory of the divine right of kings or the Nazi "leadership principle" are examples. Thus the currently popular doctrine of social responsibility appears as a nondemocratic, or even fascist, theory. As Professor Brady shows, the doctrine was commonly enunciated in Fascist Italy, Nazi Germany, and prewar Japan.[8] American businessmen sometimes attempt to deny the un-

[8] R. A. Brady, *Business as a System of Power*, New York, Columbia University Press, 1943, pp. 259-93.

democratic nature of their power by stressing the openness and freedom of opportunity in this country. They point out that corporations are controlled by managers, and managers are usually selected on the basis of ability rather than of family or wealth. Admittedly this may lead to the selection of able business leaders, but it does not alter the fact that whoever *is* selected wields great power and wields it without democratic safeguards.

The conclusion of this general line of argument is that the doctrine of social responsibility is suspect as long as businessmen retain their power and remain the sole judges of the social interest. The doctrine is regarded as simply a part of the age-old apparatus of power by which ruling classes pretend that they are the best judges of what is good for the people and that they are exercising their power benevolently in the pursuit of the general good as they define it. The doctrine of social responsibility is merely one of the myths or propaganda devices by which power is achieved and maintained.

Professor Brady, in his study of the centralized organization of business power in various countries, has said that ". . . the concept of trusteeship has always suffused the thinking of all proponents of and apologists for those systems of evolving status which have been compelled, for one reason or another, to take steps to create a favorable public opinion.[9]

Another variant of the same theme was expressed by Dr. Edwin G. Nourse, former chairman of the President's Council of Economic Advisers:

. . . the newer generation of business leaders envision for management a more tolerant and constructive role in shaping the future of the economy. Even among these leaders, however, there is a tendency to demand unilateral settlements of the basic problems of the economy rather than multilateral settlements, in which they participate frankly and cooperatively in the working out of integrated solutions. . . . The "trusteeship" concept has a fine baronial flavor generously tinctured with *noblesse oblige*. It is an aristocratic and ethical approach quite different from the democratic and scientific approach called for by the conditions of today and tomorrow.[10]

[9] Brady, *op. cit.*, pp. 260-61.
[10] *The 1950's Come First*, New York, Henry Holt & Company, 1951, pp. 73-74. Cf. also, A. T. Mason, "Welfare Capitalism: Opportunity or Delusion," *Virginia Quarterly Review*, Autumn, 1950, pp. 530-43.

In my opinion, this line of argument has considerable force. Certainly, the doctrine of social responsibility can easily become no more than a pretense or a rationalization or a propaganda device; and insincerity, hypocrisy, and subtle persuasion are in fact often present when the doctrine is advocated. However, there are important answers to this general line of argument.

The American businessman has steadily lost power in the past fifty years. He now divides his power with labor unions, consumer organizations, and farm organizations; he is fenced in by a wide variety of governmental regulations and lives in constant threat of more public control; he has submitted voluntarily to the standards of trade associations and of the community; and he has become increasingly responsive to public opinion. Indeed, the dilution of his influence over his "own" decisions has been the principal source of the businessman's dissatisfaction with modern economic tendencies and the principal basis of his feelings of insecurity. His complaints lie not in the state of his profit-and-loss accounts, but rather in the decline in power he has experienced (which also is evidence that businessmen do not live by profits alone).

The modern businessman cannot be looked upon as an absolute monarch ruling by divine right and interpreting his social responsibilities as the carrying out of his own decisions as to what is "good" for the people. The businessman, rather, is subject to the standards of the community and to the pressures exerted by various interest groups. He interprets his social responsibility as conforming to "reasonable" and socially accepted standards of the "good," and, as is often necessary, compromising among various interests that are in conflict. This is quite different, both in spirit and practice, from the view that the businessman regards his social responsibilities as including only those things which *he* considers good. In the former case, there is a giving up of power and a bowing to the social will. In the latter, there is no giving up of power—only an effort to use it benevolently, as benevolence is defined by the paternalistic holder of the power. Indeed, under modern American conditions, when the businessman falls into the latter mode of thought, he is soon reminded of his waywardness by adversely affected interest groups.

But this point must not be overstressed. The businessman is by no means completely a pawn of various pressure groups. He is still a powerful figure in American society, and when he talks of social responsibility he does often think of his obligations in terms of what is good for the people *as he sees the good* and of retaining in his own hands the exclusive power to meet or not meet these obligations. It would seem, therefore, that if the businessman is serious about his social responsibilities, he would be concerned to develop procedures by which his judgment of the good would be subjected to the criticism of other groups representing other interests, and that he would recognize an obligation to follow the good as so defined instead of restricting himself to his own limited and perhaps biased set of values.[11] As many businessmen themselves point out, the contacts of businessmen are restricted largely to people of their own kind; their experience has been limited; their points of view are specialized; and they have certain axes to grind. Therefore, businessmen are not necessarily qualified to decide what is in the public interest without provision for interaction between their judgments and those of other groups. If the doctrine of social responsibility is to become an important and dependable element in American economic life, the definition of these responsibilities must become a prerogative of more than one class or one occupational group. This is the meaning of democracy as applied to business.[12] The same statement would of course apply if we were considering the social responsibilities of labor or agriculture or investors or consumers.[13]

[11] "No man will ever be so intelligent as to see the needs of others as vividly as he recognizes his own, or to be as quick in his aid to remote as to immediately revealed necessities."—Reinhold Niebuhr, *Moral Man and Immoral Society*, New York, Charles Scribner's Sons, 1932.

[12] This theme will be developed more fully in Chapter 14.

[13] J. M. Clark, *Social Control of Business*, 2nd ed., New York, McGraw-Hill Book Co., 1939, p. 9: "Some groups are more inclusive than others, and the more inclusive the group is, the better socialized is the control which it exercises. One of the difficulties of control lies in the fact that the groups whose voice speaks loudest to a given individual are precisely those smallest groups which are farthest from expressing the interest of the whole community. Trade unions can control their members fairly effectively in matters they have at heart, but what they have most at heart is getting as much as possible out of the employer. There is need of social control of this standard by a group including laborer, employer, consumer, and public, but this group is too heterogeneous to act with the easy effectiveness of smaller groups. Many a man genuinely wants to be moral as his associates see morality and goes on doing as they do, only to suffer a painful shock when the standard of his associates suddenly has the light of a broader community standard turned upon it. Too often this test reveals merely organized group selfishness. Something of this sort happened when Charles E. Hughes made his famous investigation of the abuses of insurance in New York."

PROXIMATE VERSUS REMOTE MORAL OBLIGATIONS

Another criticism of the doctrine of social responsibility is that it would place upon businessmen an unnecessary burden which they could not hope to discharge adequately and which would deflect them from their real moral responsibilities, which consist of personal religious duties and compassion and concern for the persons with whom they come into actual contact. In this view businessmen would be relieved of the duty to relate their actions to broader social goals.[14]

As with the other criticisms of the doctrine of social responsibility, this one has much validity. It is true that many people, in their relatively futile concern for broad social reform or amelioration of distant social problems, have ignored, or felt free from, responsibilities to persons and problems nearer at hand. However, this criticism is not wholly valid because it neglects the inescapable interdependence of complex modern society; it ignores the widely ramified effects of actions by businessmen and other influential groups. Today, our neighbors (i.e., the persons whose lives we touch) are not merely those near whom we live or those whom we see in our daily work; our neighbors are scattered throughout the country and the world. The greater the power or influence of any person or group, the larger the number and the more remote will be the persons whose lives he (or they) will affect.

[14] This view, which represents a reaction against the "social gospel" and which has considerable support among Protestant groups, has been eloquently expressed by James Agee: "It is fashionable to feel, and to force upon others, an acute sense of social responsibility. . . . People have been badgered half out of their minds by the sense of a sort of 'global' responsibility: the relentless daily obligation to stay aware of, hep to, worked-up over, guilty towards, active about, the sufferings of people at a great distance for whom one can do nothing whatever; a sort of playing-at-God (since He is in exile) over every sparrow that falls, with the sense of virtue increasing in ratio to the distance. This enormous and nonsensical burden can be dropped, with best intelligence and grace, by religious men; in any case by Christians. Believing in the concern, wisdom, and mercy of God and in ultimate justice, roughly aware of how much (and little) attempts at social betterment can bring, rid of illusory responsibilities, Christians can undertake real and sufficient ones: each to do no less than he as a human being is able (and he is not apt to be a saint) for the human beings within his sight and reach and touch; and never to presume it other than antihuman to do more. Thus alone, it becomes possible to be quiet, to begin to learn a little bit thoroughly, directly, through the heart; to begin, in fact, to be human."—"Religion and the Intellectuals," *Partisan Review*, February, 1950, pp. 108-9.

It is clear, therefore, that the moral obligations of businessmen —and of all the rest of us—extend far beyond our immediate environs and embrace many persons in addition to those we meet in our daily lives. Merely because a man is actively working for broad social objectives, such as economic stabilization or elimination of racial prejudice, he is not free to beat his wife or cheat his neighbors. But conversely, merely because he discharges the moral obligations that are near at hand and obvious, he is not relieved from other obligations that are distant and less clearly seen. It is clear, therefore, that the moral obligations of businessmen, and all of us, extend out far beyond our immediate environs and beyond those persons whom we meet in our daily lives.

CONCLUSION

We have considered five arguments that are sometimes advanced in opposition to the doctrine of social responsibility. We have found that each has a degree of validity, but that no one of the arguments invalidates the doctrine.

The first argument was that under competitive conditions socially minded businessmen would be prevented from pursuing their social obligations by the failure of their rivals to be equally concerned about the public interest. In answer to this, it was pointed out that many businesses do not operate in perfectly competitive markets; that even in a competitive industry, socially sanctioned standards of business operation might be adopted.

The second argument was that when businessmen take on social obligations, their costs are likely to rise, that these increased costs will probably be passed on to consumers (or workers), and that in the end the benefits from socially oriented business policies will have resulted merely in higher prices (or lower wages). In dealing with this, it was conceded that the costs would often be shifted. However, it was pointed out that the standard of living of a country is in two parts: the final products of industry and the conditions under which these products are produced. The improvement in one part of the standard may often be at the sacrifice of the other part, and the problem is to balance the marginal returns of the two parts. Thus an increase in consumer prices may be fully justified if that increase buys better working conditions, economic stabilization, increased participation, or some other good connected with the conditions of production.

The third argument was that businessmen are too incorrigibly wedded to the profit motive to consider voluntarily their social responsibilities. In answer to this, it was pointed out that businessmen have many motives, of which profit is only one, albeit an important one. Among these motives is the desire to conform to the standards of his society. Moreover, businessmen are keenly aware of the fact that their long-run self-interest requires that they heed their social obligations.

The fourth argument was that the doctrine of social responsibility is used by businessmen, as it has been used by all ruling classes, merely as a device for retaining and justifying their power. It was pointed out that there is validity in this argument, but that the social controls to which the modern businessman is subject have greatly weakened his power, and that he is not in a position to be the sole arbiter of his social obligations. However, a fully democratic method of defining social obligations of business would require procedures or institutions by which the interests of all segments of society could be reflected in the socially accepted standards of business operation.

The fifth argument was that to impose distant social responsibilities would deflect businessmen from their immediate moral obligations. It was pointed out that moral obligations are both distant and near at hand.

In the next chapter, we shall consider another criticism of the doctrine of social responsibility; namely, that for businessmen to make decisions which are oriented toward social objectives is a violation of their legal duty to stockholders. This subject raises important questions about the nature of a corporation and its relation to stockholders and to other groups.

11

The Law and the Doctrine of Social Responsibility

The suggestion that businessmen should assume certain broad social responsibilities raises the important question whether businessmen are legally entitled to shape their policies in terms of broad social objectives as distinct from the narrower interests of stockholder-owners. The legal problem is not difficult for unincorporated businesses or even for the incorporated businesses in which ownership and management are closely identified; but it becomes acute in the typical larger corporations owned by thousands of absentee stockholders who have little knowledge of or voice in the management of their enterprises. In conventional legal theory, the directors of such corporations are trustees for the stockholders. It is their duty, as trustees, to promote the interests of the stockholders—interpreted as maximum returns on and conservation of invested capital. Any tendency to consider the interests of workers, consumers, or the public—except as these might directly or indirectly advance the interests of stockholders—is therefore a violation of a trust.

Under this theory, the directors and managers of a corporation would lack the legal right or power to pursue broad social objectives not consistent with the maximum profit of stockholders. There is, however, considerable doubt whether this rigid doctrine was ever an accurate expression of the law. Surely, today, the voluntary assumption of social responsibility by corporations has gained substantial though tacit legal acceptance. This acceptance is likely to increase in future years.

CHARITABLE CONTRIBUTIONS

It is principally in the field of charitable contributions that the law has explicitly recognized broader purposes of a corporation than mere maximization of returns to stockholders. Over the past fifty or seventy-five years, the law relating to charitable contributions by corporations has been substantially liberalized—though even in this field corporate practice has been consistently ahead of expressed legal doctrine.

In common law, it was an elementary principle that philanthropic giving by a corporation not created for charitable purposes was beyond the powers of the corporation and in violation of the rights of stockholders. In applying this principle, the courts approved donations only when direct benefit to the corporation could be shown. For example, in Ireland, Lord Justice Bowen stated in 1883: "There is, however, a kind of charitable dealing which is for the interest of those who practice it, and to that extent and in that garb (I admit not a very philanthropic garb) charity may sit at the board, but for no other purpose."[1] In the Steinway case of 1896, however, the Court stated:

> It is a question, therefore, in each case, of the logical relation of the act to the corporate purpose expressed in the charter. If that act is one which is lawful in itself, and not otherwise prohibited, is done for the purpose of serving corporate ends, and is reasonably tributary to the preservation of those ends, in a substantial, and not in a remote and fanciful sense, it may fairly be considered within charter powers. The field of corporate action in respect to the exercise of incidental powers is thus, I think, an expanding one. As individual conditions change, business methods must change with them, and acts become permissible which at an earlier period would not have been considered to be within corporate power.

The Steinway decision has been followed in later cases. According to the present law, a corporation if questioned about a charitable donation must demonstrate how that donation serves its corporate purposes. "The Court will consider the kind of corporation, the nature and location of its business, the kind of charity, the use to which the donation is to be applied, and the relation of the use to the corporate business in the light of the times. If the donation fails to meet this test, it is *ultra vires*."[2]

The issue is the remoteness or directness of benefit. The courts

---

[1] *Hutton* v. *West Cork Railway Co.*, 23 Ch. D. 654, 673 (Ct. App. 1883).
[2] Ray Garrett, "Corporate Donations to Charity," *The Business Lawyer*, November, 1948, p. 29.

usually do not question a donation when the employees of the corporation are beneficiaries, nor frequently donations to general welfare agencies and educational institutions. Although American corporations give millions of dollars each year to the American Red Cross and Community Chests, and (during the war) to war relief agencies, no court decisions have been rendered regarding corporate donations to these agencies.[3] In fact, there have been few litigated cases on the whole subject of corporate giving—which implies that giving, at least on the scale and for the purposes now practiced, has the approval of stockholders and of the community generally.[4]

As part of the general liberalization of the law regarding corporate giving, legislation permitting donations for certain purposes has been enacted in sixteen states. The first of these laws was enacted in Texas in 1917. These laws vary widely in their content, but all have the effect of extending the powers of corporate managers to make charitable donations. It is evident that corporate practice and public opinion are more liberal than the stated law.[5] It may be safely asserted that the trend is toward increasing powers, and increasing obligations, of corporations to engage in charitable giving.

PERSONNEL POLICIES

A subject closely related to charitable giving is provision of various benefits for employees as part of modern personnel policies. These include such benefits as pensions, medical care, recreational programs, and profit sharing. It is clearly evident that benefits of

[3] *Op. cit.*, p. 30.

[4] Cf. Elmo Roper, *A Report on What Information People Want About Policies and Financial Conditions of Corporations*, Vol. I, The Controllership Foundation, New York, 1948, p. xx.

[5] Beardsley Ruml and Theodore Geiger, *The Five Percent*, National Planning Association, Planning Pamphlet No. 73, August, 1951. This is a discussion of the provision of the Internal Revenue Law permitting corporations to deduct contributions for educational, scientific, and welfare purposes up to 5 per cent of net income. See also Commission on Financing Higher Education, *Higher Education and American Business*, February, 1952; Alfred P. Sloan, Jr., "Big Business Must Help Our Colleges," *Collier's*, June 2, 1951, p. 13; F. E. Andrews, "New Giant in Giving: Big Business," *The New York Times Magazine*, December 2, 1951, pp. 14, 34-38; *Company Policy on Donations*, National Industrial Conference Board, Studies in Business Policy, No. 7 and No. 49; Beardsley Ruml and Theodore Geiger, *The Manual of Corporate Giving*, National Planning Association, Washington, 1952; F. E. Andrews, *Corporation Giving*, Russell Sage Foundation, New York, 1952.

this type have become firmly established in the business practices of this country and are justified in law and in public opinion as part of the necessary costs of doing business.

BROADER RESPONSIBILITIES

When we leave the subjects of corporate giving and employee benefits and turn to the question of the broader public responsibilities of corporations, the law is relatively silent. Few cases have been brought before the courts, and no legislation has been enacted. Corporations have been left relatively free to cut prices to aid in combating inflation or to pass on to consumers an equitable share of the benefits from technological advance; to plan their productive schedules, inventories, and capital investments in order to contribute to regularization of production even when these actions will be at the sacrifice of profit; to refrain from cheap or vulgar advertising methods even when these are demonstrably more effective for sales; to refrain from forcing a competitor out of business when an opportunity to do so is present; to raise wages above the going rate; etc.

The relative absence of cases on these broader questions is presumably due to the facts (1) that corporate directors and managers have almost always acted primarily in the interests of stockholders and have been conservative and discreet in regard to actions which could not be justified on this basis, at least in the long run; (2) that stockholders have generally approved the many socially oriented policies of corporations; and (3) that stockholders have not been fully informed, or have not seen the implications of such corporate actions.

The one case which is usually cited on this subject is *Dodge* v. *Ford Motor Co.*[6] This is a complex case in which the Ford Motor Company was sued in 1919 by the Dodge Brothers, who were stockholders of the company, to force larger distribution of dividends. Henry Ford had given notice that dividends would be reduced, that the large undistributed earnings of the company would be chiefly reinvested for purposes of expansion, and that the price of his car would be reduced. He stated: "My ambition is to employ still more men, to spread the benefits of this industrial system to

[6] 204 Mich. at 507, 170 N.W. at 684.

the greatest possible number, to help them build up their lives and their homes. To do this we are putting the greatest share of our profits back in the business."

In commenting on this statement, the Court remarked:

There should be no confusion (of which there is evidence) of the duties which Mr. Ford conceives that he and the stockholders owe to the general public and the duties which in law he and his codirectors owe to protesting, minority stockholders. A business corporation is organized and carried on primarily for the profit of the stockholders. The powers of the directors are to be employed primarily for that end. The discretion of the directors is to be exercised in the choice of means to attain that end, and does not extend to a change in the end itself, to the reduction of profits, or to the nondistribution of profits among stockholders in order to devote them to other purposes.

The Ford case clearly affirmed the traditional view that the responsibility of directors is to yield profits for the stockholders— and to see that the stockholders actually get a reasonable share of these profits. Nevertheless, the Court was careful not to interfere with the proposed expansion program:

We are not persuaded that we should interfere with the proposed expansion of the business of the Ford Motor Company. In view of the fact that the selling price of products may be increased at any time, the ultimate results of the larger business cannot be certainly estimated. The judges are not business experts. It is recognized that plans must often be made for a long future, for expected competition, for a continuing as well as an immediately profitable venture. The experience of the Ford Motor Company is evidence of capable management of its affairs. . . . We are not satisfied that the alleged motives of the directors, in so far as they are reflected in the conduct of the business, menace the interests of shareholders.

One must conclude that the law, as overtly expressed in legislation and in actual cases, has not departed significantly from the basic principle that a corporation is organized for the profit of stockholders, and that it is the duty of the directors to conduct the business with this end in view. But the courts will permit the widest latitude for discretion of the directors and will not presume to dictate the operating policies of the business. They will intervene only if there is evidence of fraud, misappropriation of funds, lack of competence, or clear-cut breach of faith. Nevertheless, the basic rule is that the business be managed in the interests of stockholders.[7]

However, public opinion, business opinion, public regulation, and the general social environment within which business is conducted have changed markedly since the heyday of laissez faire. Corporate acts which fifty years ago would have been regarded as suspect and possibly beyond the powers of a private corporation organized for profit have today become part of normal operating routine, and are considered essential if business enterprises are to secure morale and efficiency among their employees and are to be well regarded by customers, suppliers, and the public generally. Examples of such acts are charitable donations, community service, employee benefits, provision of pleasant and healthful working conditions, regularization of production, cooperation with the government in national defense, charging "reasonable" prices, improving products, introducing new products (even at the cost of obsolescence of old plants), locating plants according to community needs, providing for conservation of natural resources, promoting fundamental scientific research, avoidance of inventory speculation, reinvestment of earnings, etc. Obviously, most corporations at times make decisions involving additions to cost or subtractions from revenue which are not in the interests of stockholders as conceived narrowly or in the short run. Many such decisions can, however, be said to be in the stockholders' interests in the long run, taking into account the climate of opinion and the nature of the social environment within which business operates. But there is no doubt that many corporations have, in addition, taken actions regarding prices, wages, production, etc., which, if challenged, would be hard to defend in a court of law except on the theory that a corporation can rightfully act in terms of its obligations to society at large as well as to its stockholders.

If such cases were litigated, it would be difficult to predict how any given court would judge any particular case. One might guess that the principle of the Steinway case would be followed, namely, "as industrial conditions change, business methods must change with them, and acts become permissible which at an earlier period

[7] E. M. Dodd and R. J. Baker, *Cases and Materials on Corporations*, 2nd ed., Brooklyn, Foundation Press, 1951.

would not have been considered to be within corporate power." Also a principle of the Ford case might be followed, namely, that the court should not substitute its business judgment for that of the directors. Under these principles, a wide variety of corporate actions which are not directly or immediately in stockholders' interests might be found legal and proper. The very fact that the questions regarding socially oriented policies of corporations have not been raised, during a period of revolutionary change in business practice, suggests that the public and the legal profession regard these new developments as proper and legal.[8] If actual cases were litigated, the courts could scarcely overlook the development in the practices of business and in the attitudes of the community; the courts would undoubtedly find difficulty in reaffirming the rigid doctrine that the interests of stockholders are always paramount and preclusive. To do so would run counter to a great social development which has gone unchallenged for a generation.

For example, in an age of widespread public utility regulation and antitrust laws, the courts would have difficulty in ruling illegal an attempt of corporate managers to adjust their prices in terms of a "reasonable" rate of return on capital;[9] or, in an age of widespread interest in "social security," courts would be reluctant to rule against liberal pension plans or company plans for employment stabilization; or, in an age of concern about depletion of natural resources, to rule against private conservation schemes; or, at a time of minimum wage legislation, to rule against paying premium wage rates; or, in an age of concern for housing conditions, to oppose a company plan for improving the housing of workers.

In other words, for the courts to apply strictly the principle of maximum profit for stockholders would now be grossly incompatible with the broad objectives expressed in so much of our social legislation. True, the courts might conceivably take the narrow view that corporate directors and stockholders may not engage in socially

[8] Cf. A. A. Berle, Jr., and W. C. Warren, *Cases and Materials on the Law of Business Organization*, Brooklyn, Foundation Press, 1948, pp. 1102-5.

[9] As Justice Brandeis stated in a famous dissent: "The notion of a distinct category of business 'affected with a public interest,' employing property 'devoted to a public use,' rests upon historical error." *New State Ice Co.* v. *Liebmann*, 52 Sup. Ct., 371, 383 (1932). See also Walton Hamilton, "Affectation with Public Interest," *Yale Law Journal*, 1930, pp. 1089-1112.

oriented policies unless such policies are forced upon them by legislation. But that they would actually take this narrow view seems improbable to the point of fantasy.[10]

As Professor Dodd suggests, the view of the corporation as existing only for the interests of stockholders is untenable: "Business—which is the economic organization of society—is private property only in a qualified sense, and society may properly demand that it be carried on in such a way as to safeguard the interests of those who deal with it as employees or consumers even if the proprietary rights of its owners are thereby curtailed.[11]

Conclusions

The general conclusions from this brief survey of the legal situation are (1) that the law as expressed in legislation and actual cases still regards the corporation as existing for the purpose of making profits for stockholders, and requires directors of corporations to conduct business with this end in view; (2) that the courts, however, have taken an increasingly liberal view of the discretion permitted corporate directors and of the range of policies that are considered to promote stockholders' interests; (3) that public opinion and corporate practice, as yet unchallenged in legal proceedings, have embraced the view that corporations have public responsibilities as well as duties to stockholders.

While one may conclude that corporations undoubtedly have wide latitude to adopt policies which are conceived to be in the social interest—even at the sacrifice of maximum profits for stockholders—there are limits to these powers. Surely, corporate directors may not deliberately exhaust the resources of a company in quest of broad social objectives. Rules pertaining to reasonable returns on capital, as applied to public utilities, may be pertinent here.

Possibly the directors may not even venture far beyond those social good works which are widely accepted by the community as reasonable or necessary. Thus, there is no distinct line separating those actions in the social interest which are legally acceptable and those which are not. There is a broad range of indefiniteness,

[10] E. Merrick Dodd, Jr., "For Whom Are Corporate Managers Trustees?" *Harvard Law Review*, May 8, 1932, Vol. 45, p. 1148.

[11] *Op. cit.*, p. 1162.

but the area of expected and permitted social responsibility is undoubtedly becoming broader.

A view widely held in the legal profession is that to expect corporations to assume social responsibilities is a laudable ideal but an impracticable one unless enforceable rules can be laid down to distinguish between those actions which are required and those which are permissive, and between those which are permissive and those which are forbidden. As Mr. Berle has said: "Most students of corporation finance dream of a time when corporate administration will be held to a high degree of required responsibility—a responsibility conceived not merely in terms of stockholders' rights, but in terms of economic government satisfying the respective needs of investors, workers, customers, and the aggregated community."[12] But he says further:

Now I submit that you can not abandon emphasis on "the view that business corporations exist for the sole purpose of making profit for their stockholders" until such time as you are prepared to offer a clear and reasonably enforceable scheme of responsibilities to some one else. . . . Either you have a system of private ownership or you do not. If not . . . it becomes necessary to present a system (none has been presented) of law or government, or both, by which responsibility for control of national wealth and income is so apportioned and enforced that the community as a whole, or at least the great bulk of it, is properly taken care of. Otherwise, the economic power now mobilized and massed under the corporate form, in the hands of a few thousand directors, and the few hundred individuals holding "control," is simply handed over, weakly, to the present administrators with a pious wish that something nice will come out of it all.[13]

There is, of course, a great deal of merit in this argument. However, Mr. Berle partially answered it himself in another document:[14]

Neither the claims of ownership nor those of control can stand against the paramount interests of the community. The present claims of both contending parties in the field have been weakened by the events described in this book. It remains only for the claims of the community

[12] A. A. Berle, Jr., "For Whom Corporate Managers Are Trustees," *Harvard Law Review*, June, 1932, Vol. 45, p. 1372.
[13] *Op. cit.*, pp. 1367-8.
[14] A. A. Berle, Jr., and G. C. Means, *The Modern Corporation and Private Property*, New York, The Macmillan Company, 1933, p. 355.

to be put forward with clarity and force. . . . When a convincing system of community obligations is worked out and is generally accepted, in that moment the passive property right of today must yield before the larger interests of society. Should the corporate leaders, for example, set forth a program comprising fair wages, security to employees, reasonable service to their public, and stabilization of business, all of which would divert a portion of the profits from the owners of passive property, and should the community generally accept such a scheme as a logical and human solution of industrial difficulties, the interests of passive property would have to give way. Courts would almost of necessity be forced to recognize the result, justifying it by whatever of the many legal themes they might choose. It is conceivable—indeed it seems almost essential if the corporate system is to survive—that the "control" of the great corporations should develop into a purely neutral technocracy, balancing a variety of claims by various groups in the community and assigning to each a portion of the income stream on the basis of public policy rather than private capacity.

Now, twenty years later (Mr. Berle wrote in 1932 and 1933), we have an impressive record of business decisions made with social objectives in view and of statements by leading businessmen acknowledging their social responsibilities in the broadest terms. To date, the law has not challenged this new development.

12

Toward Increasing the Effectiveness of Social Responsibility in Business Decisions

We shall now consider several conditions which must be met if the doctrine of social responsibility is to become a more significant force in shaping the decisions and actions of businessmen. These conditions are not likely to be attained fully or quickly. The mere mention and brief discussion of them suggests that the doctrine of social responsibility is subject to distinct limitations, that its effectiveness cannot be expected to increase rapidly, and that it is far from a panacea. The conditions to be discussed relate to (1) attitudes of businessmen, (2) public attitudes, (3) definition of social responsibilities, (4) scope and rigor of standards, (5) technical knowledge, (6) definition of ends, and (7) profits.

ATTITUDES OF BUSINESSMEN

The first and most essential condition, if social responsibility is to become a more effective force, is that businessmen must acquire a strengthened sense of vocation. They must accept the social implications of their calling. They must recognize that ultimately business exists not for profits, for power, or for personal aggrandizement, but to serve society. They must recognize that the freedom and the power which they enjoy has been committed to them by society on the theory that decentralization of economic decision-making contributes to social welfare through its salutary effects in unleashing the imagination, the leadership, and the enterprise of independent businessmen. Such freedom and power, of course, entail great responsibility. They must be used moderately, conscientiously, and with a view to the interests of society at large. Only thus can the widespread delegation of decision-making in matters affecting the whole community be justified—and the system of private enterprise continue indefinitely to survive. Moreover, it is not enough that businessmen be responsive to the public interest as that public interest was defined fifty or one hundred years ago. They must be attuned to the changing needs of society, and must interpret their responsibilities accordingly.

A large enterprise may be thought of as a center from which influences radiate in ever-widening circles. In the inner circle are the employees whose whole lives are bound up with the business. In the next circle are the stockholders, customers, and suppliers who are directly affected in varying degrees by the actions of the business but who seldom are closely associated with it or fully dependent upon it. In the next circle are the citizens of the community in which the business operates. If the business is socially ill-managed, these are the persons who must breathe the polluted air, or view the ugly premises, or hear the nerve-wracking noises, or bear the costs of relief and accident, or live in an atmosphere of labor-management strife. In the next circle are the competitors—both in the markets for the factors of production and in the markets for goods and services. Finally, in the outer circle is the general public, which, if the business is socially ill-managed, must suffer from the resulting economic instability, poverty, strife, vulgar advertising, selfish lobbying, etc.

The businessman produces two categories of products. The first category consists of commercial goods and services, e.g., steel, lumber, automobiles, clothing, food, etc. The second category consists of the conditions under which the production of these goods and services takes place. Included in this second category of products are the physical conditions of work, the stability of employment, the security of workers and others, the quality of the human relations, the rate of exploitation of natural resources, wage and price policies, research, location, advertising and selling practices, dividend policies, use and extension of credit, capital structure, stream and air pollution, community action, relations with government, etc. These together may be called the "social products" of business.

Both categories of products have a demand. Commercial goods and services are demanded by other businessmen and by consumers. The social products of business—the conditions under which production is carried on—are subject to the demands of persons located in the various concentric circles of business influence. Workers demand "good" working conditions, "good" wages, and security. Stockholders demand "adequate" dividends; suppliers demand "fair" prices and a steady market; local citizens demand a "good" physical and social environment; competitors demand "fair" competition and sometimes cooperation in the attainment of mutual objectives in the interests of the industry; the general public demands that the business contribute to the general social goals of abundance, progress, stability, personal security, justice, freedom, personal development, and community improvement.

If the concept of social responsibility is to become an effective force, the businessman must see that he has two kinds of products and that the ultimate success of his business will be measured by its ability to meet the demands for both kinds of products. But merely meeting demands will not be enough. Just as a businessman must anticipate demand for his commercial products, so he must anticipate the demands for his social products and provide leadership in showing how business can serve society at large. He must not be content to lag behind demand for his social products any more than he would lag behind the demand for his commercial products. To the extent that businessmen become imbued with this point of view, the concept of social responsibility can become an effective and constructive force in economic life.[1]

As has been suggested, an increasing number of businessmen are showing keen interest in their social responsibilities. This is encouraging. But the conception of their social responsibilities held by many businessmen is still narrow and for others it is little more than a grudging acknowledgment of social pressures that have become too strong to ignore. Further education of businessmen on the nature of their social role must therefore have a prominent place on the agenda of those who would reinforce the free-enterprise system.

PUBLIC ATTITUDES

A second condition of the strengthening of the concept of social responsibility is the development of public attitudes regarding the social role of business. Any attempt to achieve social control through the application of moral rules must rest upon the understanding and

[1] Cf. M. E. Dimock and H. K. Hyde, *Bureaucracy and Trusteeship in Large Corporations*, Temporary National Economic Commiteee, Monograph No. 11, pp. 108-22.

acceptance of the rules not only by those who are expected to follow them—the businessmen in this case—but also by the general populace.

All social control is achieved by a dual apparatus. On the one hand, the actors (businessmen) must be conditioned to *want* to follow the moral rules; and, on the other hand, the public must expect them to follow these rules and impose penalties if they do not. Both aspects of control rest ultimately upon the attitudes of the public. For example, businessmen are not likely to want to follow any particular moral rules unless those rules have received widespread social acceptance (including acceptance among businessmen). Without such acceptance such rules would not, indeed, be moral rules at all, and it would hardly occur to businessmen to follow them. Certainly there would be no educational machinery for inculcating these rules. Moreover, without widespread social acceptance there would be no sanctions and no method of enforcement. Businessmen would incur neither blame nor praise for following or not following the rules. They would achieve no sense of satisfaction from following them and no loss of status from disregarding them.

Clearly, if the concept of social responsibility is to be a force in our society, the public must acquire definite attitudes regarding business operations and must develop a set of generally accepted standards or rules which businessmen are expected to follow. With such accepted rules in the background, the education of businessmen would lead them to *want* to follow the rules because they would regard them as "right," and the public by the power of informal sanctions would enforce these rules.

Just as society can establish and enforce standards of right and wrong in matters of personal etiquette, dress, family relationships, language, religion and a host of other aspects of life, so it can establish and enforce standards of right and wrong in matters of business operation. But in all cases the standards are effective only to the degree that they are backed by public acceptance.

DEMOCRATIC DEFINITION OF SOCIAL RESPONSIBILITIES

A third essential condition is a reasonably clear definition of what is expected of business at any given time, place, and circumstance.

It is perhaps not necessary, or even desirable, that the obligations of businessmen be codified fully and in detail. One of the advantages of informal moral rules over formal laws is that they are more flexible and adaptable to changing circumstances. But it is important that at least general standards be clearly formulated and widely understood. Only if this is so can the businessman know what standards he is expected to follow or can public opinion be effectively applied. Even with the best of intentions, it is difficult to be moral, or to enforce moral conduct, when the content of morality is not known.

This raises the question of how and by whom the social responsibilities of business are to be defined. Many businessmen have taken the position that they, as capable leaders thoroughly conversant with business practices and problems, should define their own social responsibilities. This essentially paternalistic viewpoint is subject to question. As indicated in Chapter 10, it has been a prevalent practice of ruling classes to declare that they are exercising their power in the interests of the masses and that they (the ruling class) are best equipped to define these interests.

Businessmen and groups of businessmen should, of course, give thoughtful attention to the definition of their social obligations; they should do it as disinterestedly and conscientiously as they can; and their views should be received by other groups thoughtfully and with respect. But businessmen can hardly be relied upon as the sole arbiters of their social responsibilities. Their thinking and their values, like those of any other group, are influenced by their particular experiences and their special interests. Like the members of other groups, they tend as a group to magnify their own interests and to perceive indistinctly the interests and aspirations of others. Therefore, the views of businessmen about their own social responsibilities must be subjected to the criticisms and the judgments of other groups. Businessmen should be free to advance their ideas and to try to persuade others of their soundness, but they should not be final arbiters of the rules they are to follow. These should be worked out through the democratic process of interaction among the points of view of many interest groups. The ultimate formulation of standards should have a broad base of public acceptance. The duty of business in a democracy is not merely to meet its social responsibilities as these are defined by businessmen, but rather to follow the social obligations which are defined by the whole community through the give-and-take of public discussion and compromise.

When businessmen think of themselves as trustees mediating among the interests of stockholders, workers, suppliers, the local community, and the general public, they are close to this democratic concept. However, trusteeship, as they view it, would leave with them the power to define the interests of the various groups. In a fully democratic order, on the other hand, these various interests would be reconciled in the formulation of socially accepted standards which the businessman would then feel obliged to follow.

If the social responsibilities of business are to be effectively defined by the democratic process, new institutions—not yet fully developed in American society—may be desirable. These institutions would provide the machinery for mobilizing all points of view in formulating and communicating acceptable standards of business practice in terms of which the social responsibilities of business would be defined. The following three chapters will discuss such institutions.

Scope and Rigor of Standards

If the concept of social responsibility is to become an important element in American economic life, the standards to which businessmen are expected to conform should be set conservatively. Society should not expect sudden or large changes in business practice; the demands made should not be financially ruinous or deny the legitimate self-interest of the businessman. The temptation to impose Utopian demands on the individual businessman should be resisted.

The starting point should be the actual practices of the more forward-looking businesses, and steady but gradual improvements should be expected thereafter.

In formulating the standards, the attitude should not be one of witch-hunting or of querulous meddling in the day-to-day affairs of business. The great advantage of the private-enterprise system is that it provides for decentralization of decision-making and freedom of initiative.

The objective should be to establish general standards based upon the evolving practices of the more forward-looking and socially minded businesses and conformable to widely accepted social values, and to enforce these standards so far as possible by the power of education and public opinion.

TECHNICAL KNOWLEDGE

The concept of social responsibility can be effective as a device for social improvement only to the extent that the standards to which business is expected to adhere are appropriately related to the ultimate ends in view. This can be known only if there is valid and relevant scientific knowledge. Just as governmental policy should be appropriately designed to achieve the objects for which it is intended, so the informal standards set to guide the actions of businessmen should be suitable for the ends in view. Unfortunately, in many cases the sciences of economics, psychology, sociology, administrative behavior, etc., fall far short of providing the knowledge required. This places an important limitation on the scope and effectiveness of the concept of social responsibility.

This problem can be illustrated by an episode which occurred in 1946-47. At that time organized labor demanded increased wages on the ground that higher wages would be necessary in order to maintain mass purchasing power and thus prevent the expected postwar depression. The C.I.O. retained Dr. Robert R. Nathan, a well-known consulting economist, to prepare a report presenting the labor argument. The Nathan report[2] was widely publicized and may have had considerable effect in convincing the public that business had a social responsibility to accede to the union wage demands of that time.

The Nathan report was doubtless an able document; some day, perhaps, the scientific validity of its argument and conclusions may be demonstrated. But at the time it was written, and this is still true today, one could hardly claim on the basis of scientific evidence that a rise in wages under the conditions prevailing at that time would have prevented depression. At that time we could not even know, with any degree of reliability, whether depression threatened. So the attempt in 1946 to establish that businessmen had a social obligation to raise wages got nowhere simply because we lacked demon-

[2] Robert R. Nathan and Oscar Gass, A *National Wage Policy for 1947*, Washington, Robert R. Nathan Associates, 1946.

strable scientific knowledge on which to base such an obligation. Businessmen could and did find economists who advanced theories in opposition to the Nathan report. No one knew where the economic truth lay. Both sides used economic arguments and the authority of well-known economists to support their predetermined conclusions, and neither side could validly claim that a social responsibility either to raise or not to raise wages had been established.

The same lamentable lack of knowledge that surrounds the wage question is true of many other problems pertaining to business responsibilities. For example, we know little about incentives and therefore little about the amount of profit that is socially justifiable, or the return to capital that is necessary to maintain industry, or the executive salaries that are needed to obtain talented leadership, or the structure of wages that calls forth efficiency and productivity. We also know little about the relation between the size of business enterprises and their efficiency, their price policies, and their social effectiveness. We are unable to forecast business conditions and therefore are limited in prescribing specific policies for business firms to follow with a view to achieving greater economic stability. We have no established criteria to guide us in prescribing the most desirable rates of exploitation of natural resources, or the most desirable rates of capital accumulation. We even lack clear-cut principles regarding the location of production and the geographic distribution of industry.

To the extent that we do not know the effects of various alternative lines of action, it makes little sense to attempt to establish specific social responsibilities for businessmen. These responsibilities should be limited to matters in which there is reasonable assurance that the prescribed action will lead to desired ends.

DEFINITION OF ENDS

Perhaps even more significant than lack of scientific knowledge is the confusion about ends or goals. Most people can agree on the list of abstract economic goals presented in Chapter 2. But when these are translated into action it is found that the several goals are not always mutually independent. Economic stability sometimes must be acquired at the cost of economic progress, personal security sometimes comes at a high price measured in personal freedom, a higher standard of living may involve a sacrifice of justice or a deterioration of community living, etc. Since various people value these individual goals differently, concepts of the social responsibilities of business differ accordingly. Under these conditions, it would seem wise to restrict the social responsibilities of business to those areas in which there is wide agreement on ends.

PROFITS

Finally, if the concept of social responsibility is to become significant, it should not be made the vehicle or the excuse for an attack on the profit motive, or on profits as such. In discussions of the social responsibilities of business there is a frequent tendency to criticize profits. This criticism takes either of two forms: (1) an attack on the "profit motive" or (2) an allegation that profits are too high and should be lowered. In any case, it is usually assumed that businesses should meet the costs of their expanding social obligations out of profits. There are elements both of danger and of futility in these attitudes toward profits, and it is doubtful that the emphasis on profits and the profit motive is the most useful approach to the problem of the social responsibilities of business.[3]

Attacks on the profit motive are common especially in the writings of moralists and religious leaders. It is held that the quest for profit is based upon selfish motives, and that these ought to be replaced by altruistic motives of service to society. The slogan "production for use" is advanced in opposition to the present practice of production for profit. This line of thinking is surely based on a misconception of the nature and function of profit.[4]

It is true that the profit motive is based upon selfishness, but in this it is no different from the rent motive, the interest motive, the wage motive, or the consumer motive. When a landowner shifts his land from corn production to wheat production because he expects the return from wheat to be higher, few moralists would criticize him. When an investor sells A. T. & T. stock and buys General Motors, because he expects General Motors to pay higher dividends, this is ordinarily considered legitimate. When a worker

[3] Cf. P. F. Drucker, *The New Society*, New York, Harper & Brothers, 1950, pp. 52-73.
[4] Kenneth E. Bounding, *Economics of the Peace*, New York, Prentice-Hall, 1945, pp. 236-40.

moves from the South to the North, because he thinks wages are higher in the North and employment opportunities better, no one upbraids him. When a young man considers carefully his choice of occupation on the basis of expected remuneration, he is usually praised for his foresight and providence. When a consumer chooses to buy more cheese when the price of beef rises to $1 per pound, this is said to be good economy. All economic decisions such as these are made typically with self-interest as the predominant motive. Yet they are not considered morally questionable. But when a businessman chooses a particular line of production, or enters a particular market area, or replaces one kind of machinery with another, or expands his scale of operation, or makes any other of the myriad decisions that may affect his costs or his markets, if he is thereby seeking profit, this kind of self-interest becomes an unworthy objective. If we are to attack the profit motive of the businessman, surely we must be consistent and attack also the rent motive, the interest motive, the wage motive, and the consumer motive.

There are several difficulties in relying heavily on the service motive in any of these cases. First, in view of the moral limitations of men, the service motive is less reliable and consistent than the motive of self-interest. Second, individuals are often not in a good position to know how they can best serve society, and their decisions based on the service motive may often hit wide of the target. Third, to ask people to weigh all their economic decisions by calculating the social interest would place an intolerable strain on them. They need short-cut methods of reaching decisions that do not involve all the complexities of relating every individual action to the social interest. The price system provides this short-cut method. With all its imperfections, it is a marvelous device for registering social valuations and thus providing a system of easily recognizable signals by which individuals can reconcile their own self-interest and the social interest.

When a farmer shifts from corn production to wheat production, he ordinarily does so because the price of wheat has risen relative to the price of corn or because the cost of producing wheat has fallen relative to the cost of producing corn. A selfish motive leads him to make the shift. But is this not also in the social interest? The increase in the price of wheat means that wheat has become more valuable—is needed more urgently—perhaps because new uses for it have been found, because consumers' preferences have shifted toward wheat, or because too little of it had been produced for the given demand. When the farmer shifts to wheat production, then, he is acting in the *social* interest. On the basis of a price signal, he is led to make an adjustment in the social output which will add to the total satisfactions received by society from its production. The same argument would apply if he had made the shift because the cost of producing wheat had declined. If the cost of producing wheat falls relative to the cost of producing corn, society will be better off to substitute wheat for corn in some of the marginal uses of the latter. In this way, the quantity of the factors of production required to meet the needs of the society for grain can be reduced and some of these factors can be transferred to the production of other things. In this case, too, the farmer, by following his price signals, has served both himself and society.[5]

The same general line of argument can be applied to the decisions of investors. When an investor shifts from A. T. & T. to General Motors because the dividends of the latter are prospectively higher, he is helping the automobile industry to get more capital,[6] an industry which should expand because either the demand for its product has risen or its cost of production has fallen. The investor is following price signals and thereby serving society. Similarly, when a worker moves from the South to the North in search of higher wages, he is following price signals by leaving work where the value of his services is lower and going to work where the value of his services is higher. When a young man chooses carpentry, a trade in which his prospective earnings will be $5,000 per year, in preference to bookkeeping, in which his earnings are likely to be $3,000 per year, he is attempting to enter that occupation in which the value of his services will be at a maximum. And if a consumer chooses to substitute cheese for beef when the price of the latter rises to $1 per pound, he is trying to achieve economy by using less of his income for food so that he will have more left over for other uses.

[5] This argument is based on the theory of welfare economics. It is not possible to present here all of the qualifications of this theory. For a more complete discussion, see H. R. Bowen, *Toward Social Economy*, New York, Rinehart & Company, 1948, Parts IV and V, especially pp. 120-55.

[6] The resulting higher price of General Motors stock would make more favorable the terms on which General Motors could float new securities.

What has all this to do with the profit motive of businessmen? Just this: when businessmen follow the profit motive they are merely following social valuations as expressed in the prices at which they can sell their products and the prices at which they can buy productive services, materials, supplies, and their other requirements. For example, if there are big profits to be made in manufacturing nylon hosiery, this is an indication that society has placed a high valuation on this product in relation to its cost. This is society's way of saying that more of it should be produced. When the businessman follows this signal, he is following not only his own interest but that of society as well.

It is true that the businessman may, on occasion, disagree with social valuations as expressed in prices. He may feel that certain kinds of goods are not "worth" their market price because their consumption contributes only unimportant, or even undesirable, satisfactions. He may feel that certain types of workers, in view of the unpleasantness or difficulty of their work, are "worth" more than the market offers. Moreover, he may feel that some workers should receive more than their market wages simply because the market fails to provide them with a decent living. He may easily criticize many other prices as distorted valuations and as sources of injustice. But how far should he go in trying to substitute his own personal judgments on these matters for the broader social judgments reached through interaction of the choices of many peoples? The answer is clear. The practical and the democratic thing for him to do is to rely primarily on profit as his guide in deciding his business actions.

The profit motive can be objected to legitimately when the quest for profits results in restrictive monopoly, exploitation, fraud, misrepresentation, political bribery, waste of natural resources, economic insecurity, etc. It is the *abuse* of the profit motive, not the motive itself, that comes under criticism.

We do not condemn the sex motive *as a motive*; rather we criticize excesses, perversion, and licentious conduct. So, in attempting to identify and formulate the social responsibilities of businessmen, we cannot reasonably attack the profit motive as such but only abuses of it. What we aim for is a profit motive that knows limits, that operates with moderation, that is tempered by consideration for social ends. But still we must rely on the profit motive to guide production into the most fruitful industries and to encourage efficiency.[7] Even in a socialist economy, the profit motive would be relied upon in the sense that production would be shunted away from those industries in which costs are in excess of product prices and toward those industries in which product prices are in excess of costs.[8]

The second attack on profit is the frequent allegation that profits are too high and ought to be lowered. This attack also must be qualified carefully before it can be accepted. To the extent that profits are excessive because of the abuses just mentioned (and there is no doubt that some profit is derived from antisocial conduct), then all can agree that profits ought to be lowered at least to that extent. But when it is demanded that profits be lowered even further, there are grave questions not only as to whether such a policy is desirable but whether it is possible in an economy of private enterprise.

I shall assume that we mean by *profits* the total share of the national income paid to equity owners or reinvested for them after allowance for return at the market rate to all land and capital employed in business enterprises. This definition conforms to the economist's (but not the accountant's) concept of profit. Under this definition, there is some question whether profits in the aggregate are positive or negative in amount. In any given year, some businesses make profits and others suffer losses. In some years, the aggregate losses of those businesses which have failed to make a profit exceed the aggregate profits of the profitable businesses. In other years, the aggregate profits of the profitable firms exceed the losses of the unprofitable firms. Over the long run, it is uncertain whether combined profits and losses are positive or negative. Therefore, the demand that profits be lowered may be a demand that something which fluctuates around zero should be reduced on the average to a negative amount. This could only mean a reduction in the return for the use of capital and land.

[7] Cf. J. M. Keynes, "The End of Laissez Faire," in *Essays in Persuasion*, New York, Harcourt, Brace & Company, 1932, pp. 320-21.

[8] A considerable literature has been developed on this subject. See for example, Oskar Lange, F. M. Taylor, and B. E. Lippincott (ed.), *On the Economic Theory of Socialism*, Minneapolis, University of Minnesota Press, 1938; A. C. Pigou, *Socialism vs. Capitalism*, London, The Macmillan Company, 1937; A. P. Lerner, *The Economics of Control*, New York, The Macmillan Company, 1947.

But the economist's concept of profit is not that of the common man who regards as profits the total share of the receipts of business firms which are paid to the several classes of owners (bondholders, stockholders, proprietors, etc.) or reserved for them by reinvestment in the business. To the common man, the term "profit" refers to the return to "capitalists" in the broad sense. When he asks that profits be cut, he is asking essentially that a smaller share of the national income be paid to capitalists in the form of interest and dividends or reserved in undistributed profits, and a larger share be paid to workers (either in higher wages, better working conditions, or lower prices). He is raising questions about the fundamentals of the private-enterprise system. Should property receive its full share of the national income as determined by the market price of its use, or should its share be reduced to less than the market would give it?

Most economists would agree that the allocation of capital and land to different uses should be accomplished by means of market prices (rents and interest rates) expressing the relative demands for the use of various assets. In this way, each asset would tend to be placed in its most productive use and the market would be "cleared"; whereas, if lower prices were established, some less productive uses might attract capital and land while more productive uses were forced to do without. The question is: Must the prices required for economical allocation also determine the amount of income paid to the owners of capital and land? The negative answer to this question is essentially the socialist position. The essence of socialism is to separate the allocational functions of factor prices from the distributional functions. The positive answer to the question is, of course, the capitalistic position. The intermediate answer is that we permit factor prices to perform both allocational and distributional functions, and then we temper the resulting distribution of income by means of taxation and public subsidies.

If we accept the capitalistic solution (this study is based on the assumption that the system of private enterprise is to be maintained), then we are estopped from demanding lower returns to land and capital by the need to use price as a guide to allocation. Efficiency requires that rents and interest rates be determined in the market on the basis of relative demands and supplies.

But leaving the allocational problem aside, there is the further question whether it is possible, within the framework of a private-enterprise system, to reduce the returns to capital and land. It is common knowledge that the efforts of labor unions to increase labor's share of the real national income have been disappointing. Increases in money wages have apparently been matched by increases in prices so that labor's share of the national income has remained relatively constant at around 65 to 70 per cent of the total. And there is even a serious question as to the possibility of reducing the profits of business firms by means of taxation. There are some economists and many businessmen who believe that taxes on business net income often result in higher prices and that the taxes are consequently shifted in substantial amounts to workers or consumers.

One may argue, of course, that businessmen *should* be willing to accept lower profits, but experience to date suggests that it will not be easy to change significantly the division of the national income between the shares of labor and of property. Those who are interested in progress toward the acceptance of social responsibility by business will not expect too much in the form of reductions in the relative incomes of property owners. Efforts to redistribute income through personal taxes and subsidies seem more promising than trying to cut the profits of business. Much more will be accomplished toward constructive social action on the part of business if the costs of this action can be counted along with other costs in the determination of prices. At any rate, it does no good to try to mix up the effort to cut profits with the effort to get business to assume other responsibilities. These are separable problems, and each should be handled in ways that are most appropriate. For example, in eliminating sweatshops, the additional labor costs, if any, must be met either by reducing employers' profits or by raising their prices. In the latter way the job gets done; whereas, if the cost must be met out of profits, one questions whether the sweatshop would ever be eliminated. If profits are cut, there is no incentive on the part of the employer to make the desirable changes in working conditions; whereas, if prices can be raised and profits maintained, the employer has less reason for resistance. If it also happens that profits are too high, that is another question which can be handled in its own way without jeopardizing the objective of cleaning up the sweatshops.

All this does not deny that in many individual cases, through restrictive monopolistic practices and other abuses, profits are too high and ought to be reduced. And it is a clear responsibility of businessmen to refrain from such abuses, and to act with restraint and good conscience when they find themselves in possession of unusual power over the market.

Conclusion

In this chapter, we have considered the conditions which must be met if the concept of social responsibility is to take an important place in American business life. The main conclusion of this discussion is that there are limits to what can reasonably be expected of business. Too much should not be attempted. Specifically, it was suggested that workability of social responsibility depends upon favorable public attitudes; standards that are democratically defined, reasonable in relation to current business practices, based on sound technical knowledge, and appropriately related to ends; and avoidance of unreasonable attacks on the profit motive and on profits as such.

13

Proposals: Changes in Business
Organization and Practice

The American people are in favor of continuing the system of
private enterprise. They wish to preserve the freedom, the decentralization of decision-making, the flexibility, the incentives, the
initiative, and the opportunity which this system provides. And
they wish to reduce governmental regulation of business to the
practicable minimum. On the other hand, and perhaps more
urgently, they hope to avoid the instability, the insecurity, the injustice, and the social inefficiencies inherent in a system of unregulated and irresponsible private enterprise. Their aim is to evolve
forms of social control under which business will remain essentially
free and yet will serve the broader interests of society.

There is no simple or ready-made formula for achieving this
aim. There is no "ism," which will provide the solution. The aim
can be realized in part by allowing free play to self-interest as
tempered by competition, in part by governmental regulation and
intervention, and in part through the voluntary assumption of social
responsibility by businessmen and groups of businessmen. This
third method involves, in a nonpolitical sense, the democratization
of business essentially under private management. Insofar as this
third method is effective in bringing private business into conformity with evolving social needs, governmental regulation is unnecessary.

This chapter will present several constructive proposals for increasing or extending the effectiveness of social responsibility as a
factor in business management. These are relatively simple measures, some of which have already been tried or are in the process
of development. An individual business might adopt any of them
voluntarily without in any way jeopardizing its status or its freedom of action.

Composition of Boards of Directors

First, the composition of boards of directors could be consciously modified to include one or more directors who represent the points of view of workers, suppliers, consumers, the local community, or the "general public." Various proposals along this line have been made.[1] It has frequently been suggested that groups other than stockholders should have the right to select one or more directors. The recent German plan of "codetermination" is an extreme form of this idea.[2] It has also been suggested that some directors should be appointed by a designated public agency.

Another much more modest proposal has recently been made by Beardsley Ruml.[3] He suggests: "As a first step, one director be elected or re-elected and he be asked to act as 'trustee' for one of the three parties at interest, other than the stockholders. Such a director-trustee might be assigned the interests of either the customers, or the vendors, or the employees, depending on the nature of the company's business. He would be the nominee of the management and of the existing board of directors and would be elected in the usual way by the owners of the company, the stockholders. During the experimental period of whatever length, no public announcement would need to be made that such a policy had been adopted." If the experiment worked out well, "the next step would be a director-trustee for each of the other interests—all depending on the nature of the company and whether the groups are important enough in the particular case to warrant specialized consideration."

Mr. Ruml suggests that these trustee-directors be paid because their duties would be more exacting than the duties of directors

[1] For example, R. H. Tawney, *The Acquisitive Society*, New York, Harcourt, Brace & Howe, 1920, pp. 102-3; George Goyder, *The Future of Private Enterprise*, Oxford, Basil Blackwell & Mott, 1951, pp. 97-99; and E. A. Duddy, "The Moral Implications of Business as a Profession," *Journal of Business of the University of Chicago*, April, 1945, pp. 72-73. Compare also W. O. Douglas, "Directors Who Do Not Direct," *Harvard Law Review*, 1934, pp. 1305-34; H. Maurer, "Boards of Directors," *Fortune*, May, 1950, pp. 107-8, 122-32; National Industrial Conference Board, *Compensation and Duties of Corporate Directors*, Studies in Business Policy, No. 16, New York, 1946; M. E. Dimock, *Bureaucracy and Trusteeship in Large Corporations*, Temporary National Economic Committee, Monograph No. 11, 1940.

[2] See Chapter 14.

[3] "Corporate Management as a Locus of Power," New York University School of Law, Third Annual Conference on the Social Meaning of Legal Concepts.

have traditionally been. His concept of the duties of the trustee-directors is suggested when he says, "Let us suppose that this first director-trustee has been asked to act for the customers of the company. Although he owes his nomination to his fellow directors, and his election to the stockholders, nevertheless he has accepted a trusteeship—a trusteeship which has been created voluntarily by those choosing him so to act as trustee. Now as he sits on the board, the interests of the customers of the company are his single interest. It is his duty to know what these interests are and to see to it that they are considered when matters affecting them are decided upon."

There is merit in Mr. Ruml's proposal. It would require no new legislation and no sharp break with custom. Indeed, some corporations already have public directors. It would be consistent with businessmen's professed recognition of their function as trustees for the various groups whose welfare is linked with the business enterprise. It would provide an opportunity for gradualism and experimentation and would afford an easy transition to more thoroughgoing changes if they should prove desirable.

REPRESENTATION OF THE SOCIAL POINT OF VIEW IN MANAGEMENT

In view of the fact that management is ordinarily more effective in the decisions of a company than the board of directors, Mr. Ruml's proposal might well be extended to management. Persons might be appointed in the higher echelons of management whose duty it would be to represent the public interest. If Mr. Ruml's director-trustees were to be full-time paid employees in close daily contact with management, they doubtless would serve the purpose. But if they were not to be actually in and of management, there would be need for representation of the several interests within management itself.

There are several possibilities. For example, staff officers of high rank might be appointed to represent workers, customers, suppliers, the local community, and the "general public" in deliberations on company policy. These officers would presumably carry on continuing studies of the company's operations to determine how its social performance might be improved, and they would make and advocate recommendations on the basis of these studies. An alternative would be to modify and extend existing staff functions. This would be perhaps a more practicable method and would take advantage of existing evolutionary trends in business practice.

The department of public relations affords an example of a staff function that might so be modified and extended. The function of "public relations" was initially introduced into American business as businessmen recognized that public attitudes toward a company (or toward business generally) may affect its supply of capital and labor, the demand for its products, and the treatment it receives at the hands of courts, legislative bodies, and regulatory agencies. The original conception of this function was to seek public favor through various publicity techniques and through personal contact with leaders of public opinion and agencies of public control. The public-relations director was supposed to beat the drums for the company and its policies, regardless of the merits of those policies.

As the public-relations function has matured, however, leaders in the field and many businessmen have become increasingly aware that favorable public attitudes depend quite as much on the nature of a company's policies as on the publicity techniques used to "sell" these policies. Accordingly, public relations has become a factor in policy determination and the public-relations function increasingly has become one of advising on policy from the point of view of its effects on public attitudes. It is not a great jump from this conception of the public-relations function to that of spokesman or trustee for the public interest.

Another function for which the same kind of evolution is possible is that of economic research. Economists and economic-research departments were attached to enterprises when businessmen became acutely aware of the fact that the fortunes of their companies were closely tied to developments in the total national or world economy. The function of economists was to advise management on current and likely future developments so that the enterprise might adjust to these developments. But an economist is (or should be) by training a man who considers events primarily from the point of view of the *total* economy rather than of the single enterprise. Therefore, it requires no great imagination to visualize the business economists of the future as interpreters not only of the influence of the total economy upon interests of the enterprise, *but also of the*

effects of the decisions of the enterprise upon the total economy.
Thus, business economists might well become spokesmen for the
public within business management.[4]

Similar possibilities exist for other staff officials, for example,
the expert on human relations, the psychologist, the director of
community relations, the director of training, and others. Perhaps,
some day, a new official known as the "manager of the department
of social responsibility" might be created to coordinate the activities
of the various officials who represent various aspects of the public
interest. There are, of course, many ways by which the various
groups whose interests are closely linked with a business might
be represented in management. Different companies might evolve
different methods or might reach the same methods by different
routes. The main point is that such interests should have some
effective influence within management itself, and that management should be experimenting with new devices to achieve the
desired breadth of representation in managerial decisions.

THE SOCIAL AUDIT

Another possible institutional change which might help to
strengthen the social point of view in business management would
be the *social audit*. Just as businesses subject themselves to audits
of their accounts by independent public-accountant firms, they
might also subject themselves to periodic examination by independent outside experts who would evaluate the performance of the
business from the *social* point of view. The social auditors would
make an independent and disinterested appraisal of a company's
policies regarding prices, wages, research and development, advertising, public relations, human relations, community relations,
employment stabilization, etc. They would then submit a comprehensive report to the directors and to the management with evaluation and recommendations. Such a report would be for the
information of responsible officials and not a public document.
Social audits might be made every five years rather than annually,
as is usually the case with the accounting audit.

[4] Cf. Chamber of Commerce of the United States, *Business Management and
Economic Analysis,* Report of the Committee on Economic Policy, Washington,
1947.

The social audit would be made by a team of persons who are (1) oriented toward the social point of view, (2) conversant with business practices and problems, and (3) technically trained in fields such as law, economics, sociology, psychology, personnel, government, engineering, philosophy, and theology. It is conceivable that special teams of auditors would be recruited for each separate job. Or it is possible that one or more auditing organizations might be formed which would regularly engage in the business of appraising the operations of corporations from the social point of view. Such an organization might be a private firm organized for profit, like the ubiquitous business consulting firms. Or, better, it might be an independent cooperative organization, created by a group of business corporations each of which would agree to underwrite a share of the expense for a specified number of years and each of which would agree to subject itself to audit at specified intervals.

The social audit would have several advantages: (1) it would provide a recognized method for bringing the social point of view to the attention of management; (2) the appraisal of individual corporations would be made by persons outside the company who would have a more disinterested and detached view of its activities than company employees; (3) the creation of a specialized group of social auditors would give an impetus to the consideration and development of recognized social standards for corporate practice; (4) the fact that the report on the audit would be made to the company and not to the public would make possible complete frankness and at the same time would make the scheme more acceptable to businessmen.

To my knowledge the concept of the social audit has not been suggested previously. But there are signs of institutional development in this direction. For example, some companies have been surveyed by management consultants with social performance as one of the factors under consideration. Also, many companies have invited professors, clergymen, and others to survey their operations with a view partly to "educating" the surveyors and partly to gaining suggestions as to how social performance might be improved. From these beginnings, the formal social audit would be a natural evolutionary development.

Economic and Social Education of Managers

As pointed out in Chapter 7, businessmen are almost unanimous in their belief that education of the American people in certain "fundamentals" of economics is imperative. They are perhaps less aware of the fact that they too are in need of education. By this I do not mean to imply that businessmen are as a group uneducated or ill-informed. The reverse is true. And year by year, the educational level, the intellectual breadth, and the cultural attainments of American businessmen are steadily rising. They are, collectively, one of our most talented and capable groups. Nevertheless, there is need for them to understand more completely their own functions in society, the conditions necessary to smooth functioning of a free-enterprise system, the problems of government, the facts and problems of international relations, the needs and aspirations of the masses of our people, the nature of the great social movements of our age, etc. Only with understanding of this type are they fully qualified to assume the power and responsibility involved in guiding the destinies of great enterprises affecting the lives and welfare and future of a whole nation. Only this kind of understanding will endow them with the perspective, the humane attitudes, and the statesmanship which their great power and influence so patently require.

If businessmen are to become well-educated "philosophers of enterprise," they must be given opportunities during their careers to read, to discuss, to reflect, and they must be given incentives to avail themselves of these opportunities. There is no pat formula for ensuring that businessmen will become more broadly educated men. It is chiefly a matter of the social environment in which they work and the standards which that environment sets. However, there are certain specific things which businesses might do—in many cases are already doing—to encourage the development of an executive class with broader perspectives and greater social understanding. Among these things are (1) attention to broad educational background and interests of men who are selected for executive training programs and who are considered for promotions; (2) provision of discussion groups, seminars, classes, and lectures for executives; (3) encouragement of executives who wish to take graduate university courses on a part-time basis; (4) provision of leaves of absence for executives to undertake formal university study. The educational programs for executives offered by the Schools of Business of Harvard University and the University of Chicago are notable examples of the kind of educational opportunities in which many businessmen should participate.[5]

In pointing to the need for broader background and social understanding it is not suggested that businessmen should stop their daily work to become economists and social philosophers. There is still need for technical competence in business. The exigencies of competition will surely continue to demand that businessmen work hard at their primary jobs of production, sales, finance, etc. The requirements of these tasks will surely absorb so much of the energies of many businessmen that they will have neither the time nor the inclination to think about or to act upon the broader implications of their work. Nevertheless, in every enterprise there is need at the top level for the leavening influence of executives who have broad perspective and social understanding. In the final analysis this can be achieved only through education in the broadest sense. Business, therefore, should set an example when it proposes that other groups should become more literate in matters social and economic.[6]

PARTICIPATION OF MANAGERS IN GOVERNMENT

An important influence in the social orientation of businessmen has been their increasing acquaintance with government and its problems. Businessmen have been called upon to serve on innumerable advisory committees; many have temporarily worked for the government in the armed forces or in civil capacities; and many have had intimate contacts with government through war and defense production. This development appears to be gaining under the Eisenhower administration. No one would argue that businessmen have been uniformly happy about their experiences in and with government. Yet there is no doubt that these experiences have broadened their vistas and increased their social understanding. At the same time, the contacts between business and government

[5] Compare also the Niemann fellowships for journalists.

[6] Mr. Edward L. Bernays has suggested that labor might "educate" management, as well as management "educate" labor. "How to Build Industrial Peace and Prevent Strikes," *Advanced Management*, December, 1947, pp. 154-58.

have been effective in bringing the business point of view to government. The results of this interaction have thus far been sufficiently rewarding to suggest that business enterprises should as a regular policy enable some of their executives to accept assignments in government, either in advisory capacities or in temporary full-time work. The result would be increased understanding on both sides, and perhaps an improvement in the operation of both business and government.[7]

PUBLICITY

There is a marked tendency among our leading corporations toward releasing more information about their activities and toward removing the atmosphere of mystery, secrecy, and stuffy formality that has traditionally surrounded business affairs. Many companies are searching for ways of presenting the story of their operations in human and understandable terms so that the public may become more fully aware of what business is and does. This is a desirable trend and should be continued and broadened to include more companies. Business, while private in the sense that it is nongovernmental, is public in the sense that its activities affect everyone. The businessman should be fully accountable not only to his board of directors, his stockholders, and the tax collector, but also to workers, consumers, suppliers, the community, and the general public. The public has a right to know how the managers, who call themselves "trustees," have discharged their trusts. They have a right to know this in considerable detail. This calls for widespread public reporting of the affairs of so-called private companies. News of dereliction or of statesmanlike conduct in business should be as widely publicized as similar news regarding public officials.

Publicity has two valuable effects. First, when managers know that their actions are to be publicly scrutinized, they are likely to exercise greater care in meeting their social responsibilities than if their activities are carried on in secret. Second, when the public can know about the behavior of companies, it is in a position to distinguish between those companies which have faithfully met their

[7] Cf. F. W. Taussig, "The Love of Wealth and the Public Service," Presidential Address to the American Economic Association, Publications of the American Economic Association, Third Series, Vol. VII, 1906, pp. 1-23.

social obligations and those which have failed to live up to accepted standards, and is then in a position to exert moral pressure toward higher standards of performance.

Three arguments are advanced in opposition to full publicity on business operations. First, it is held that business is *private* and that to invade a company in search of news is a violation of privacy. This traditional view is rapidly disappearing. Today the wage negotiations, price policies, and expansion plans of large companies are regularly covered in the news. A much fuller job of business reporting, however, would be desirable.

Second, it is sometimes argued that secrecy is necessary to secure competitive advantages. It is doubtful, however, that secrecy is in the public interest even for this purpose. As economists know, the greater the knowledge of participants in a market, the greater the chance that prices and outputs consonant with social welfare will be achieved. Many larger companies have become less concerned with secrecy. Nevertheless, the desire to withhold information from competitors remains as an important barrier to full publicity of business operations.

Finally, third, because of the danger that publicity will be used sensationally and irresponsibly, many companies try to shield their operations from the public gaze. They fear that facts will be misunderstood, misinterpreted, and misused. Sometimes, so the argument runs, information is used in ways detrimental to the interests of the company in its negotiations with workers, suppliers, and others; or sometimes it is used by demagogues to cast discredit on the company, or upon the private enterprise system.

It is of course true that facts are often distorted and misused. This is hardly an adequate argument, however, for suppressing them. As has been amply demonstrated in the past, the suppression of information also leads to misunderstanding, misrepresentation, and suspicion; and the frank presentation of facts often allays suspicion and criticism. Whether they like it or not, the actions of businessmen are of public concern and a full accounting to the public is required. Businessmen are public figures to whom great power and responsibility are given. Like all public servants in a democracy they must expect to have their actions discussed and criticized. No one can expect to rise to a position of great power without becoming an object of public discussion and on occasion—rightly or wrongly—a target of criticism. It is better to be able to answer the criticism with facts and information than with generalizations and slogans. Proper regard for their position in modern society will impel businessmen to reveal full information about their actions and to conduct their operations so that they need have no reluctance to report them fully or even to have them the subject of investigation by fair-minded outsiders.[8]

BUSINESS CODES

Many individual businesses and trade associations have formulated codes of good business practice. These have been expressed in varying degrees of generality and have had varying degrees of influence upon actual business conduct.[9] Businesses and trade associations might well give further consideration to the development of codes of business ethics and to making such codes more specific and concrete. There is great need for continuing efforts to formulate standards and to revise these standards as economic and social conditions change.

RESEARCH

Business occupies an important if not dominant place in research in the natural sciences. But in the social sciences, it has barely begun to think about research in any fundamental sense. Industry, for example, will spend millions of dollars to find a better technical

[8] Cf. R. H. Tawney, *The Acquisitive Society*, New York, Harcourt, Brace & Howe, 1920, pp. 123-6; W. H. Hutt, "The Sanctions for Privacy Under Private Enterprise," *Economica*, August, 1942, pp. 237-44; Louis D. Brandeis, *Other People's Money*, New York, Frederick A. Stokes Company, 1932, pp. 92-108; John T. Flynn, *Graft in Business*, New York, Vanguard Press, 1931, pp. 304-5; Charles W. Eliot, *Great Riches*, New York, Crowell & Company, 1906, pp. 34-37; Harold D. Lasswell, "Educational Broadcasters as Social Scientists," an address before the annual convention of the National Association of Educational Broadcasters, November 13, 1951 (mimeographed), pp. 4-6; John Fischer, "The Lost Liberals," *Harper's Magazine*, May, 1947, pp. 385-95; J. M. Keynes, *Essays in Persuasion*, New York, Harcourt, Brace & Company, 1932, p. 318; H. S. Dennison and J. K. Galbraith, *Modern Competition and Business Policy*, New York, Oxford University Press, 1938, p. 119; M. E. Dimock, *op. cit.*

[9] E. L. Heermance, *Codes of Ethics*, Burlington, Vermont, Free Press Printing Co., 1924; E. L. Heermance, *Can Business Govern Itself*, New York, Harper & Brothers, 1933; "The Ethics of the Professions and Business," *The Annals of the American Academy of Political and Social Science*, May, 1922.

method of cutting steel or to develop a plastic material of specified properties. In comparison, it spends pennies on research in psychology, sociology, economics, or government—fields in which it has an enormous stake. Research in the natural sciences, it is true, often yields a profit to the particular company engaging in the research, in that patentable methods and products are developed which produce a specific income. Research in the social sciences, while it sometimes contributes to lower costs or greater sales (e.g., research in human relations, employee training, or advertising), usually does not produce an identifiable income for a particular company. Nevertheless, for industries or for business as a whole, research in the social sciences may pay off handsomely.

From the point of view of carrying out its social responsibilities, business individually and collectively should give generous support to objective research designed to assist in the formulation of standards for good social performance by business firms. Such research would at the same time assist government in developing its policies for regulating business. With an ongoing research program conducted under conditions in which objectivity similar to that which characterizes its technical research is maintained, business would be in the position to offer much more than the all-too-frequent unsubstantiated opinion when called upon to consult with government. For example, research on the economic effects of varying degrees of competition or of varying types of market structures would provide guidance both to individual businessmen and to governmental antitrust policy. Similarly, research on methods of employment stabilization, on factors influencing the quality of human relations, on factors influencing worker efficiency, on the relation of various kinds of wage policy to inflation or deflation, etc., would be of enormous help in formulating standards for business conduct and in guiding public policy. Businessmen, moreover, are the custodians of tremendous quantities of records and data which are not now readily available to research workers. Their active support of research in the social sciences would thus open vast new sources of data.

For three reasons, it would seem wise for research in the social sciences, as sponsored by business, to be conducted in special independent institutes rather than in individual companies: (1) Basic research in the social sciences is not ordinarily profitable in the usual sense, even though it may be of enormous benefit to entire industries or to the business community as a whole; therefore, if conducted within individual companies it would tend to be submerged whenever there was need to cut costs. (2) Rightly or wrongly, social-science research by individual business firms tends to be under a cloud of suspicion. The research would ordinarily command respect only if done in organizations set up in such a way as to promote objectivity. (3) Social-science research of the type suggested could be conducted efficiently only in large organizations having all of the modern facilities for data collection and analysis, having a wide range of specialized personnel, and having freedom from short-run operating responsibilities.

For some types of social-science research pertaining to particular industries, existing trade associations, if they have, or can regain, a reputation for reasonable objectivity, might become the sponsors. Other types of research would best be done by institutes having no industrial affiliation. The research program of the Committee for Economic Development is a possible precursor of this type of institute.

CONCLUSION

In this chapter we have considered several proposals for increasing the responsiveness of business management to the social interest: (1) changing the composition of boards of directors, (2) greater representation of the social point of view in management, (3) the social audit, (4) education of managers, (5) participation of managers in government, (6) greater publicity of business affairs, (7) development of business codes, and (8) research in the social sciences. These proposals are of a relatively modest character representing further evolution of trends already clearly observable and involving no sharp break with tradition. The spirit of these proposals is one of gradualism and experimentation. It is not necessarily intended that all these proposals should or would be adopted concurrently, although there are no inconsistencies among them and development along all the lines suggested might go on simultaneously.

14

Proposals: The Industry Council Plan

One of the more ambitious proposals for ameliorating the conflict and insecurity of modern economic life is the *industry council plan*. This proposal has been most fully developed by Catholic writers; therefore, its discussion would best begin by a consideration of Catholic economic ideas.

CATHOLIC ECONOMIC IDEAS

In many respects, Catholic attitudes toward economic questions are similar to those expressed in Protestant pronouncements. For example, Catholic doctrine, as applied to American conditions, opposes the extremes of both laissez-faire capitalism and communism; it emphasizes the concept of stewardship and social responsibility in the use of personal talents and private property; it criticizes the profit motive as a sole or dominant motive in economic life; it favors wide distribution of power and property, and "justice" in the distribution of income; it upholds the right of labor and farmers to organize; it advocates the cooperative movement; it is concerned about the concept of vocation; it advocates a "living wage" and good working conditions; it emphasizes the dignity of man and the importance of his being treated with respect in economic relationships; it condemns discrimination among persons on the basis of race; it favors provisions for security of persons against the contingencies of life; it advocates protection of the family: it demands "just" prices; and it eschews detailed blueprints applicable to all times and places.

The Roman Catholic Church is unique among religious organizations in the thoroughness, the authority, and the systematic exposition with which its economic ideas are presented. In addition to the long tradition of economic thought going back to St. Thomas

164

Aquinas and beyond, and in addition to the several papal encyclicals of modern times, Catholic writers of several countries have produced a voluminous and detailed literature expressing the Catholic position on economic affairs.[1] This literature develops fully the idea, only vaguely suggested by Protestant writers, that the solution of our economic ills lies in the direction of broad and responsible participation of all groups in economic decisions.

The Catholic proposal is to reorganize economic life on the basis of cooperation rather than class struggle and on the basis of control by voluntary groups representing interested parties rather than control by either excessive competition or excessive public regulations. The purpose is to achieve teamwork among all parties in economic life. As Father Cronin has stated, "the basic weakness of modern society is that we have abundant means for pressing special interests and claims, but we are deficient in organizing to secure common interests and mutual concerns.[2] The solution, he says, "is a restoration of smaller social units in both economic and political fields, with real power inhering in these groups. At the same time their activities must be coordinated so as to secure essential social ends. In the economic sphere, this can be done partly by competition and the market and partly by limited state intervention. But the bulk of the coordinative process should be committed to the self-governing social groups which represent the diverse interests in economic life. . . . The best answer to individualism and statism alike is the multiplicity of buffer societies, hierarchically arranged,

[1] One of the most complete and up-to-date statements of the Catholic position as applied to the United States is J. F. Cronin, *Catholic Social Principles*, Milwaukee, Bruce Publishing Company, 1950. This book can be highly recommended for those seeking a general knowledge of the Catholic position on economics. It also contains an excellent bibliography. See also John A. Ryan, *Distributive Justice*, New York, The Macmillan Company, 1916; John A. Ryan, *A Better Economic Order*, New York, Harper & Brothers, 1935; Oswald von Nell-Breuning, *Reorganization of Social Economy*, Milwaukee, Bruce Publishing Company, 1950; *Five Great Encyclicals*, New York, Paulist Press, 1943; Joseph C. Husslein, *The Christian Social Manifesto*, Milwaukee, Bruce Publishing Company, 1939; J. F. Flubacher, *The Concept of Ethics in the History of Economics*, New York, Vantage Press, 1951; B. W. Dempsey, "Roots of Business Responsibility," *Harvard Business Review*, July, 1949, pp. 393-404; Heinrich Pesch, *Lehrbuch der Nationalökonomie*, (5 vols.), Freiburg Herder, 1905-23; Pesch Commemorative Issue, *Social Order*, April, 1951.

[2] Cronin, *op. cit.*, p. 215.

with a maximum of power at the lower levels, while higher groups step in only when needed to coordinate and regulate in the interests of the common good."[3]

THE INDUSTRY COUNCIL PLAN

Specifically the Catholic proposal is to organize *industry councils,* the membership of which would vary according to the functions to be performed. These councils would be officially recognized by the government but would not be public agencies. They would be organized at the level of industries, occupations, or professions, of geographic areas, of related groups of industries, of the whole country, and even of the entire world. There would also, presumably, be councils of managers and workers within individual plants or companies. These would not properly be regarded as "industry councils" but rather as preparatory or underlying organizations. The organization and structure of industry councils would be determined according to the particular functions to be performed and according to the interests that would be affected by the performance of these functions. They would, so far as possible, be organized around the common interests of the various groups represented rather than the divergent or conflicting interests. They would deal with the problems of the industry or region or national economy or world economy with a view to social welfare. They would perform policy-making and judicial functions and, subject to general supervision by the state, would be empowered to enforce their decisions. They would advise with the government in the framing of its laws and administrative procedures affecting economic life.

At the level of individual plants or individual enterprises, the industry councils would be composed of representatives of labor and management.[4] They might consider common problems relating to production, markets, expansion of the business. It is not clear whether working conditions and wages would be considered, because these give rise to divisive issues. Some writers favor inclusion of these matters and others prefer (at least at first) to handle them through present machinery. At the level of whole industries or

[3] *Op. cit.,* pp. 217-9.
[4] These would be subsidiary to "industry councils" proper, which would be organized at the level of entire industries and groups of industries.

groups of industries, problems of fair competition, codes of ethics, trade practices, sources of raw materials, and labor standards would be considered. On these councils would be representatives of labor, management, and the public. Industry councils in agriculture would deal with planting quotas, soil-conservation practices, and farm credit. Regional industry councils, with broad representation, might deal with regional planning and development or with regional problems such as land use, transportation, and diversification. National industry councils would coordinate the activities of the various subsidiary councils, would consider comprehensive planning—especially for economic stability—and would advise with the government on its programs affecting economic life. International councils would consider international trade, regional development, and kindred subjects. The industry councils at the various levels would presumably evolve from or build upon the many trade associations and other organizations now functioning in our modern economic life.

The essential difference between the industry councils and the present organizations is that the former would be organized to represent all interested parties and would be designed to consider the social interest, whereas the present organizations are devoted predominantly to furthering the interests of particular groups and classes often without regard for the common welfare. Presumably, any tendency of the industry councils to work against the common interest would be checked by the provision that their actions would be reviewed by industry councils at the higher levels and finally by the government. Their object, however, would be to relieve government of the function of detailed supervision and control over economic life by delegating this work to subsidiary organizations consisting of the people directly concerned.

Catholic writers are sensitive to two criticisms. First, it is sometimes suggested that the comprehensive industry council plan resembles the economic organization under Italian fascism. They answer this criticism by pointing out that the industry council plan was perverted in Mussolini's Italy by the existence of a dictatorship in which authority and control was handed down from above, whereas the industry council plan as proposed would represent a kind of democratic economic government in which initiative and power would be widely delegated and diffused among organizations at the grassroots representing all classes of people.

Second, it is sometimes suggested that the industry council plan is only another NRA, an organization which, in retrospect, has had few consistent supporters. In answer to this, it is pointed out that the NRA was a creation of government imposed suddenly without opportunity for the kind of evolutionary development that would be necessary to create a stable organization of this kind. It failed to give representation to labor, and it concentrated on problems of pricing and output determination with results unfavorable to the public interest. The industry council plan, on the other hand, would evolve gradually from existing organizations; would give representation to labor; would concentrate on trade practices and codes of ethics rather than on prices and production which would be determined largely by private initiative and regulated so far as practicable by competition.

The industry councils, in other words, would be concerned primarily with the *environment* in which private business is to be conducted, with the standards, with the rules of the game and the enforcement of these rules, rather than with the detailed conduct of business.[5] For example, the present Pope, Pius XII, is explicit in stating that "the owner of the means of production, whoever he be—individual owner, workers' association, or corporation—must always—within the limits of public economic law—retain control of his economic decisions."[6] According to this view, we would suppose that the industry council is not to take over the detailed management of economic affairs. Some writers, however, suggest that the councils would regulate wages, prices, output, and other detailed aspects of business management.

The industry council plan is a far-reaching scheme for the reorganization of economic life. That such a plan could have been consistently advanced over a long period of years by a succession of popes and by leading Catholic scholars surprises most people who have not been close to Catholic thought. Perhaps most Americans—

[5] Catholic writers are not necessarily in agreement on the extent to which the councils should regulate prices, wages, and outputs. See, for example, Francis J. Haas, *Man and Society*, New York, Appleton-Century, 1930.

[6] *Address to Catholic Employer*, May 7, 1949, quoted from Cronin, *op. cit.*, p. 205.

even those who are members of the Catholic Church—are still not aware of the proposal or do not understand its full implications.[7]

Though the industry council plan has not had a profound impact upon economic thinking in America outside a fairly small circle of intellectuals, there are signs, both here and abroad, of great interest in ideas of the same genus. One of these is the CIO proposal.

THE C.I.O. PROPOSAL

The Congress of Industrial Organizations (C.I.O.) under the leadership of its late president, Philip Murray, has advocated a system of industry councils resembling those proposed by Roman Catholic writers.[8] At the 11th Constitutional Convention of the C.I.O., held in 1949, a formal resolution was approved calling upon the government "acting as agent for the people" to undertake a comprehensive "public planning program" with reference to economic stabilization, housing, agriculture, social security, monopoly, collective bargaining, and the like. The resolution criticized the present concentration of industrial control "by a handful of industrial managers who, in many cases, are not even the owners of the factories and shops in which we work," and proposed that the planning activities be "carried through with democratic participation of all economic groups at the industry, regional, state, and community levels." These "industry councils" would be organized in all the

[7] One Catholic pamphlet states: "The proposal, though long familiar to the Pontiffs on Vatican Hill, is an innovation to the modern mind. As a matter of fact, it is so radical that even Catholics hesitate to urge it. . . . The probability of its acceptance is meager. Not because the proposition is without soundness or merit, but because it presupposes human beings who are willing and ready to think and act as human beings. No blueprint of any kind can change a human heart. . . . The blame for the failure to gain a hearing and the charge of impracticability, however, should be lodged in the proper place. The fault is not with the Papal proposals. It rests in the lives of men who persistently demand the untenable privilege of exercising all the rights of human beings while rejecting utterly the very basic responsibilities upon which those rights are predicated." —Supreme Council, Knights of Columbus, *What Is the Catholic Attitude?* pp. 19-20. See also G. J. Schnepp, "A Survey of Opinions on the Industry Council Plan," *American Catholic Sociological Review*, June, 1951, pp. 75-83.

[8] Catholic writers do not uniformly welcome direct comparisons of the C.I.O. plan and their own. Some Catholic writers fear that they may be unjustly associated with interpretations and recommendations by the C.I.O. with which they do not necessarily agree. Especially, they fear that the C.I.O. would place more power in centralized planning groups than they would approve.

basic industries. They would be composed of labor, management, consumer, and government representatives, and a similar representative board including farmers, with over-all national authority. The councils should extend through the entire industrial structure, functioning at all levels, national, regional, local, and in the individual factory and mill. They should be given the necessary legal powers of fact gathering, inquiry, and access to industrial records.[9] They would consider problems associated with production, investment, employment, technology, wages, hours, prices, quality of goods, labor-management relations, natural resources, raw-material supplies, plant size and location, and others.[10]

The C.I.O. proposal is perhaps the most elaborate plan for economic reform now being seriously advocated by any leading *economic* group in America.[11] However, the plan is still nebulous, and it is doubtful that it has the support of any large portion of the rank-and-file membership.[12]

EVALUATION OF THE INDUSTRY COUNCIL PLAN

Modern society is characterized by a multiplicity of economic organizations, including corporations, trade associations, labor unions, civic and regional organizations, farm organizations, and professional associations. These organizations are each striving to advance the welfare and interests of their own members, often with imperfect or secondary concern for the social welfare. Because the interests of these various organizations are often in opposition, their activities tend to be conflicting and socially divisive. Moreover, their competition frequently takes the form of a struggle for political power with unfortunate effects upon government.

[9] Congress of Industrial Organizations, *Daily Proceedings of the Eleventh Constitutional Convention*, November 3, 1949, pp. 50-55.

[10] *Op. cit.*, pp. 56-57.

[11] An unusually significant American example of an industry council within a particular industry is furnished by the Millinery Stabilization Commission, Inc. This is an organization consisting of management and labor, with strong public representation, in the millinery trade of New York. See Millinery Stabilization Commission, Fifth Report, New York, 1951. See also J. D. Munier, *Some American Approximations to Pius XI's Industries and Professions*, Catholic University, Washington, 1950.

[12] Cf. Daniel Bell, "Labor's Coming of Middle Age," *Fortune*, October, 1951, p. 137.

The essence of the industry council plan is to bring about such an evolution of these economic organizations that their membership would no longer be confined to particular interest groups but would include all interested parties. These modified economic organizations—the industry councils—would then focus their attention on common interests, would facilitate mutual understanding of problems and points of view, and would promote cooperation for the social interest in place of struggle for the self-interest.

The industry council plan is directed toward worthy objectives. There is genuine need in modern society, as persons of many persuasions concede, for broader participation in private economic decisions, for greater tolerance and mutual understanding among various economic groups, for genuine discussion of public economic policy by members of interested groups, for formulation of widely acceptable standards for economic behavior, and for greater awareness by decision-makers of their social responsibilities. At the same time, many would agree that economic decision-making should be decentralized so far as practicable; in particular, that the tendency to centralize decision-making in the federal government should be reversed. The industry council plan has drawn public attention to these needs, and offers concrete proposals for meeting them. Gratitude is due the Catholic leaders and thinkers who have advanced the plan and developed its practical implications. Nevertheless, the industry council plan presents difficulties—in both theory and practice.

First, the industry council scheme, if fully developed, might lead to an enormous proliferation of organizational activity involving endless meetings and debates and requiring a tremendous secretariat. This would entail economic cost in time, energy, and money, and might result in the creation of a vast bureaucracy not unlike that of socialist societies. The plan, because of its comprehensiveness and its infinite ramifications, would thus be subject in part to the same criticisms as are made of detailed government economic planning. For the same reasons, the industry councils might operate to stifle initiative, to regiment individual action, to reduce the flexibility and adaptability of economic life, and to involve the economy in complicated procedures and endless red tape.[13]

[13] Proponents of the plan point out, in opposition to this criticism, that many of the functions that would be performed by the industry councils are now

Second, the industry council plan would be difficult to inaugurate in that it would run counter to so many vested interests in present organized groups. This, of course, is not an argument against the plan, as such, but against its practicability. American businessmen are jealous of their "right to manage," and resist encroachments of organized labor, government, and other groups upon their traditional prerogatives. They prefer the concept of stewardship under which they retain the power to define their social responsibilities. Similarly, the success of the industry council plan would result in a partial loss of function on the part of labor unions and their leaders, and also in a reduction in their independence and freedom of action. The same might be said of farm organizations.

Third, even assuming the successful organization of a comprehensive structure of industry councils, it is not clear that this would greatly reduce the amount of conflict between powerful economic groups—unless this conflict were suppressed in the totalitarian manner. It might merely add another arena within which pressure groups would operate. In addition to the present arenas, there would be the industry councils where each group would be trying to exert influence and pressure. Power politics are not necessarily changed or eliminated merely by the erection of a new organizational edifice.

Fourth, the industry council plan as proposed would be composed primarily of business, labor, and agriculture—i.e., producer interests—and would not necessarily provide effective expression of the general public interest or of the consumer interest. It is true that public or consumer representation is suggested; also that at the upper levels of the structure of councils the public interest would be seen more clearly than at the lower levels. Yet it is not evident that the public or consumer interests would be expressed more effectively than at present through government. The "general public" or "consumers" lack the kind of powerful organized expression that characterizes "producers," for the simple reason that most individuals are more directly concerned about their producer interests—which are definite and obvious—than about their consumer interests—which are indefinite, complex, and diffuse. This raises questions whether the industry councils would become socially sanctioned organizations for collusion among particular groups of labor,

carried on by government, trade associations, labor unions, and other organizations. It is suggested, therefore, that the industry council plan would not necessarily increase bureaucratic tendencies in modern economic life or stifle initiative.

business, and agriculture at the expense of the general welfare rather than instruments for consideration and advancement of the public interest.

These possible difficulties in the industry council plan would not be too serious if the participating groups would sincerely and effectively accept the fundamental ethical principle that the public interest has precedence over particular interests. The successful operation of the industry council scheme, like most proposals for economic reform, would rest ultimately upon the attitudes of men and upon the social environment within which they act.

The essential question in evaluating the scheme is this: Would the industry council plan provide an institutional framework within which men would be led more easily to recognize the public interest, would have greater motivation to accept their social responsibilities, and would be encouraged or even coerced to act in accordance with the general interest? It is possible that this question may be answered affirmatively. If the plan resulted in broad participation in economic affairs, if it led to discussion and mutual understanding among persons of various classes and interests, if it led to serious consideration of standards for economic behavior, if it provided informal social sanctions (even without laws and formal penalties) against antisocial behavior, and if, at the same time, it did not degenerate into some totalitarian scheme, it would contribute enormously to the creation of a unified and cohesive society and to a smoothly functioning economy.

On the other hand, as its sponsors readily admit, the industry council plan is no panacea which can be started at will by holding mass meetings, inventing slogans, and displaying "blue eagles." It would have to evolve slowly through extension and development of present institutions, and through experimentation and selection. At each step, it would need to be critically examined to discriminate between collusion for the purpose of exploiting the public and cooperation for the purpose of serving the public. Such discrimination presents problems so insuperable that many would prefer to seek the objectives via outright public regulation or by restoring and enforcing competition rather than by taking chances with a device so uncertain in its ultimate results.[14]

My own conclusion is that, while the industry council plan may

[14] See William Miller, "A Catholic Plan for a New Social Order," *Social Action*, February 15, 1951, pp. 3-43.

not be the ultimate answer to all problems of modern economic life, it offers prospective advantages sufficient to warrant modest and tentative experimentation with it. As a beginning, the functions of industry councils should surely be limited to discussion and recommendation. They should provide a forum in which all parties at interest would have an opportunity to get acquainted, to understand each other's points of view, to consider mutual problems, and to try to arrive at mutually acceptable recommendations. Their power, if any, should be *moral* power—not legal power.

Broadly representative groups within individual companies—at the grassroots—might be helpful especially in providing opportunities for broader participation of all interested parties, in developing more complete and mutual understanding among these parties, and in working out solutions to problems of common concern.

On the other hand, for consideration of the broad problems of public and private economic policy, the organization of a permanent national economic council representing all segments of business, labor, agriculture, the professions, consumers, and others might be a forward step.[15] Such a council would provide a forum in which economic issues such as monetary policy, taxation, fiscal policy, foreign-trade policy, labor legislation, and the like could be debated and recommendations formulated. It could also provide a forum in which the specific economic and social responsibilities of business, agriculture, labor, and other groups could be considered and recommendations or standards formulated. Thus, it might consider the duties of businessmen and other groups with respect to wages, prices, employment stabilization, collective bargaining, advertising, lobbying, and many other subjects.

A national economic council should be a permanent institution with regular meetings. Its deliberations should be conducted in the manner of a parliamentary body. It should have a full-time secretariat, a research staff, organs for dissemination of its findings, and facilities for determining the extent of its influence upon public and private economic policy. It should be launched under auspices and

---

[15] The National Planning Association is an organization which is intended to function somewhat along these lines. It has not yet achieved the influence and prestige that an effective national economic council should have. The Brookings Institution, the New American Assembly program of Columbia University, and perhaps other existing organizations or programs might conceivably evolve in the direction of a national economic council.

conditions which would give it prestige without at the same time creating excessive optimism as to the extent of its possible immediate achievements. It would be a mistake to call such a congress for some limited session of a few weeks' duration. Years, not weeks, are required to create the mutual understanding and the breadth of viewpoint necessary for constructive action by any organization representing many diverse interests.

In this respect, a clear analogy can be drawn between a national economic council and the United Nations. Both types of organization represent conflicting interests with deep-seated prejudices and enormous difficulties of effective communication. One cannot expect rapid progress toward mutual understanding among parties so sharply divided. On the other hand, just as the ultimate hope of world peace is cooperative action through an organization like the United Nations, so the ultimate hope of a sound economy within the United States may lie in the creation of institutions within which interest groups may learn to compose their differences by the democratic techniques of discussion conducted with the will to reach agreements.[16]

In view of the possibilities of constructive and lasting benefit from industry councils both at the grassroots and at the national level, businessmen might well consider joining in experimental

[16] In discussing a possible labor-management conference, the President's Council of Economic Advisers has expressed the view that if such a conference is to be successful, "preparatory work would be as necessary as in the case of international conferences. The area within which there is some real chance of agreement should be ascertained by extensive preliminary inquiry, and an agenda should be prepared and agreed upon through which fruitful subjects might be carried to a conclusion and the conference not led into disagreements upon points not yet within the area of possible agreement. Such an agenda should not concentrate upon those legislative efforts through which management or labor has in the past endeavored to obtain some advantage over the other. Nor should it endeavor to arrive at specific wage or price agreements. It should concentrate upon those discerning analyses of conditions throughout the economy, both immediate and long-range, from which might be deduced some standards that management and labor could later apply in the course of their negotiations. These standards would not be binding; they would be primarily informational in character. But from them might emerge, after a testing period of time and experience, a better reasoned and therefore more workable formulation of wage policies to be applied through collective bargaining. Agricultural representatives also should participate in any such conference, because industrial wage and price policies cannot be dissociated from the problem of agriculture's share in the output of the whole economy."— Council of Economic Advisers, *Third Annual Report to the President*, December, 1948, p. 25.

efforts to create such organizations. Such deliberative organizations at the level of the individual company and at the level of the national economy would be free from most of the difficulties of the more comprehensive industry council plan as advocated by Catholic churchmen.

15

Other Proposals

In this chapter, we shall consider several proposals (or actual developments) less comprehensive than the industry council plan, but nevertheless related to the industry council idea. Some of these have to do with the decision-making process in individual enterprises and others are concerned with the formulation of national economic policies. The general theme which runs throughout most of these proposals is that business and economic policy should be formulated in joint consultation with various interest groups concerned. They are presented here, not necessarily for advocacy, but to illustrate the kind of thinking that is developing in many quarters.

The idea that there should be broader participation in business decisions—that businessmen should share their powers with other groups—has been frequently expressed over the past fifty years. The interest of some Protestant leaders and groups in broadening the base of business decision-making has already been mentioned.[1] And these ideas have also been advanced by many other social critics and observers. Often, the doctrine of broader participation is expressed as a *concern* without any indication of how it is to be implemented. Frequently it is not made clear whether the participation is to be restricted to matters of basic policy or to detailed business decisions, or whether it involves actual devolution of power and responsibility or only improved communication among interest groups. And frequently little attention is directed toward the considerable administrative problems that would confront businessmen if they were to make their policies or decisions in joint consultation with other groups. Nevertheless, the doctrine of broader participation apparently appeals to many persons of widely different experiences and viewpoints.[2]

[1] See pp. 41-43 and Chap. 14.

[2] Perhaps the most consistent advocate of a broader base for the determination of business policy is Dr. Ordway Tead. See his *Personnel Administration* (with H. Metcalf), New York, McGraw-Hill Book Co., 1933, pp. 484-505; *New*

DEVELOPMENTS IN WESTERN EUROPE

In Western Europe there has been a definite movement toward broader participation (especially of workers) in the control of industry, and several interesting experiments are in progress.

In England, these ideas go back at least to the early 1920's. At that time guild socialism, a form of socialism which stressed industrial self-government, was being advocated by a highly articulate and influential group. At that time also, the Whitley Committee recommended the setting up of "joint industrial councils" representing labor and management. Many such councils were organized, some temporarily. Today more than a hundred are in operation. Sir Godfrey Ince, Permanent Secretary of the Ministry of Labor and National Service, rated these councils as very important when he said:

Their regular meetings to discuss matters not in dispute, have helped employers' associations and trade unions to think of their problems in common, and to see each other as partners rather than as bitter rivals.

Adventures in Democracy, New York, McGraw-Hill Book Co., 1939, pp. 142-224; Democratic Administration, International Committee of the Young Men's Christian Association, New York, Association Press, 1945; and The Art of Administration, New York, McGraw-Hill Book Co., 1951. Other articles and books in which the doctrine has been discussed are J. M. Clark, Alternative to Serfdom, New York, Alfred A. Knopf, 1948, pp. 121-53; J. M. Clark, Guideposts in Time of Change, New York, Harper & Brothers, 1949, Chapter VII; Russell W. Davenport, "The Greatest Opportunity on Earth," Fortune, October, 1949; Peter F. Drucker, The Future of Industrial Man, New York, John Day Company, 1942; J. M. Keynes, "The End of Laissez Faire," in Essays in Persuasion, New York, Harcourt, Brace & Company, 1932, pp. 313-14; S. H. Slichter, "Social Control in Industrial Relations," Commercial and Financial Chronicle, January 26, 1950, p. 15; John Calder, Capital's Duty to the Wage-Earner, New York, Longmans, Green & Company, 1923; Charles P. McCormick, The Power of People, New York, Harper & Brothers, 1949; James F. Lincoln, Incentive Management, Cleveland, Lincoln Electric Company, 1951; W. L. Mackenzie King, Industry and Humanity, Boston, Houghton Mifflin Company, 1918; B. A. Javits, How the Republicans Can Win in 1952, New York, Henry Holt & Company, 1952; J. Spedan Lewis, Partnership for All, London, Kerr-Cris Publishing Company, 1948; George Goyder, The Future of Private Enterprise, Oxford, Basil Blackwell & Mott, 1951; Peter F. Drucker, The New Society, New York, Harper & Brothers, 1950; Neil Chamberlain, "What Is Management's Right to Manage?" Fortune, July, 1949, pp. 68-70; Morris L. Cooke and Philip Murray, Organized Labor and Production, New York, Harper & Brothers, 1940; Clinton S. Golden and Harold J. Ruttenberg, Dynamics of Industrial Democracy, New York, Harper & Brothers, 1942.

These councils are one of the major factors contributing to the record of industrial peace . . .[3]

Since the end of World War II, the Labor Government has established "working parties" in eighteen industries, each "party" composed of leaders of labor and management and of experts who were jointly to develop plans for modernization of their respective industries. The Industrial Organization and Development Act of 1947 provides that these working parties or industrial development councils be continued on a permanent basis.[4] One of the great issues in contemporary Britain is the extent to which labor shall be represented in the management of nationalized industries.

In the Scandinavian countries, joint collaboration of industry, labor, and the government has been commonplace for many years. In Sweden, for example, a basic agreement between employers' associations and the trade unions was reached in 1938 after two years of meetings and discussions.[5] Also in Sweden, as a result of agreements reached in 1946 and 1947, "enterprise councils" were established for firms employing twenty-five or more workers. The enterprise council is an "organ for information and joint deliberation, its tasks being (1) to maintain a continuous cooperation between the employer and the employees for bringing about the best possible production, (2) to enable the employees to acquire insight into the economic and technical conditions as well as the results of the enterprise, (3) to work for security of employment and for safety, good health, and contentment at the workplaces, (4) to promote the occupational training carried on by the enterprise, and (5) generally to further good production and working conditions within the enterprise." The councils have access to the records of the firm, and are consulted on its plans.[6]

In Western Germany, a plan known as "codetermination" (*Mitbestimmungsrecht*) embodied in several state laws and in the Fed-

[3] "Development of British Industrial Relations," *Monthly Labor Review*, January, 1951, p. 28.

[4] Jean A. Flexner, "British Labor under Labor Government," *Monthly Labor Review*, October, 1948, p. 370.

[5] This suggests that the 1945 Labor-Management Conference in the United States, which lasted only a few weeks, was perhaps a feeble first effort.

[6] A *Survey of Social and Labour Conditions in Sweden*, Stockholm, Swedish Employers Confederation, 1947, p. 47. See also Jean A. Flexner, "Labor-Management Relations in Scandinavia," *Monthly Labor Review*, May, 1951, pp. 528-32.

eral law of April 10, 1951, provides for direct labor participation in the management of individual enterprises. In this case, labor representatives sit on the boards of directors—five labor members on boards of eleven persons.[7]

Similar developments are to be found in other countries of Europe and elsewhere. It is unfortunate that in the present study these developments could not have been investigated in detail. In any continuation of the studies of which this volume is a part, a thorough examination of the widespread movement in thought and action toward broader participation in the direction of industry would be highly rewarding.

THE GOYDER PLAN

Mr. George Goyder, a British businessman and Christian leader, in a book, *The Future of Private Enterprise*,[8] has recently advanced a proposal for changing the legal structure of the corporation "to define the rights and duties" of the parties interested in or affected by business operations so that industry will be able to act "responsibly with a minimum of intervention by government."[9] He argues, as do many American businessmen, that business owes obligations to workers, capitalists, the community, and the consumer. And, he says, businessmen are hindered in discharging these obligations by the corporation law which specifically recognizes only the duty to shareholders. "Profitability needs to be defined in terms which include the interests of all the parties to industry, and not merely the interests of one of them."[10] In doing so, it is necessary that management not be hampered or subject to detailed restrictions, and that its responsibilities be clearly defined.[11]

[7] *The World Today* (Royal Institute of International Affairs), June, 1951, pp. 249-62; W. H. McPherson, "Codetermination: Germany's Move Toward a New Economy," *Industrial and Labor Relations Review*, October, 1951, pp. 20-32; Rev. J. F. Cronin, *Joint Labor-Management Control of Industry*, Office of U. S. High Commissioner for Germany (mimeographed), May 7, 1951; Eberhard Müller, *Recht und Gerechtigkeit in der Mitbestimmung*, Stuttgart, 1950.

[8] Oxford, Basil Blackwell & Mott, 1951.

[9] *Op. cit.*, p. 7. See also R. H. Tawney, *Equality*, New York, Harcourt, Brace & Company, 1929, pp. 237-38.

[10] *Op. cit.*, p. 29.

[11] To accomplish these objectives, he proposes (p. 93) that the general objects of the corporation be redefined in corporation law or charters to include the following obligations: "(a) to the company itself: its development, financial stability

Then he suggests that the method of defining the duties toward various groups and of distributing the company's profit be settled in advance in the company's charter. This would include a provision for the method of determining wages and dividends and of fixing prices. It would include general provisions regarding working conditions, workers' rights, and worker participation. (The workers would be members of the corporation and would have representation on the board of directors.) And it would include "a clause stating that it shall be a General Object of the Company to distribute surplus reserve, after paying a prescribed level of dividends and after providing for certain specific reserves, for one or more of the following objects: (a) To provide a bonus to workers, (b) To assist the locality by providing funds for the improvement of its social, educational, and recreational amenities without thereby seeking to exercise control over the community through them . . . (c) To provide funds for the interests of the industry as a whole, for research and development . . . and for any other purpose calculated to benefit the business. . . ."[12]

Many of Mr. Goyder's proposals are patterned after the Articles of Incorporation of the Carl Zeiss Foundation established by Ernst Abbe in 1896 to govern the activities of the famous German optical firm. The interesting provisions of these articles are printed in full in the Appendix of Goyder's book.

THE FISCHER PLAN

In an article, "The Lost Liberals,"[13] John Fischer has proposed drastic institutional changes which would link big business and government into a close partnership. This plan is noted here to indicate a more extreme proposal, short of full socialization, for greatly increasing social control over business.

Under the Fischer plan, the government, through the Council of Economic Advisers, would study the structure of American industry

---

and future growth, (b) to the shareholders (to pay regular dividends in accordance with the company's articles), (c) to the workers of the company (to provide stable employment under good conditions so far as possible), (d) to the consumers of the company's products (to make good bread or shoes or whatever it may be at fair and reasonable prices)."

[12] Op. cit., pp. 95-96.
[13] Harper's Magazine, May, 1947, pp. 385-95.

and identify the dominant corporations. Congress would then confer on these corporations "special status and responsibilities"—perhaps through mandatory federal incorporation.[14] They would be required to agree "never to use their vast quasi-monopolistic powers to restrict output, extort unjustified prices, or rig cartel agreements with foreign concerns. They would also be required to conduct their affairs in a goldfish bowl, just like any other public institution." The President's Council would "keep their records and day-to-day operations under constant scrutiny." When actions in opposition to the social interest were discovered, the Council would publicize these infractions. Publicity would thus be the principal means of control. In cases where publicity was not sufficient, the Council would turn to the courts. Executives guilty of serious offenses would be barred from ever again holding positions in the large corporations.

Mr. Fischer suggests that the large corporations would be called upon not only to conduct themselves honestly but also to participate in general economic planning on matters such as investment, wages, prices, dividends, use of credit, etc. Labor would be represented along with business and government in such planning activities. And the same system of rewards and penalties would be used to ensure compliance with social requirements relating to economic planning as would be used to ensure honesty.

Clearly this is a bold and even radical scheme for which public opinion—particularly business opinion—is not prepared. The Fischer plan has not been worked out in detail. It was meant by its author to be suggestive of a possible line of approach and not as a blueprint. Therefore, it is perhaps unfair to criticize the plan. The author himself suggests: "Some extreme left-wingers no doubt would seize upon it as a first step toward a Communist society, while their counterparts of the extreme right might try to convert it into a corporative state. Constant vigilance would be necessary to keep either the government from trying to run the Two Hundred Corporations, or the Two Hundred Corporations from getting ambitious to take over the government."

These are surely pitfalls to be avoided in such a plan. A par-

[14] On federal incorporation, see "The Domestic Economy," *Fortune*, December, 1942 (supplement), p. 13.

ticular danger is that the scheme might degenerate into arbitrary control of business by an agency of the government acting without well-defined rules. It would, of course, be intolerable to subject business to vague mandates enforceable, without recourse, by an agency of the state. This would indeed smack of totalitarianism. It would resemble the German amendment to corporate law, passed in 1937 under Hitler, which read: "The management on its own responsibility must so conduct the company as to advance the welfare of the enterprise of its personnel and the general advantage of the state and of the people."[15] The last part of this amendment— seemingly so innocuous—was the very legal device used to subject business to the arbitrary will of the state.

In view of the dangers inherent in a scheme like the Fischer plan, any future proposal for its adoption should be examined with utmost attention to safeguards.

THE PROTESTANT DETROIT CONFERENCE

As indicated earlier, Protestant thinking is veering in the direction of concern for broader participation in economic affairs. At the National Study Conference on the Church and Economic Life held in Detroit in 1950, this interest was clearly expressed when the Conference delegates accepted, and "commended to the churches for study and appropriate action," a statement from which the following quotations are made:

The problem of making organized groups responsible overshadows all our economic considerations. . . . We favor, as one means of making power blocs and pressure groups more responsible, the fuller development of voluntary groups carrying out research and discussion in economic affairs, so that pertinent facts as to the effects of group action may be known to the groups and to the public. A voluntary group for securing mutual understanding among leaders of power groups, as well as for bringing public opinion to bear in behalf of the common good, might be a national congress or conference of individuals drawn from the ranks of business, agriculture, labor, the professions, and the general public. Such a conference, meeting as individuals with a wide variety

[15] Quoted from Allen W. Dulles, "Businessmen's Responsibilities to the World," in *The Responsibilities of Business Leadership*, H. F. Merrell, editor, Cambridge, Harvard University Press, 1948, p. 82.

of experience, but not as official representatives of special interests, could have a great influence upon public opinion. To aid in making more effective these national conferences, we strongly recommend the establishment and regular meetings of local groups, representing all phases of our community life, wherein these vital economic problems may be discussed fully and real understanding developed.[16]

At the same conference, Walter Reuther, president of the United Automobile, Aircraft, and Agricultural Implement Workers of America (C.I.O.), suggested a national conference of labor, management, agriculture, and other functional groups at which pressing national problems would be discussed.[17] And Noel Sargent, secretary of the National Association of Manufacturers, proposed "encouragement of joint consideration of economic and social problems by various groups, but avoidance of governmental compulsion which would eliminate freedom of choice by workers, business executives, investors, farmers, and housewives."[18]

THE NATIONAL LABOR-MANAGEMENT CONFERENCE

In 1945, President Truman called a national labor-management conference which met in Washington and was attended by leading representatives of organized labor and business. In his opening address, Mr. Truman emphasized that this was not a "government conference" but rather a group of private and responsible citizens called together to consider joint solutions to the problem of alleviating industrial strife. Most observers of this conference declared it a failure, not only because the members could not agree on fundamental issues but also because the conference failed to kindle the interest of the American people or to provide machinery for future and continuing consultation between the leaders of labor and management. One of the issues on which sharp differences appeared was the division of functions and responsibilities between management and labor. Management adhered to its "right to manage"

[16] Federal Council of Churches, *National Study Conference on the Church and Economic Life* (Detroit), *General Statement and Topic Reports*, New York, 1950, pp. 19-20.
[17] Federal Council of Churches, *National Leaders Speak on Economic Issues*, New York, 1950, p. 19.
[18] *Op. cit.*, p. 29.

and held that unions should not try to encroach on managerial prerogatives. Labor, on the other hand, indicated interest in broader participation in the affairs of business, including matters not directly related to wages and working conditions.

The conference had been suggested in a letter of Senator Arthur H. Vandenberg to the Secretary of Labor (July 30, 1945). The Senator, fresh from the San Francisco United Nations Conference, felt that conciliatory solutions to the problems of international relations which had seemed so eminently successful at San Francisco might be equally applicable to domestic industrial warfare. Later experience, however, indicated that the achievement of mutuality is not easy either in international or domestic affairs.

ADVISORY COUNCILS

It has sometimes been suggested that the federal government should establish joint advisory councils from which it would seek advice in the formulation and administration of economic policies. This proposal has, of course, obvious kinship with the industry council plan (at the national level) as outlined in the preceding chapter. The important difference is that the joint advisory councils would be more directly creatures of the government.

These advisory councils, which would consist of representatives of business, labor, agriculture, consumers, and other interested groups, would consider economic and social questions of mutual interest, and transmit their findings and recommendations to the appropriate governmental agencies. It has sometimes been suggested that for each field of Congressional action or for each administrative function there might be an appropriate advisory committee consisting of representatives of all interested groups. It has been suggested also that these specialized councils might be federated into a kind of national economic congress in which broad economic and social issues would be considered and recommendations formulated.

There have been many examples of citizen advisory councils in government, for example, in the NRA, OPA, WPB, Department of Commerce, and many other agencies. The National Labor-Management Conference of 1945 was also an example. The Selective Service Boards and the Voluntary Credit Restraint Committees[19] are examples of the use of citizen groups in carrying out administrative functions.

Those who recommend the joint advisory councils argue that consultation with interested parties is an indispensable part of public policy formation and administration. Such consultation is necessary, they say, in order that realistic policies may be developed, and in order that the parties at interest may understand and comply with these policies. It is conceded that there is today much consultation in the formulation and execution of governmental policies. However, it is argued, most of it takes the form of pressure by particular interest groups. Each is striving to attain its relatively narrow ends. Only in exceptional cases do the several interest groups, together with representatives of the government, sit down for joint deliberation on mutual problems. Thus the bulk of the consultation today is dominated by a spirit of self-seeking and seeming disregard of the social welfare. The government becomes the agency through which the various points of view are reconciled or compromised. There is no machinery by which the interest groups themselves can compose their differences, or understand each other's points of view. It is concluded that in the interests of good government and social cohesion it would be desirable to develop institutions through which *joint* consultation with interested parties would be possible.[20] Under such a plan, it is said, the various groups would become accustomed to considering their social problems together and a spirit of cooperation between government and private groups might be fostered. Understandings might be reached and differences reconciled in a way that would enhance social harmony and increase governmental efficiency. The ultimate objective would be development of a spirit of mutual cooperation between government and private groups, and of a widespread attitude that public and

[19] See "The Bankers Do a Job," *Fortune*, October, 1951, pp. 93-94, 203; "Experiment in Self-Control," *Business Conditions* (Federal Reserve Bank of Chicago), August 1951, pp. 2-4, 13-15. Another interesting example of joint action between government, labor, and industry is the so-called Agreed Bill in Illinois. On several occasions, representatives of labor and industry have reached agreement on proposed labor legislation, which has then been introduced and passed by the general assembly. See Gilbert Y. Steiner, *Legislation by Collective Bargaining*, University of Illinois, Institute of Industrial and Labor Relations, 1951.

[20] Cf. J. M. Clark, *Guideposts in Time of Change*, New York, Harper & Brothers, 1949, pp. 198-99.

private economic activity are joined in the achievement of a common end, namely, social welfare.

EMPLOYMENT ACT OF 1946

A variant of the joint advisory council idea was included in the Employment Act of 1946. In this act, the Congress declared "that it is the continuing policy and responsibility of the Federal government to use all practicable means . . . to coordinate and utilize all its plans, functions, and resources for the purpose of creating and maintaining . . . conditions under which there will be afforded useful employment opportunities . . . for those able, willing, and seeking to work . . ." This declaration was carefully hedged by the qualifications that the goal of "maximum employment" was to be reconciled with "other essential considerations of national policy" and was to be sought "in a manner calculated to foster and promote free competitive enterprise and the general welfare." To implement this policy, a new agency, the President's Council of Economic Advisers, was created, and a procedure for the preparation, transmission, and consideration of the President's economic reports was established. In essence, the Council of Economic Advisers was to become a sort of coordinating general staff in the field of economic policy.

In the discussions which led up to the Act, it was frequently suggested that efforts should be made to coordinate the activities of private business, labor, agriculture, and government to the end that these combined activities would add up to full employment and economic stability. Along this line, the Act itself provided that in carrying out the declared policy the federal government was to have "the assistance and cooperation of industry, agriculture, labor, and State and local governments," and was empowered to "constitute advisory committees and . . . consult with such representatives of industry, agriculture, labor, consumers, State and local governments, and other groups, as it deems advisable." In its first annual report to the President, the Council of Economic Advisers elaborated the theme that mutual cooperation and coordination of private and governmental activities was to be one of the primary purposes.[21]

[21] Council of Economic Advisers, *First Annual Report to the President*, December, 1946, pp. 15-17.

But the bold and unequivocal statement of purpose and intent contained in this first report was not duplicated in subsequent statements of the Council and was not put into practice. The Council, of course, consulted widely with officials of various governmental agencies, with leaders of private business, labor, and agriculture, and with other citizens. It did not, however, provide strong leadership in developing mutual consultative relations between government and private groups of a type calculated to evolve toward the integration of public economic policy and voluntary private decisions. It is possible that the Council of Economic Advisers might have made a more useful contribution, and that it might have been less vulnerable politically, if it had attempted to carry out the function, so clearly called for in the Employment Act of 1946 and so clearly acknowledged in its First Annual Report, of achieving effective and mutual consultative relations between government and private groups.

EDUCATION AND RESEARCH

As has been repeatedly suggested in this book, the basic problem in achieving greater effectiveness of social responsibility as a factor in business management is to create a favorable social and moral environment—an environment in which businessmen will be impelled, by their own moral sensibilities and by the demands society makes upon them, to have increasing regard for the social interest.[22] There are tasks, therefore, for churches, universities, writers, scholars, and others who have a part in shaping the climate of ideas and attitudes.

The churches are ideally suited to take leadership in an effort to create a favorable moral atmosphere. They are suited to this task partly because moral education is part of their business and partly because they include—or should include—in their membership persons drawn from all classes of society.[23] Churches and religious

[22] For an interesting account of the relationship between business conduct and social environment, see H. M. Robinson, *Relativity in Business Morals*, Boston, Houghton Mifflin Company, 1928. Cf. also D. E. Lilienthal, *This I Do Believe*, New York, Harper & Brothers, 1949; G. R. Taylor, *Are Workers Human?* Boston, Houghton Mifflin Company, 1952.

[23] The Report of the Amsterdam Assembly of the World Council of Churches reads: "The Church can be most effective in society as it inspires its members to ask in a new way what their Christian responsibility is whenever they vote

leaders have already accomplished much (as indicated in Chapters 5 and 14). They might, however, become more vigorous and more specific in their teachings relating to the application of morals to everyday living. Since a large part of everyday living takes the form of economic activity, such teaching inevitably would relate to economic life. To carry out this educational function, with promise of great achievement, the churches would need a continuing program of research and study on the moral aspects of economic and social life, and they would need a large corps of leaders trained in economics and other social sciences.[24]

With research and leadership as a foundation, the churches could successfully undertake broad educational programs for clergy and laymen; they could prepare literature, conduct conferences, sponsor permanent councils, mediate disputes, testify before Congressional committees, and do all the many things that an effective program of education requires. The ultimate purpose of this activity would be to show people how ethical principles can and must be applied in detail to all aspects of everyday life, and that life cannot be divided into areas where ethics are relevant and where they are inapplicable.

It would be tempting to hope that a program of education in economic and social ethics might engage the cooperation of a wide range of Protestant denominations and might be an object of cooperative efforts on the part of Protestants, Catholics, Jews, and other ethically motivated groups. It would be tempting also to hope that this educational effort would reach the rank and file of clergy-

---

or discharge the duties of public office, whenever they influence public opinion, whenever they make decisions as employers or as workers or in any other vocation to which they may be called."

[24] "Historic Christianity is in the position of having the materials for the foundation and the roof of the structure of an adequate morality. But it is unable to complete the structure. Its faith in a meaningful world, having a source beyond itself, is the foundation. Its faith in the end and the fulfillment is the roof. The walls, the uprights, and the diagonals which complete the building are the moral actions and ideals which are fashioned by the applications of religion's ultimate insights to all specific situations. This application is a rather sober and prosaic task, and a profound religion with its insights into the tragedy of human history and its hope for the ultimate resolution of that tragedy is not always equal to it. Accustomed to a telescopic view of life and history, it does not adjust itself as readily as it might to the microscopic calculations and adjustments which constitute the stuff of moral life."—Reinhold Niebuhr, *An Interpretation of Christian Ethics*, New York, Harper & Brothers, 1935, p. 166.

men and laymen and not be restricted to scholars in the theological seminaries, participants in national conferences, or leaders of inter-denominational and interfaith activities. One would hope that two-directional communication would be established on these mat-ters between the rank and file and the leadership.

There are also other groups which could contribute to the crea-tion of a favorable social and moral climate. For example, schools and colleges—without attempting to impose doctrinaire views—might emphasize, more than has been customary, the role of ethics in social life. The collegiate schools of business particularly might carry forward the excellent work they have begun in acquainting students with the concept of social responsibility. The agencies of mass communication could perform a service by giving greater publicity to the activities and decisions of private businessmen. Cooperative groups might intensify their efforts to introduce the consumer point of view into business operations. Intellectuals might devote themselves to working out the philosophical foundations of an emergent welfare capitalism in which economic life is conducted largely through mutual cooperation among various economic groups and government without detailed government regulation.[25]

Purposes so broad and so far-reaching cannot be achieved easily or hurriedly. Indeed, it is doubtful that they can ever be achieved completely. In the meantime, crises in international relations or in domestic economic affairs may so involve us in detailed economic control by government that the methods of cooperative self-deter-mination in economic affairs will remain only in the memory of an older and disillusioned generation. At the present moment in history, we must not accept collectivism as inevitable. We must retain and renew our faith that we shall be able to surmount future crises without destroying or impairing our free institutions. We shall be more fully equipped to meet future crises if the spirit of individual self-determination and social responsibility permeates our economic and social life.

[25] Cf. J. M. Clark, *Alternative to Serfdom*, New York, Alfred A. Knopf, 1948, pp. 118-53; also Russell W. Davenport, "The Greatest Opportunity on Earth," *Fortune*, October, 1949, pp. 66, 208.

Concluding Statement

In this and the preceding two chapters, many proposals have been presented for increasing the effectiveness of social responsibility as a factor in business management. In Chapter 13, we considered certain proposals for changes in business organization and practice—things that businessmen might do voluntarily in their effort to discharge their social responsibilities more effectively. These proposals would require only modest changes in present practice and would not impair freedom of initiative or self-determination on the part of businessmen. In Chapter 14, we considered the industry council plan, which would increase the participation of workers, consumers, suppliers, and others in economic and business affairs. In this chapter, we considered several proposals which would provide joint consultation on business decisions and on national economic policy. Some of these would call for direct leadership of government.

Each of the proposals considered was intended to achieve one or more of the following purposes: (1) to strengthen the sense of social responsibility on the part of businessmen; (2) to provide institutions through which this sense of social responsibility could be made more effective; (3) to encourage the formulation of specific and practicable standards for the guidance of business decisions; (4) to promote discussion, mutual understanding, and cooperation among the several interest groups; (5) to broaden participation in business decisions; (6) to develop teamwork between government and various interest groups in the formulation and administration of public and private economic policy; and (7) to create a social climate in which socially oriented behavior becomes necessary to businessmen and others in the pursuit of their own self-interest.

The proposals vary in immediate objectives, in method, and in the degree of reform implied. Each individual will find some of them more acceptable than others, or judge some more practicable than others. Altogether, they indicate a wide range of thinking on the problem of making our economic system more responsive to the goals of our society.

In particular, the proposals differ in the degree to which they would curb the businessman's freedom of initiative and self-determination. Many businessmen feel that those proposals which would require strong leadership by government would in the long run constitute a threat to the freedom (power) of enterprise. Many businessmen also feel that those proposals which would increase the participation of workers, consumers, and others in the conduct of economic and business affairs would also tend to curb the freedom of business. In both of these judgments they may well be correct. Even when nothing more than consultation is proposed, there is an implied threat to the businessman's hegemony. The very act of consultation would subject businessmen to moral suasion which they could scarcely disregard. Consultation, by its nature, is almost certain to influence the actions of the parties; if it does not, it is meaningless and soon breaks down.

That broader participation in the conduct of economic and business affairs would limit the freedom of action of businessmen is a possibility that is often overlooked by those who advocate such participation. Many businessmen are skeptical of schemes which would result in a weakening of their freedom, not only because of the fear of losing power but also because of a serious concern regarding the administrative problems that would inevitably arise as participation became broader, as decision-making became less unified, and as responsibility became divided.

This suggests that those proposals will be most useful which involve research, education, voluntary actions by businessmen, and consultation among interest groups on broad questions of national economic policy and on basic ethical principles for the conduct of private business. The primary tasks are (1) to find areas of agreement regarding basic principles, and (2) to create a moral environment in which businessmen will want to follow these principles and will find it in their long-run interest to do so.

16

Ethical Issues Relating to the Distribution of Income

One is tempted to try to state precisely and systematically *the* social responsibilities of businessmen. Doubtless many readers will expect just this and will regard the absence of such a statement as a major omission. Nevertheless, I have resisted the temptation.

A concrete and workable system of ethical precepts applicable to the myriad forms of business conduct can scarcely be worked out by any one person. It can be developed only through the democratic process of thoughtful and patient discussion among persons who represent the several parties at interest, who are experienced in the practical problems of business life, and who are trained in ethics, economics, law, and other relevant disciplines.[1]

But even through discussion carried on with the best of good will, an ethical system cannot be worked out easily or quickly. Many years will be required, during which tentatively accepted principles can be tested as they are applied to concrete cases. The development of a moral code for business that can win wide acceptance and social sanction necessarily involves somewhat the same evolutionary process as characterizes the development of the law. And great care should be taken to ensure that the code will produce desirable results; wide acceptance either by businessmen or even by the community at large is no guaranty of this objective. We should not assume, however, that we are starting in this process from zero. Even under laissez faire, there was a system of moral rules for business.[2] And with the decline of laissez faire has come the social acceptance of new rules—some embedded in law and

[1] Cf. E. A. Duddy, "The Moral Implications of Business as a Profession," *Journal of Business of the University of Chicago*, April, 1945, p. 67.

[2] See pp. 17-18.

others adopted informally as part of our mores. But with lingering laissez faire ideas, we have not proceeded far toward a conscious recognition of the new informal moral rules or toward their systematic codification. And we have scarcely begun to consider seriously how these informal rules might be desirably modified or extended.

In view of these considerations, it would seem more useful in the final chapters of this book to try to *state* the more important ethical issues rather than to try to settle these issues. This and the following chapter, therefore, may be regarded as preliminary agenda rather than as a statement of conclusions.[3]

The Problem of Income Distribution

Many ethical issues relate to the distribution of business income. Frequently they become acute in controversies as to whether business profits are too large and as to how business profits should be distributed among the several claimants. Such issues cannot usefully be approached, however, merely by considering the disposition of net profits. Many of them can be analyzed clearly only in terms of the total pattern of receipts and expenditures of the business. Each receipt or expenditure of a business for any purpose represents a transaction with some individual or firm in which the amount received or expended might conceivably have been larger or smaller. The basic issues pertaining to the distribution of income are directly related, therefore, not alone to net profit but to the total configuration of the company's receipts and expenditures. There are moral issues involved in each receipt and in each expenditure.

The traditional way of looking at the relation between receipts and expenditures has been to regard expenditures as a *cause* of receipts. That is, each expenditure is made by the firm only because it is calculated to "produce" equal or greater additions to receipts. In classical economic theory, each expenditure was assumed to be pushed to the point where the final (marginal) dollar of outlay would be matched by an additional (marginal) dollar of revenue. At this point of adjustment, profit would be maximum; beyond it, profit in relation to outlay would be reduced. Also, it has been traditional in economic thought to assume that the various

[3] Cf. W. A. R. Leys, *Ethics for Policy Decisions*, New York, Prentice-Hall, 1952.

prices received and paid by the firm are beyond its control in the sense that they are independently determined in the market. This idea rests upon the assumptions of (1) free mobility or choice of all sellers and buyers of goods and productive services, (2) markets in which large numbers of competing buyers and sellers are interacting, and (3) sufficient time for all relevant adjustments to be made.

The classical approach to the theory of a business is no doubt useful, especially as a first approximation to tendencies that work themselves out in the long run. But actual business behavior takes place in the short run within markets which are far from perfectly competitive, and with sellers and buyers who are not completely mobile. In business operations, demands are frequently made by several groups of claimants appearing as pressure groups. Moreover, at any given time, the prices and costs of the firm are not independently determined by impersonal market forces, but are partly within the control of the firm—at least in the short run.

The primary condition the firm must meet even in the fairly short run (though not in every single year) is the basic condition of survival; namely, that total receipts be at least equal to total expenditures. In order to meet this condition, the firm must pay out whatever sums are necessary to provide the rewards and incentives needed to keep its organization intact in the short run and to maintain its market. In the disposition of any receipts over and above these minimal costs, the firm has considerable freedom of choice. These receipts will be divided into two major categories; (1) sums used to provide the rewards, incentives, and reserves necessary to maintain the business in the *long run,* i.e., to provide for long-run survival,[4] and (2) pure profits used for the growth of the enterprise and for distribution to stockholders and possibly other claimant groups. We shall take up the ethical problems involved in the disposition of receipts to each of these categories.

LONG-RUN COSTS

Perhaps the most difficult ethical issues pertaining to the distribution of business income occur in connection with decisions as

[4] On occasion, the question of whether the firm should survive may be a relevant and important ethical issue—for example, if the firm is producing something for which the demand is inadequate to enable it to pay going wages, if it is producing something which is harmful to consumers, or if it is irremediably inefficient.

to precisely what costs must be incurred in order to provide for the long-run survival of the business. These include the payments required to maintain a continuous flow of labor, capital, natural resources, supplies, and executive talent to the company; the costs involved in maintaining markets and good will; and the reserves to provide for capital replacement and for contingencies.[5] One's judgment as to the correct amount to be allocated to these various costs would be determined by an appraisal of the rewards and incentives necessary for maintaining the steady flow of supplies and productive services, by an evaluation of the risks and uncertainties which the company faces, by an estimate of the physical length of life of its capital assets and their rate of obsolescence, etc. These are matters largely of subjective judgment. We tend to settle many of them through the conventions of accounting procedure; we form habits of thinking about these things in terms far more precise than is justifiable. Since the judgments are based on future unknowns, they are never more than best guesses.

Questions such as the following arise—questions having important ethical overtones: What rate of interest and dividends should be paid to provide adequate incentives for maintaining the capital of the enterprise and attracting new capital? What kinds and amounts of executive compensation and benefits are necessary to provide incentives and to recruit able leadership?[6] What prices should be paid for raw materials and for parts and supplies purchased from other firms in order to maintain a steady flow of these essentials? How rapidly should debt be liquidated in order to main-

[5] See Peter F. Drucker, "The Function of Profit," *Fortune*, March, 1949, pp. 110-20.

[6] A problem in the distribution of corporate income that is minor as far as dollar amount is concerned, but major in its effect on public attitudes, is the compensation and privileges of executives. The high salaries, bonuses, expense accounts, retirement privileges, stock options, lavish offices, and other amenities provided for executives are regarded by many as unnecessary and extravagant uses of corporate income. It can be argued that these are essential to the provision of adequate incentives and to the maintenance of a steady supply of high-quality business leadership. It is held that the competition among companies for executive talent makes such large compensation a necessary cost of doing business. On the other hand, it is argued that the executive group through its control over the corporation is able to set aside for itself a disproportionate share of the total income of the business. The question of what constitutes adequate and justifiable executive compensation is surely an important ethical issue in modern business life. See "Do Executives Work for Fun," *Fortune*, March, 1952, p. 85.

tain financial solvency? What wages, working conditions, and labor benefits should be offered to provide adequate incentives to labor and to attract new workers? What advertising and selling appropriations are justified to maintain the market? How much should be expended for research and product development? What reserves for depreciation and obsolescence should be set up and how much should be spent for the maintenance and replacement of plant and equipment? When the company is subject to high corporate income taxes or excess profits taxes, are any expenditures justified that would not be justified otherwise? What expenditures for public relations and community welfare should be made in order to give the company a favorable reputation so that it can attract workers, maintain customers, and enjoy good relations with government? What reserves should be set aside in prosperity to tide the business over bad times?

These are difficult questions for which there can be no definite answers and no simple rules or formulas for providing definite answers. The answers are to be found only in the subjective judgments of humans beings who appraise the present condition of a business in the light of estimates about highly uncertain events in the distant future. Many of the controversies between businessmen and workers over the division of income between profits and wages are based upon differing judgments as to the amounts of various kinds of outlays which are required for the continued survival and prosperity of the firm. Businessmen are inclined to emphasize the necessity of high executive salaries, high dividends, and large selling expenditures; workers are inclined to question expenditures, reserves, and dividends which seem to them excessive and to serve no obvious short-run economic purpose. Businessmen, in a period of high profits, are likely to consider the possibility that depreciation allowances may be inadequate for replacement at current prices, or that profits may include substantial inventory valuation gains which can be quickly wiped out at a turn of the business cycle, or that high profits in one year must be considered in relation to possible low profits in other years. Workers, on the other hand, sometimes look merely at the reported profit figure for the single year.[7]

[7] The following statement of an influential labor leader, contained in a letter to the author, illustrates the labor point of view: "How large a profit can a

If the many questions as to what outlays are necessary for the continued survival of a business, i.e., what shall be regarded as the necessary long-run costs of the enterprise, could be satisfactorily settled, most people would presumably agree that a company should be permitted and even encouraged to meet these costs.[8] This would then provide a basis for the distribution of the great bulk of the firm's total receipts. But suppose total receipts were more than sufficient to meet all costs as so defined. What disposition should be made of the excess, which in the economist's language would be called "pure profit"?

DISPOSITION OF PURE PROFITS

When a firm is in a position to earn pure profits, it is faced with a difficult problem as to how these profits should be disposed. There are several rival claimants: consumers, workers, officers, stockholders, suppliers, the community, and the company itself. And there is a tendency for at least several of these claimants to use pressure-group tactics in pushing their demands.

Lower Prices to Consumers? A strong case can be made—a case that appeals to many economists and to many businessmen—for eliminating pure profits by reducing the prices charged to consumers.[9] It is argued that if the company is meeting all of its costs in the sense of providing working conditions as good as those gen-

---

Christian business conscientiously vote for itself? It does take such a vote, when it sets prices it will charge and the wages it will pay. I know that workers would be willing to forgo wage increases if the corporations would limit themselves to reasonable profits such as 6 per cent. Consumers would not gripe about prices if they thought the profit was reasonable. As long as the fat boys insist on their present rate of profit on invested capital and on the gravy trains that are altogether too common during a war economy, there will be constant criticism and recurrent drives to improve the income of the worker through higher wages and to improve the status of the consumer through lower prices."

[8] It may be argued that some of the costs that are necessary from the standpoint of an individual company are not socially desirable, for example, certain types of expenditures for competitive advertising and for public relations activities. This implies rather that the social environment within which business operates might be changed, than that business should not incur costs necessary to its long-run survival.

[9] For an eloquent discussion of this view, see Edwin G. Nourse, *Price-Making in a Democracy*, Washington, Brookings Institution, 1944; also Edwin G. Nourse and Horace B. Drury, *Industrial Price Policies and Economic Progress*, Washington, Brookings Institution, 1938.

erally prevailing, rewarding capital at the going rate, paying suppliers as much as they can get elsewhere, etc., then the consumer is being exploited if he is charged more than the cost of production, and it is to the consumer that pure profits should be paid. This is in accordance with the familiar proposition of welfare economics that when price exceeds (marginal) cost, welfare can be increased by lowering price, thereby permitting more of the product to be produced and consumed.[10] Moreover, when a profitable firm cuts its price, competitors are stimulated to become more efficient. On the whole, the disposal of pure profits to consumers in the form of lower prices has much to commend it. But this solution presents several difficulties.

First, it may have adverse effects upon concentration of control within an industry. Typically, the various firms of an industry do not have equal costs. Inequality of costs may be due to differences in location, in access to raw materials, in quality of labor or equipment available, in skill of management, in scale of operations, etc. If the firms with lower costs distribute their pure profits in the form of lower prices to consumers, they will then capture a larger share of the market. This would not be serious if the low-cost firms should be smaller enterprises. Indeed, it would be advantageous from the point of view of efficiency if production were transferred from less efficient to more efficient firms. But if the low-cost firm should be a giant enterprise, the effect of lowering its prices might be to squeeze out smaller rivals, and to increase still further the size of the giant.[11] The resulting tendency toward concentration of the industry into the hands of one or a few large firms would be regarded by some, at least, as an undesirable effect.

A second possible objection to distributing pure profits to consumers is that this would dissipate an important source of new capital for the enterprise. It has become customary for business firms to reinvest substantial portions of their earnings in the business. In this sense, the firm itself becomes one of the claimants for

[10] The increase in production would involve a transfer of labor, capital, and land from other industries where the value of their product was less to this industry where the value of their product is greater, thus increasing the total national product. For a discussion of this proposition, see H. R. Bowen, *Toward Social Economy*, New York, Rinehart & Company, 1948, pp. 120-55.

[11] Several large firms are said to have been in this position during the recent postwar period.

a share of the profits. This raises an ethical question as to the extent to which present consumers, or other claimants, should be required to help finance the growth of an enterprise. There are some who argue that a company should raise all of its new capital from the sale of securities in the market and should not plow back its earnings. In this way, it is said, each new capital issue of the firm would be forced to meet the test of the market and to compete with alternative opportunities available to investors rather than be made by directors with funds under their exclusive control. This was, at least in part, the theory underlying the famous but short-lived undistributed profits tax of 1936. The opposing argument is, of course, that a prosperous company should grow, that the most practicable and readily available source of funds is current profits, and that the management of the enterprise is in a better position than the "capital market" to know about its needs for capital.

A third possible objection to the distribution of pure profits exclusively to consumers is that it might tend to retard improvements in working conditions, labor welfare, and community welfare. The standard of living of a country cannot properly be counted solely in quantities of consumer goods and services. It must be counted (although the statistics invariably omit this) also in the conditions under which these goods are produced, that is, in the effects of this production upon the lives of workers and others. Profits often appear as a result of technological advances which reduce the cost of production. Such technological progress can be transmitted to society in the form of greater quantities of goods and services. It can also be transmitted wholly or in part in the form of improved working conditions, labor welfare, and community welfare.

Ordinarily society would wish to receive part of the gain in each of these forms. But if all pure profits were to be paid out to consumers in the form of lower prices, nothing could be available for these other purposes, and progress in working conditions, labor welfare, and community welfare might be retarded.

A fourth argument against giving the consumer the whole of pure profits in the form of lower prices is that profits—even unusually high profits—are a necessary part of our incentive system and should be paid to stockholders. According to this view, capitalists are often called upon to assume great risks. They can be induced to do this only if they are permitted to reap the rewards as well as to bear the losses. If, when large rewards are possible, they cannot be realized by capitalists, the effect on incentives becomes like that of a proposition of "heads I win, tails you lose." In opposition to this argument, the point is sometimes made that, although capitalists who incur great risks should be able to reap the profits, yet the stockholders of long-established and secure companies, whose founders and promoters have long since passed from the scene, are hardly entitled to enjoy returns in excess of those needed to maintain capital under the risks now confronting the companies. The interesting suggestion has been offered by an English businessman that there should be no limit on rate of profit but only on the length of the period over which profit is to accrue to stockholders. He suggests the redemption of the stock by the company at the end of fifty years.[12] An alternative suggestion would be to convert stock to fixed interest-bearing securities at the end of fifty years or some such period.[13]

Distribution to Workers? Having considered some of the issues involved in distributing pure profits in the form of lower prices to consumers, let us consider another frequent proposal; namely, that pure profits should be distributed to workers in the form of higher wages. Sometimes this proposal is advanced in the following form: (1) in theory it is best to make the distribution in the form of lower prices to consumers; (2) however, consumers are not so powerful a pressure group as workers; (3) therefore, distribution to workers involves less social conflict than distribution to consumers; (4) since workers represent a large portion of the total population, this is at least a rough approximation to distribution to consumers, who by definition make up the entire population; (5) moreover, there is an

[12] George Goyder, *The Future of Private Enterprise*, Oxford, Basil Blackwell & Mott, 1951, pp. 114-15. See also William Temple, "Begin Now," in *Christian Newsletter*, August 7, 1940.

[13] Another argument, often advanced by businessmen, is that prices should be reduced, not necessarily as a way of eliminating excessive profits, but as a way of increasing profits in the long run. According to this view, it is not only good social policy but also good (profitable) business to offer low prices and thus to achieve large volume, rapid turnover, and high profits. But this argument still leaves open the question of what to do with the profits once they have been earned, one possibility being to cut prices still further. For an excellent statement of the "rapid turnover" argument, see Jack I. Straus, "The Responsibilities of the Businessman to the Consumer," in *Responsibilities of Business Leadership*, H. F. Merrell, editor, Cambridge, Harvard University Press, 1948, pp. 49-54.

element of distributive justice in this solution since workers on the whole are in the lower-income brackets.

There is much to commend this argument. Historically, a large part of the gains from technological progress has been transmitted to society in the form of higher wages. But this solution also presents ethical issues such as the following: Is it just for the wages of workers in high-profit firms to be higher than wages in low-profit firms? Should the entire pure profits be distributed in the form of higher money wages, or should some be distributed in the form of better working conditions, labor welfare, and community welfare? Should some of the pure profits be applied to expansion and development of the company? Should stockholders who may have borne great risks have a share? In other words, the questions that can be raised regarding the distribution exclusively to consumers can also be asked regarding the distribution exclusively to workers.

To Suppliers? Another major group of claimants, in addition to consumers and workers, are the suppliers of a company. Most of the ethical issues in the relations between a company and its suppliers relate to possible short-run exploitation based upon imperfect mobility of suppliers. In the present context, however, we assume that the company is paying its suppliers prices that will ensure long-run maintenance of supplies. The present issue, then, is whether a part of pure profits should be distributed in the form of higher prices to suppliers. Perhaps the great majority of persons would answer in the negative. When the suppliers are farmers, however, there is sometimes a tendency to suggest, on ethical grounds, that some of the profits should be disbursed in the form of higher prices paid. The conflict between farmers and the "business interests" has, of course, been one of the great issues in American history. It reached its most acute form during the Granger period of the late nineteenth century and again during the 1920's and 1930's. Great social movements have arisen on the basis of the real or alleged exploitation of farmers by the railroads, by "Wall Street," or by big corporations—generally. Comparisons of prices received by farmers for their raw produce with prices paid by consumers for the same produce in processed form have often been offered as evidence of this exploitation. When the grievances of farmers were not, or could not, be redressed by appeal to the business interests, governmental intervention was invoked, with the resulting railroad regulation, agricultural price supports, and other public aids to agriculture.

WHO SHALL BE THE RESIDUAL CLAIMANT?

Still another important issue in the distribution of corporate receipts pertains to this question: What recipients should be paid at stable rates, year by year, and what recipients should be residual in the sense of absorbing the impact of fluctuations in business activity? It can be argued that each group of recipients is entitled to a degree of stability. For example, many people apparently believe that wage rates and the conditions of labor should not fluctuate up and down according to the profitability of the company. Also, it is often argued that there should be stability of employment, or of total wages paid, from year to year. True, there are many advocates of profit sharing; yet one of the strongest arguments against this practice is that it results in a variable and unpredictable income for the worker.[14] Similarly, many would argue that community-welfare programs depending upon support from business should receive relatively stable amounts regardless of the profitability of business. Similarly, the view is gaining increasing acceptance that dividends should be paid at relatively stable rates from year to year because many individuals and institutions depend upon dividends for their livelihood. It is probable, in fact, that corporations have on the whole been more solicitous for stability of dividends than for stability in the amount of annual wages paid to labor. There are few who would argue that prices charged to customers should vary from year to year according to profits, or that prices paid to suppliers should fluctuate in relation to profits, and it is sometimes held that even the quantities purchased from suppliers should be stabilized over long periods.

The interest of the various claimants in stability of returns from the corporation suggests that the company itself become the principal residual legatee of corporate profits. The share which would

[14] For a complete discussion of profit sharing, see Kenneth M. Thompson, *Profit Sharing*, New York, Harper & Brothers, 1949. Also, "The Pitfalls of Profit Sharing," *Fortune*, August, 1951, pp. 104-5, 137 ff; and W. H. Wheeler, Jr., "How I Would Introduce a Profit Sharing Plan to a Board of Directors," *Michigan Business Review*, January, 1952, pp. 14-17.

be expected to vary most directly with profits would be the corporation's own share, namely, earnings available for reinvestment in the company. These would vary widely from year to year (in some years they might be negative) while other shares would remain more or less stable. This suggests that a condition of stability of return to outside claimants is that in good years, when pure profits are positive, part of these profits should be retained within the enterprise. But this raises the question whether they should be held indefinitely in the enterprise or merely held as reserves for the payment of outside claimants during unprofitable years.[15]

CONCLUSIONS

It is evident that we do not now have a definite and practicably applicable set of ethical principles to guide businessmen in the distribution of their receipts among the several claimants. Perhaps it can be agreed that a company should allocate to costs of various kinds at least enough (1) to ensure a flow of labor, capital, supplies, and executive talent; (2) to maintain its market; and (3) to tide itself over bad years and to provide for contingencies.[16] But there is room for the widest disagreement as to what these permitted costs might be in any case. Moreover, if there is an excess of profit over and above costs, there are few principles—except the principles of expediency in a world of pressure groups—to guide the distribution of the excess to the various claimants.

This is a sorry situation in that some of the most divisive issues of modern life pertain to the distribution of the receipts of business enterprises. It is time that we attempt to achieve a set of principles for guidance in this matter. It is all very well for the businessman to announce that he is a trustee mediating among the interests of the several claimants. But a trustee who is operating in the absence of a set of concrete and practically applicable principles can do little more than make arbitrary decisions, and cannot easily be held ac-

[15] If additions to plant and equipment are financed substantially from earnings, the result may be variations in capital investment tending to accentuate the business cycle. This suggests that in years of relatively low profits the firm should seek investment of outside sources of funds to supplement its impaired internal resources.

[16] Presumably, if the receipts of a company are consistently insufficient to make this possible, the firm should eventually withdraw.

countable for his actions. Moreover, in this kind of situation, any of the claimants (including businessmen) can advance any kind of extreme demand without fear of contradiction *in principle*.

Almost any set of principles on which there could be reasonable agreement and social sanction would be preferable to no principles at all. And principles which men of experience, technical competence, varied interests, and good will could accept as just and sound would be still better. The conclusion is clear: we need careful study and discussion of the *principles* to guide businessmen in the distribution of their receipts among the several claimants.

The need is greatest, of course, in connection with the thorny problem of determining the proper division of receipts between profits and wages. On this subject, Peter Drucker has pointed out that "unless two contending parties of equal weight have a principle of decision in common, their bargaining is not likely to end in peace and harmony but in deadlock, frustration, mutual recrimination and bitterness—precisely what we are having now."[17]

Similarly, Professor Sumner H. Slichter has stated:

The greatest immediate need of collective bargaining is to develop principles to guide adjustment of wages. Thus far, collective bargaining has been largely the process by which the two sides rationalized positions already taken. Employers have invariably had reasons why wages should not be increased; unions have invariably had reasons why wages should be increased. . . . It is obvious that collective bargaining will not long command the respect of thinking men if it continues to be a mere attempt of the parties to rationalize positions which are taken without regard to the effect upon the community.[18]

George Goyder has said that ". . . unless there is an agreed policy with respect to the distribution of profits in a company there cannot

[17] Peter F. Drucker, *Concept of the Corporation*, New York, The John Day Company, pp. 200-201. Mr. Drucker suggests (p. 202) that the success of our labor policy during World War II was due to the fact that we did have a principle, namely, the Little Steel formula.

[18] Sumner H. Slichter, "Raising the Price of Labor as a Method of Increasing Employment," *Review of Economics and Statistics*, November, 1949, p. 287; see also Sumner H. Slichter, *Basic Criteria Used in Wage Negotiations*, Chicago Association of Commerce and Industry, 1947; John T. Dunlop, "Fact-finding in Labor Disputes," *Proceedings of the Academy of Political Science*, May, 1946, pp. 67-69; J. M. Clark, *Alternative to Serfdom*, New York, Alfred A. Knopf, 1948, pp. 129-36; J. M. Clark, *Guideposts in a Time of Change*, New York, Harper & Brothers, 1949, pp. 115-46, 187.

be full confidence between the parties. This does not mean that the directors should bind themselves in advance to distribute profits in exactly such and such a proportion. It means that the lines on which distribution is to take place must be the subject of prior agreement in principle."[19]

With increasing tendencies toward price leadership and wage leadership among a few large companies and a few large labor unions, special responsibility for leadership in the development of principles falls upon a fairly small number of businessmen and labor leaders.

There are, in summary, serious difficulties in developing a set of principles to guide the distribution of corporate income. In the first place, the ends of distributive justice, economic stability, and economic progress are probably in conflict, and some compromise among these ends may be necessary. Secondly, we are sadly lacking in reliable knowledge of the effects of various distributive policies on incentives, economic stability, and progress. Therefore, part of the task is to establish a more reliable foundation for the distributive principles. In this, the collaboration of social scientists and other technically trained persons will be required.

[19] Goyder, *op. cit.*, pp. 109-10.

17

Other Ethical Issues Facing Businessmen

HONESTY AND LAW OBSERVANCE

A group of ethical issues applicable to businessmen may be treated under the heading of "honesty and law observance." These include such matters as truthfulness in selling and advertising, honest weights and measures, avoidance of financial manipulation for the benefit of "insiders," observance of contracts, disclosure of full and accurate information to the tax collector, maintaining legally required conditions of safety and sanitation, observing price-control regulations, etc. These matters form the socially acceptable elements of what has traditionally been called "business ethics."[1]

In broad general principle, there is little question as to what constitutes probity in these matters. It does not follow, however, that merely because the general principles are clear, businessmen uniformly observe them. Some businessmen have been guilty of gross and obvious violation of these principles. But the real difficulty lies not in the gross violations but in the subtle transgressions arising

[1] The following are some samples of the literature on business ethics: Richard C. Cabot, *Adventures on the Borderlands of Ethics*, New York, Harper & Brothers, 1926, Chapter 3; Norman Hapgood and others, *Every-day Ethics*, New Haven, Yale University Press, 1910; Arthur T. Hadley, *Standards of Public Morality*, New York, The Macmillan Company, 1907; James M. Lee, *Business Ethics*, New York, Ronald Press Company, 1926; Everett W. Lord, *Fundamentals of Business Ethics*, New York, Ronald Press Company, 1926; Edward D. Page and others, *Morals in Modern Business*, New Haven, Yale University Press, 1909; Edward D. Page, *Trade Morals*, New Haven, Yale University Press, 1914; Max Radin, *Manners and Morals of Business*, Indianapolis, Bobbs-Merrill Company, 1939; H. B. Reed, *The Morals of Monopoly and Competition* (Private Edition), University of Chicago Libraries, Chicago, 1916; F. C. Sharp and P. G. Fox, *Business Ethics*, New York, D. Appleton-Century Company, 1937; Carl F. Taeusch, *Professional and Business Ethics*, New York, Henry Holt & Company, 1926; and Carl F. Taeusch, *Policy and Ethics in Business*, New York, McGraw-Hill Book Co., 1931.

from the difficulty of applying these principles to the complexities of everyday business life.[2]

To take only one example, let us consider the problem of applying the canon of "truthfulness in advertising and selling." It is by no means easy to establish the boundary between truthfulness and deception. For instance, does ethical behavior require a businessman to tell his customers about the undesirable as well as the favorable features of his product? Is it ethical to package a commodity so that the quantity *seems* larger than it really is? Is it ethical to exploit the propensity of consumers to judge quality by price? Is a businessman justified in making a sale when he knows that a product more suited to the consumer's needs can be obtained elsewhere? Can a businessman with good conscience imply through his advertising the superiority of his products over competing brands when there is in fact no superiority? These are a few questions, selected from a much longer list, to illustrate that the boundary between truthfulness and deception in advertising and selling cannot easily be drawn.

Similar problems in the detailed application or interpretation of general principles are found in connection with many other aspects of business practice. It is not always easy to distinguish an ethical from an unethical financial procedure, to define an "honest" tax return, to determine whether a business is complying with safety requirements, or to decide whether it is following price regulations. These issues can be resolved only through careful consideration of concrete conditions, industry by industry, and sometimes case by case.

Working Conditions and Labor Benefits

Working conditions include both physical and psychological features of the job. Physical conditions (which may have psychological effects also) include such things as light, heat, ventilation, noise, provision for health and safety, speed and arduousness of work, monotony, hours, etc. The psychological conditions of labor include such things as opportunity to get ahead, provision for growth and

---

[2] See E. H. Sutherland, "White-Collar Criminality," *American Sociological Review*, August, 1940, pp. 138-55; M. B. Clinard, *The Black Market: A Study of White Collar Crime*, New York, Rinehart & Company, 1952.

development, opportunities for creative satisfactions, security against major contingencies, participation in the enterprise, a sense of belonging, friendly personal relations with coworkers and managers, respect for human dignity, a sense of the social significance of work, etc. Labor benefits include such things as pensions, recreation, vacations, health insurance, etc. All of these things together are an important influence determining the quality of the life and the personality of the worker. His standard of living may be thought of as consisting partly of the goods and services he buys with his wages and partly of the conditions under which he spends a major share of his life in earning these wages. One of the most important ethical issues confronting businessmen is this: What kind of working conditions and labor benefits should be provided? Or, as the issue is frequently faced, what demands in these areas should be acceded to?[3]

Three general principles can be formulated. First, many things to improve working conditions—especially the psychological aspects—are not costly. They pertain to the point of view, the manner, and the attitudes of management. It costs no more to smile than to frown, or to be respectful, friendly, and considerate than to be arrogant, officious, and high-handed. Businessmen have no reason for not continuously searching for the many ways of improving working conditions in their enterprises that do not add substantially to costs.

Second, it frequently happens that improvements in physical and psychological working conditions and in labor benefits are self-financing in the sense that the costs involved are more than matched by additions to productivity. When this is the case, these improvements are in the interests of all, including businessmen. For example, if labor produces as much or more in an eight-hour day than it does in a ten-hour day, there is little excuse for working ten hours. Or if plant cleanliness contributes to productivity more than it costs, there is little excuse for a dirty plant. Modern production

[3] On working conditions and human relations in industry there is, of course, an enormous literature. The following are some outstanding contributions: Elton Mayo, *Human Problems of an Industrial Civilization*, New York, The Macmillan Company, 1933; F. J. Roethlisberger, *Management and Morale*, Cambridge, Harvard University Press, 1941; F. J. Roethlisberger, *Management and the Worker*, Cambridge, Harvard University Press, 1947; T. N. Whitehead, *Leadership in a Free Society*, Cambridge, Harvard University Press, 1936.

engineering has made great strides in showing how higher productivity can be achieved through improved working conditions and benefits. But the relationship between conditions of labor and productivity is not a simple one. It is related not only to the objective conditions of labor but also to the attitudes of workers and others toward these conditions. These attitudes, in turn, are affected by the generally prevailing conditions of labor and by judgments as to what conditions are acceptable or appropriate for the given time and place.

In an age when standards of sanitation are primitive, for example, workers were not perturbed by what we today would regard as shocking sanitary facilities. But with the prevailing standards today, a dirty washroom may cause a failure of morale, may result in serious inefficiency, may even provoke a strike; and merely by cleaning up the washroom a dramatic improvement in morale and productivity may ensue. High worker productivity is related to current standards of working conditions and benefits; losses in productivity are likely if a firm lags behind, and gains may result if it exceeds accepted standards. This raises the question of what the *standards* ought to be at any time.

Presumably, since the provision of better working conditions and larger benefits is costly, these can be provided only out of funds which might otherwise be paid as wages. Therefore, the question becomes one for workers to decide. Do they prefer better working conditions and more benefits, or do they prefer more wages? Here we reach the third principle, namely, that this is a matter which should be left largely to the decision of labor groups in consultation with employers; i.e., it is a matter for collective discussion and bargaining. It is even possible that some employers would offer higher wages with less elegant working conditions and less generous benefits; whereas other employers would offer lower wages and more elaborate amenities and greater benefits. Workers with different valuations of the two classes of compensation might choose from among employers according to their preferences. The doctrine, sometimes advanced, that all employers should offer all possible amenities and benefits for workers is clearly false if, as a matter of fact, workers prefer higher wages to more amenities and benefits. It would seem useful, nevertheless, for worker and employer groups to be continuously exploring the problem and considering how working conditions and benefits, relative to wages, could be adjusted to the advantage of workers.

For example, a problem like this might be considered: Is it worth while for a company to spend a million dollars for improvements in safety which, on an actuarial basis, would be calculated to reduce serious injuries by one per year? Would the workers prefer to take their chances with present safety devices and draw higher wages, or would they prefer greater safety and lower wages? Thoughtful and frank discussions of such questions by interested parties with the advice of technical experts might result in the achievement of a more satisfying balance between wages and working conditions and benefits. It is also possible that such consideration of these matters would have the effect of encouraging workers to take a larger share of their increasing wages in the form of higher standards on the job rather than in the form of higher standards of living at home. It is possible that in our society, oriented as it is toward consumer goods, welfare would be enhanced if more were spent for job satisfactions and less for consumer satisfactions. Perhaps companies with pure profits should devote some of their surplus to experimentation in the improvement of working conditions and benefits. Such companies could afford to innovate, to test the effects of new improvements in working conditions, and to offer leadership in demonstrating how working conditions and benefits might fruitfully be improved.[4]

EFFECTS OF BUSINESS LIFE UPON EXECUTIVE AND WHITE-COLLAR WORKERS

Many of the considerations pertaining to working conditions and labor benefits as applied to the manual workers apply also to executive and white-collar workers. However, there are some special ways in which business life leaves its imprint upon the character and personalities of the latter group, and some special issues arise.[5]

[4] On the cost of fringe benefits, see Chamber of Commerce of the United States, *The Hidden Payroll*, Washington, 1949. According to this study, nonwage payments represent an addition to labor cost in the plants surveyed of 15.4 per cent.

[5] For an excellent early statement of this problem, see F. Ernest Johnson and Arthur E. Holt, *Christian Ideals in Industry*, New York, The Methodist Book Concern, 1924.

First, there is a marked class structure within most enterprises. It takes the form not only of differences in rank and authority— which are characteristic of any organization—but also of special privileges and differentiation of classes by means of an elaborate symbolism. Executive groups, for example, often have special dining rooms where the décor and the food are in marked contrast to the dining facilities (if any) provided for other employees. Similarly, executives have elaborate offices and retinues of messengers, servants, and assistants. Executives sometimes have special bonuses, special retirement provisions, special expense accounts, special vacation privileges—not to mention handsome salaries—and they are set apart from other employees and treated with great deference and respect. Often, among the lesser officialdom, lesser privileges of the same general type are in evidence. A significant issue is whether so obvious social stratification within the business enterprise can be justified on either ethical or practical grounds.

Second, a whole range of problems centers around the incentive system for individuals in the higher echelons of corporate hierarchies. The prevalence of strain, inability to relax, nervous breakdown, ulcers, and coronary disorders is well known, and threatens to become a national problem. This raises the question whether the much-vaunted productivity and progress of the American system of free enterprise, led by a class of highly motivated and almost supercharged businessmen, may not be attained at a cost that is too high in human terms. Perhaps our business life places undue emphasis upon pushing, getting ahead, being aggressive, and beating the other fellow. Perhaps it places undue demands upon the time and energy of those who get caught up into its incentive system and into its pattern of behavior.[6]

Third, American business—and perhaps American life generally —seems increasingly to encourage superficial human relationships in which the parties have ulterior motives. The object of many human relationships becomes that of selling something, gaining "influence," "knowing the right people," "making contacts," or "getting in good with the boss."[7] Friendship or pseudo-friendship is

[6] Francis Williams, "The Moral Case for Socialism," *Fortune*, October, 1949, p. 122.

[7] Cf. David Riesman, *The Lonely Crowd*, New Haven, Yale University Press, 1950; and W. H. Whyte, Jr., "Groupthink," *Fortune*, March, 1952, pp. 114-17, 142-46. Plays and novels such as *Death of a Salesman* (Arthur Miller), *Awake*

used widely for pecuniary purposes. The parties simulate friendly and intimate behavior by indulging in easy backslapping and use of first names. As a part of this process, lavish entertainment has become a part of normal business operations. And even wives and families of business executives are brought into the round of activities known as "sales" or "public relations."[8] One may readily ask whether some of the human relationships and personality characteristics fostered by modern business practice are of a desirable sort.

SOCIAL COSTS AND SOCIAL VALUES

Another set of issues, with which economists are familiar, pertains to the costs of enterprise which are borne by society in one form or another but which are not necessarily paid by the corporation, and to the values which the corporation may create but for which it does not necessarily collect.[9]

The uncompensated social costs may include such detriments as smoke, odor, dirt, noise, stream pollution, risk of explosion, defacing the landscape, constructing ugly buildings, contribution to urban congestion, etc. Firms are required by law to eliminate some of these costs to some extent, but frequently important social costs remain. The question is: What should a company do about them? Economists are generally agreed that all costs of production should be covered. This suggests that the detriments leading to social costs should be eliminated or that the enterprise should compensate whoever may be affected. Then the questions are raised as to which procedure should be followed in each case, and how the amount of compensation should be settled and to whom it should be paid.

But business firms also create social values. Sometimes they erect structures which improve the landscape and enhance the attractiveness of the community; they engage in educational work; they ad-

---

and Sing (Clifford Odets), and Point of No Return (John P. Marquand) express this theme. See also Shepherd Mead, How to Succeed in Business Without Really Trying, New York, 1952.

[8] W. H. Whyte, Jr., "The Wives of Management," Fortune, October, 1951, pp. 86-88, 204 ff.; W. H. Whyte, Jr., "The Corporation and the Wife," Fortune, November, 1951, pp. 109-11, 150 ff.; E. W. McLemore, "Manifesto from a Corporate Wife," Fortune, March, 1952, pp. 83, 194.

[9] K. W. Kapp, The Social Costs of Private Enterprise, Cambridge, Harvard University Press, 1950; A. C. Pigou, Economics of Welfare, 4th ed., London, The Macmillan Company, 1932.

vance knowledge through research; they provide off-season work for farmers; they contribute to community projects, etc. Thus, in considering compensation for social costs, it is desirable to take into account also the social values created by business firms. The ethical issue can be thus stated: each business should consider carefully both the social costs involved in its operations and the social values it creates, and do what it can in the light of its competitive situation to compensate for the net social costs for which it is responsible. The manner of compensation should be determined in consultation with those affected. For example, if the social cost is an unpleasant odor in the community where the plant is located, the problem would be to decide whether the community would prefer the elimination of the odor, let us say at the cost of a million dollars, or the use of that sum for a community improvement project, let us say the building of a hospital.[10]

It is, of course, difficult for a firm to receive compensation for the social values it creates when these exceed social costs. Yet it might be argued that a firm should be on the alert to manage its affairs so that the social values it creates are as great as possible. When these values are not costly, as is sometimes the case, the firm surely has a responsibility to select those policies which will add to social values. For example, if two sites for the location of a plant are under consideration, and are equally desirable from the commercial point of view, the company has an obligation to choose that one which will afford the most social benefit or the least detriment.[11]

ADVERTISING, SELLING, AND MASS COMMUNICATION

Some of the businessman's greatest responsibility lies in the area of his sales activities. It goes without saying that his sales claims should be honest and that he should not corrupt the integrity of his sales employees by asking them to make false or misleading representations to customers. But there are many more subtle ethical issues connected with his sales operations. Should he conduct selling in ways that intrude on the privacy of people, for example, by

[10] There are many issues pertaining to the effect of social costs on property values. If a nuisance impairs property values in the vicinity of a plant, should the property owners or the residents of the area be compensated?

[11] Cf. "Whose Mistake at Nashua?" *Fortune*, November, 1948, pp. 98-100.

door-to-door selling or by sending salesmen who appear unannounced, and without appointment, and insist upon taking up the time of prospective customers? Should he use methods involving ballyhoo, chances, prizes, hawking, and other tactics which are at least of doubtful good taste? Should he employ "high-pressure" tactics in persuading people to buy? Should he try, through his selling and advertising appeals, to make people dissatisfied with what they have? Should he try to hasten the obsolescence of goods by bringing out an endless succession of new models and new styles? Should he appeal to and attempt to strengthen the motives of materialism, invidious consumption, and "keeping up with the Joneses"? Should he emphasize sex in his advertising appeals? Should he attempt to set himself up as the arbiter of good taste and "proper" living standards through his advertising and selling activities? Should he assume responsibility for the good taste, the artistic value, the educational contributions, and the recreational value of his radio and television programs and his printed advertisements?[12] Should he exert influence over the social and political ideas expressed in the media of mass communication which his advertising supports?[13]

These are clearly difficult and important questions. They can be answered from any one of three general points of view: (1) that it is the job of businessmen to produce only in response to a given consumer demand, and that they should not attempt to influence that demand except by offering information to consumers as to availability of various kinds of goods from which consumers can choose; (2) that businessmen can legitimately attempt to influence consumer demand, but that the power this gives them over our standards, values, and wants—over our entire culture—is so great that they must use this power with restraint and a deep sense of responsibility for the social welfare; (3) that businessmen are not and should not be the guardians of our morals and attitudes and should be free to employ any sales techniques which the public will accept in the sense that they will respond by buying goods.[14] If the first or the second point of view is accepted, there is need for

[12] See The Commission on Freedom of the Press, A Free and Responsible Press, Chicago, University of Chicago Press, 1947, pp. 90-96.

[13] See Sidney Hook, "Bread, Freedom, and Businessmen," Fortune, September, 1951, pp. 117, 174 ff.

[14] Sometimes this third position is based on the conviction that advertising and selling activities are not strongly influential in shaping our culture patterns.

careful consideration by interested parties and technical experts of the principles which should guide businessmen in their selling activities.

ECONOMIC STABILIZATION

In recent years, it has often been proposed that businessmen should try to conduct their operations in a way calculated to contribute toward general economic stability. That this proposal should be advanced is not surprising. A major portion of the employment of the country is within private business firms. And fluctuations in total employment take the form chiefly of fluctuations in the amount of employment offered in the many individual enterprises. Therefore, one possible approach to the problem of economic fluctuations is to attempt to stabilize the employment offered by individual firms. This is a sort of "grassroots" approach to stabilization policy.

A more sophisticated variant of this idea is based upon the widely accepted theory that a major cause of economic instability is fluctuation in the rate of spending by business enterprises—especially for inventories and for plant and equipment. It is held that if businessmen could stabilize their expenditures for these purposes (or even vary their spending countercyclically), the result would be greater stability for the total economy.

With either of these approaches, it is held that businessmen, whose combined decisions spell prosperity or depression for the economy, have a deep responsibility to plan their operations with a view to their effects on general economic stability. This general line of thinking was in the minds of the sponsors of the Employment Act of 1946, and it has appeared from time to time in the literature on stabilization policy.[15]

[15] Perhaps the most ambitious inquiry into the subject was made by the Conference on Regularization of Business Investment held under the sponsorship of the National Bureau of Economic Research in November, 1951. At this conference numerous papers were presented by leading economists. See also Herman Feldman, *Stabilizing Jobs and Wages*, New York, Harper & Brothers, 1940; Joseph L. Snider, *The Guarantee of Work and Wages*, Harvard University Division of Research, Boston, 1947; Morris A. Copeland, "Business Stabilization by Agreement," *American Economic Review*, June, 1944, pp. 328-39; H. G. Moulton, *Controlling Factors in Economic Development*, Washington, Brookings Institution, 1949; Jack Chernick, *Economic Effects of Steady Employment and Earnings*, Minneapolis, University of Minnesota Press, 1942.

There is no doubt that fluctuations in economic activity are strongly influenced by the decisions of individual businessmen, and that if businessmen could adjust their operations with a view to contributing to total economic stabilization the results would be salutary. But this would not be easy. Just as governmental stabilization policy often flounders because of the inability to diagnose the economic situation correctly and because of imperfect knowledge of the remedies (even when the diagnosis is correct), so private business policy also is handicapped. The case of 1947 provides an excellent example of these difficulties. At that time, there were two conflicting diagnoses: one that depression was imminent, and the other that inflation threatened. And, on the assumption that the diagnosis of imminent depression was correct, there were two conflicting opinions as to what should be done about wages: one that wages should be held steady or even reduced, and the other that wages should be increased. It seems apparent that in our present state of knowledge about the causes and cures of economic instability we must not thoughtlessly ask the businessman to assume responsibilities which he cannot reasonably be expected to discharge even with the best of good intentions.

Having expressed this note of deep skepticism, it is possible to suggest, however, some things that businessmen might do, indeed have done to promote economic stability.

One of the first, most obvious, and least controversial things a business might do is to maintain a sound financial structure so that its capital structure, caution in the use and extension of credit, and pression and be forced to liquidate its inventories or even its capital assets in a distressed market. This suggests care in the make-up of its capital structure, caution in the use and extension of credit, and prudence in its reserve and dividend policies.[16] One should hasten to add, however, that if businessmen were to overdo these things, prosperity and dynamic growth of the economy might never happen. Their problem is to achieve a reasonable balance between security and progress.

Second, there is undoubtedly much that businessmen could do

[16] Cf. W. E. Upjohn Institute for Community Research, *Full Employment Through Business Enterprise*, Kalamazoo, 1950. For Swedish experience see Arne Bjornberg, "Full Employment in Sweden," *Commercial and Financial Chronicle*, August 18, 1946.

to reduce fluctuations in their outlays for plant and equipment. If they took a sufficiently long-run view, they might even be able to adopt long-term schedules of capital improvements which they would expect to carry out almost regardless of variations in business conditions. In some cases, they might even try to work out a counter-cyclical pattern of capital outlays. They might do something also about retarding maintenance activities in a boom and expanding them in depression. Similarly, they might attempt to introduce new products and new methods during depression periods rather than in boom times. All of this might be good business in the sense that capital assets can be acquired and new promotions carried out more cheaply during depression than during prosperity.[17] But it is asking a great deal of businessmen to suggest that they should expand and assume new risks when business conditions and prospects are poor, and should restrain themselves when business is good. Businessmen, like most of us, are inclined to make outlays when they can "afford" them and not when they feel financially pinched. Moreover, businessmen are often forced into expansion during a boom period by the action of competitors. If one's rivals expand during a boom and threaten to capture a larger share of the market, the inevitable reaction is expansion to maintain one's competitive position. This is not to say that long-range planning and stable rates of investment are undesirable or even unattainable, but to suggest that not too much can be expected through voluntary private action.[18]

[17] For example, the construction of Rockefeller Center during the 1930's was undoubtedly sound from both commercial and social points of view.

[18] Professor Walter W. Heller has recently completed a study of investment decisions in which he reached this conclusion:

"The suggestion that instability is deeply imbedded in our business structure finds much support in this study. Probing failed to reveal within the pattern of current business conduct anything which appears to offer a firm foundation on which to build greater stability of capital expenditure. Like all of us, business executives strongly desire greater stability. But the size and nature of the enterprises they direct do not appear to offer an incentive to stabilize their own activities in the interests of a more stable economy. The firms are not large enough to take their cue from the impact of their actions on the economy as a whole. Quite logically, the profit motive dictates that 'general business conditions' should be viewed as a determinant—not a resultant—of their actions.

"Another factor which makes for instability is the characteristic of flexible management and speedy decision making. It is true that this is good insurance against bureaucratic stagnation, but it also intensifies the cumulative nature of fluctuations in capital expenditures.

"Finally, management investment policies are so closely geared to realized

Four other proposals for private business policy toward economic stability deserve mention. The first is that expenditures for advertising and selling should be adjusted countercyclically.[19] It is well known that advertising and selling expenditures are larger during boom periods than in depression. The suggestion is made that this should be reversed in order to encourage buying in slack periods and to place less stress on sales during booms when sales are easy anyhow. This is a plausible argument, but not necessarily a strong one. There is some doubt as to whether countercyclical advertising would be an important stabilizing influence. Moreover, we again run squarely into the problem of business motivation and the effect of competition. The businessman advertises in order to be able to sell goods. The amount he can afford to spend depends on potential profit he can expect from the additional sales. In good times, this potential profit is larger than in depression; therefore, from his point of view it pays to spend more for advertising in good times than in bad. An individual businessman might, of course, be willing to pass up the profits to be made from advertising in a lush market; but if his competitors do not see it this way his forbearance will result in their capturing a larger share of the market. Therefore, despite his good intentions, he might be forced to follow the cyclical pattern of advertising expenditures. This argument does not apply, however, to institutional advertising, which might well be arranged countercyclically—except for the practical fact that businessmen feel they can "afford" it in good times but not in bad times.

Another proposal is that businessmen should adopt inventory policies calculated to contribute to stability or at least not to aggravate instability. This implies avoidance of inventory speculation,

profits that such stability-promoting proposals as slack-period plant construction and equipment purchases and conscious inventory stabilization simply do not seem to fit into the pattern of thinking. The appeal such proposals might have in the way of lowering the cost of acquiring plant and equipment and inventories is overshadowed by the greater risk believed to be involved in making commitments that are not geared to profits already made or easily in sight.

"In short, this study indicates once again that private economic motivation generates far more instability than stability, and that the residual job of stabilization left to government will be large."—"The Anatomy of Investment Decisions," *Harvard Business Review*, March, 1951, p. 102.

[19] For discussion of this problem, see Joel Dean, "Cyclical Policy on the Advertising Appropriation," *Journal of Marketing*, January, 1951, pp. 265-73. See also G. Rowland Collins, *The Advertising Appropriation and the Business Cycle*, Schools of Business, New York University, 1948.

holding inventories down in good times and not liquidating them precipitously in bad times. There is much to be said for this proposal both in terms of private business policy and social policy.

A third proposal is that, when relations with competitors and labor unions permit, businesses should adjust their prices and wages according to the requirements of the economic situation. It is likely that wage and price policies in private business firms are important factors determining the degree of economic stability. However, there is wide disagreement among professional economists as to just what wage and price policies are desirable at various stages of the business cycle. For example, some economists advocate wage reduction during a depression in order to lower costs and increase profit incentives; others advocate wage stability in order to maintain mass purchasing power. Some advocate wage stability in an inflationary period; others, that wages should rise with the cost of living. Similarly the doctors disagree on price policy; some suggest flexible prices with reductions during depression periods and increases during boom periods, and others advocate price stability. Until expert opinion is more fully crystallized and more firmly founded, there is little that can be said about the businessman's responsibilities regarding wage and price policies through changing business conditions. Indeed, this is one of the most important unsolved economic problems of our time.

A special form of the proposals regarding price policy is that during periods of inflation (e.g., in the years following World War II), businessmen should hold prices below market levels on the grounds that it would help (1) to stem the tide of advancing prices, and (2) to make governmental price controls unnecessary. There is no doubt that many businessmen have in recent years held prices below market levels—as the shortatges of many commodities have so eloquently testified. They have done this for a variety of motives, among them the desire to avoid regulation, fear of adverse public reactions to high prices, and sincere belief that to advance prices would be economically unsound. Yet any impartial observer would conclude, on the basis of the experience of recent years, that voluntary restraint by businessmen cannot usefully be relied upon as a major defense against inflation.[20] This is not to deny that the for-

[20] See Ralph E. Flanders, "Economics Collides with Ethics," *American Economic Review*, May, 1948 (supplement), pp. 357-67; Hearings Before the Joint Committee on the Economic Report, June 24 to July 17, 1947; *Current Price*

bearance of businesmen has been helpful, but only to suggest that it would be unwise, and indeed unfair to the business community, to expect them to hold the line against inflation the causes of which are not of their making.

All of this suggests that the things which businessmen can reasonably be expected to do toward economic stability are relatively limited. Nevertheless, there are things they can do, and these things should be done whenever possible. And as economic knowledge advances, it is likely that there will be more things businessmen can do in the interests of economic stability.[21] Our argument suggests, however, that, for the time being at least, economic stability is a problem that must be tackled chiefly by governmental measures. This means that the businessman has a deep responsibility to cooperate with government in its efforts to develop and carry out effective stabilization policies. Businessmen should make their contribution constructively toward the development of sound public policy, and should cooperate fully in coordinating their activities with the public policy adopted. Since the maintenance of economic stability is so vital to the preservation of the system of private enterprise, it is in their own interest, as well as the public interest, for them to do so.

It is to be hoped in the process that the element of the "vicious circle" can be remedied—the tendency of businessmen and others to assume that serious business fluctuations like those of the past will occur in the future and to base their plans on this expectation. This leads them to take a short-range view of the future, to adopt only those investments which promise a quick pay-off, to try to make a "killing" when business is good, to curtail operations at the first sign of depression, to try to profit from speculation over the phases of the cycle, to hold back on capital expansion that is needed to supply the country's needs in periods of full employment, etc. The fear of instability, in other words, leads to action which tends to accentuate instability. If government and business would develop a cooperative program of stabilization in which confidence could

---

Developments and the Problem of Economic Stabilization; Report of a Subcommittee of the Joint Committee on the Economic Report, *Profits,* 1949; Report of the Joint Committee on the Economic Report, *December* 1949 *Steel Price Increases,* 1950.

[21] Cf. Arthur Smithies, "Federal Budgeting and Fiscal Policy," in *A Survey of Contemporary Economics,* Howard Ellis, ed., Philadelphia, The Blakiston Company, 1949, p. 208.

be placed, businessmen could then make their plans on the basis of less fearful and pessimistic estimates of the future, and they could then afford to pursue policies which would help make this brighter future a reality. It would seem to be one of the prime obligations of business to try to make this possible.[22]

The discussion of economic stabilization thus far has focused entirely on the great swings in economic activity which we know as booms and depressions. There is another type of instability, namely, seasonal fluctuations in employment and economic activity, about which private business can do, and does, a great deal. For example, firms can regularize production throughout the year by such devices as the following: stabilizing the rates of production and allowing inventories rather than employment to vary seasonally, adopting or developing new products to be produced in slack seasons, and integrating operations with other industries having different seasonals. Often these devices are good business as well as good social policy because they keep the organization intact, improve worker morale, attract more efficient and steadier workers, etc. Along this line some firms are experimenting with the guaranteed annual wage or guaranteed annual employment. All of these practices are obviously desirable, although they are more adaptable to some industries than to others. Many businessmen have shown, however, that with imagination and courage much can and ought to be done toward reducing seasonal and short-run fluctuations in business activity.

Finally, one additional business problem pertaining to economic instability is to determine upon which workers the incidence of unemployment shall fall when the working force is cut. This raises a host of ethical issues. Strict economy usually calls for laying off the least efficient workers. Union policy often requires the laying off of workers with the least seniority. Some would argue that married women or persons with outside means of support should be first to go, or that persons without dependents should be cut off ahead of those with dependents, or that the retirement age should be advanced. If the layoffs are due to the decline of an industry or occupation rather than to general depression, it may be appropriate to lay off those first who can most easily learn a new trade. Another possible approach to the problem is to spread employment by shortening the length of the work week. The question of who should

[22] Cf. Walter W. Heller, op. cit., pp. 102-3.

bear the brunt of a decline in employment is clearly a difficult one which is made even more acute by the fact that the employment of the executive group is ordinarily not affected by the ups and downs of business activity.

RELATIONS WITH GOVERNMENT

There have always been significant ethical issues for businessmen in their relations with government; but today when government is often their biggest customer and frequently controls their prices, costs, labor relations, and sources of materials, the ethical issues become more acute simply because the stakes are larger. There are two classes of ethical issues here: those pertaining to the *objectives* which a business may legally pursue in its relations with government, and those pertaining to the *methods* which it may use in seeking its objectives.

The objectives of a business in its relations with government include favorable changes in general public policies, such as taxation, labor legislation, price controls, tariffs; and special grants or concessions for the particular firm, such as franchises, contracts, favorable court decisions, subsidies, special tax concessions, material allocations, foreign intervention to protect an investment, etc.

The methods may range from mere requests for aid to lobbying, publicity, campaign contributions, "knowing the right people," entertainment, gifts, bribes, and promises of future jobs to "cooperative" officials.

We have heard a great deal in recent years about both the objectives and the methods sometimes employed in the relations of business with government.[23] We have particularly heard lurid accounts of fur coats, "five-percenters," gay social affairs, and the like, all of which are presumed to be part of the "influence" business in Washington. It is easy to conclude from these newspaper stories that all or most businessmen pursue unworthy objectives by corrupt methods. This is far from the truth, though unquestionably serious abuses exist.[24]

[23] Hearings before a Subcommittee to Study Senate Concurrent Resolution 21 of the Committee on Labor and Public Welfare, 82nd Congress, 1st Session, *Establishment of a Commission on Ethics in Government*, June 19 to July 11, 1951.

[24] Cf. Temporary National Economic Committee, *Economic Power and Political Pressures*, Monograph No. 26, Washington, 1941.

But before one can usefully consider the questions of what objectives a business may ethically pursue and what methods it may rightfully employ in its relations with government, one must consider the basic theory of government in a democracy. There are two views.

The first (which has been called *"neo-laissez faire"*[25]) is that every individual or interest group should be permitted to state its case, to persuade, to cajole, to apply pressure, and to do whatever seems necessary (short of bribery and perjury) to gain its ends. Since other opposing individuals and groups would have the same privilege, the progress of any one group toward ends unpalatable to others would stimulate the others to apply countervailing measures. If particular groups should be overwhelmed by stronger rivals, coalitions of weaker elements could be organized to neutralize the power of the stronger. In any conflict of interest between economic groups the public will be bombarded by propaganda from both sides; legislators will be buttonholed by lobbyists from both groups; influential people will be entertained by both sides. As a result of this mutually defeating competitive effort, the opposing interests will be balanced, and no one group will be able to exert undue power for any extended period of time. The process is similar to that by which a balance of power may be achieved in international relations or to that by which justice is achieved in litigation, where each side is permitted to present its "case" as best it can.

The theory of neo-laissez faire is reasonably plausible as an objective description of the way government actually functions. Whether it is equally plausible as a theory of how government *ought* to function is another question.

The second view on the functioning of democratic government holds that the constant conflict among warring groups, which we witness every day and which is regarded as the norm in the theory of neo-laissez faire, is intolerable for several reasons. First, it divides society into conflicting and ideologically estranged groups and threatens to destroy social cohesion and unity. Second, there is no assurance that the hit-and-miss competitive process really produces

---

[25] I am indebted to Mr. Nelson Cruikshank for this term. Cf. also, J. K. Galbraith, *American Capitalism, The Concept of Countervailing Power*, Boston, Houghton Mifflin Company, 1952. In citing Mr. Cruikshank and Professor Galbraith, I do not imply that either of them endorses the theory of *neo-laissez faire*.

a reasonable or just compromise among the several warring interests. Even if it is admitted that a workable compromise might be achieved in the long run, the long run for this purpose is even longer than the economist's long run; and that—it is argued—is too long to wait for justice to prevail. Third, there is no assurance that one group or one coalition will not gain a mastery over the others and impose its will on them. Accordingly, the conclusion is reached that the only solution to the problem of government is the solution of *cooperation* among the several groups. Cooperation in this sense calls for the working out of their problems through discussion, mutual under-standing, and consideration for the common good rather than through conflict, power politics, and preoccupation with the self-interest. It is held that we need new institutions, industry councils for example, to facilitate the settlement of social conflict by co-operative methods.[26]

The basic issues regarding the relations of business—or any other group—to government must be considered in terms of these two theories of the democratic process. In the world as we know it, which does seem to operate pretty largely along the lines of neo-laissez faire, it would be idle to suggest that businessmen ought not try to convert people to their point of view, and ought not press for their interests. While anyone would wish to draw the line, so far as his methods are concerned, somewhere this side of outright per-jury or bribery, it would be futile and unjust to expect businessmen to withdraw from the political arena unless they could be persuaded that others would also withdraw. And so the fundamental issue is this: Can we develop new institutions through which the several groups can settle their conflicts by the methods of cooperation? Many ethically motivated people would argue that this should be our objective, and that it is a responsibility of businessmen and other groups to seek for cooperative solutions. As part of this ap-proach, close working relationships between government and the various interest groups (including business) would be achieved. There would be mutual consultation on problems of public policy and cooperation of the interest groups in the execution of public pol-

[26] That group harmony may be a prelude to totalitarianism has been ably pointed out by W. H. Whyte, Jr., "Groupthink," *Fortune*, March, 1952, pp. 114-17, 142-46.

icy.[27] The goal would be an integrated society in place of a collection of warring factions. Is this goal visionary and impracticable?[28]

OTHER ISSUES

There are several other ethical issues facing American businessmen of which space will permit only brief mention. These issues are treated summarily, not because they are unimportant or because the solutions are easy, but because their nature is relatively obvious.

1. A great deal of attention has been given to the obligations of businessmen in their human relations with workers and others inside the enterprise. The question can also be asked: What obligations do they have in their human relations with customers, suppliers, government officials, and other persons outside the enterprise? Doubtless the same spirit which should activate dealings with members of the corporate family should also prevail in their dealings with others.

2. Significant ethical issues arise in connection with competitive relationships. How vigorously should businessmen compete? Is a "live and let live" policy compatible with the free-enterprise system? Should a firm eliminate a rival or prevent the entry of a rival? On what matters is cooperation among competitive firms permissible? Should a competitor who has met a misfortune be helped? What information should be withheld from competitors? Is spying on competitors legitimate? When is it permissible to attract key personnel from competing firms? Are agreements not to hire away another's personnel legitimate? Should patents be licensed to competitors? How large should a company allow itself to become? Under what conditions are mergers permissible? These are, of course, extremely difficult questions, the answers to which must be derived from one's answer to a more fundamental issue, namely, to what extent should we rely on competition among independent firms for control of business? Perhaps the majority opinion in the United States would be that firms have the obligation to compete

---

[27] Samuel Courtauld, "An Industrialist's Reflections on the Future Relations of Government and Industry," *Economic Journal*, April, 1942, pp. 1-17.

[28] Many writers are skeptical of public programs involving voluntary cooperation of business with government on the ground that they place too much moral stress on businessmen. See, for example, Albert G. Hart, *Defense Without Inflation*, New York, Twentieth Century Fund, 1951, pp. 155-57.

vigorously and that competition should be encouraged, fostered, and even required by law. In Europe, on the other hand, competition is less highly regarded, and control of business is sought through cartel and other trade organizations operating under governmental surveillance rather than through competition.

3. Another range of questions centers around the responsibilities of a business toward future generations as distinct from the present generation. How rapidly should the company add to its plant and equipment?[29] How much should it invest in research and development? How rapidly and in what manner should it utilize nonreplaceable natural resources? What provision should be made for replacement of timber, fish, and other reproducible natural resources? Is the destruction of arable land through strip mining ethically defensible? These are extremely difficult questions because there are no clear principles to determine precisely how the interests of future generations should be balanced against those of present generations, or to what extent private business should be called upon to look out for future generations. It can be argued that it is desirable for a business to take a long view in its decisions, because a long view is likely to coincide more nearly with social interests than is a short view. It can also be argued that obviously wasteful use of natural resources is morally indefensible, and that businessmen should be continuously searching for more economical methods of using them and striving to find reproducible substitutes. In general, however, there are limits to the expenditures, or forbearance, which can reasonably be expected of businessmen. Consequently, the interests of future generations probably must be handled largely through governmental policy—with which businessmen should be expected to cooperate.

4. Another question relates to the degree and kind of influence which businessmen should attempt to exercise over charitable, religious, and educational institutions which they support or which they serve as board members. This raises a host of issues pertaining to freedom of speech, thought, and teaching and to the terms under which social services are to be provided. Perhaps many would argue that businessmen should be extremely circumspect in their relation-

[29] This has been a prominent public issue in recent years with respect to the steel industry. Government has been pressing the industry to expand its facilities, in the interest of national defense, beyond what the firms have felt was justified in terms of their own interests.

ships with these organizations, or perhaps that they should, as a matter of principle, exercise any influence they may have jointly with representatives of other groups.

5. A related and perhaps more fundamental question is: What position should businessmen take in defending the traditional American freedoms in a time when these are under serious attack? One suspects that businessmen have been more diligent in their defense of freedom of enterprise than in their concern for the related freedoms of thought, of speech, and of religion.[30] And there is another similar question: What are businessmen's responsibilities toward the elimination of prejudice and discrimination?[31] Why is it, asks Sidney Hook, "that the fight for civil liberties, for academic freedom, for minority rights is left largely to bishops, lawyers, and professors?"[32]

6. Since a large portion of all scientific research is done under the sponsorship of business enterprises, what responsibilities do businessmen have for the promotion of pure research, the advancement of scientific knowledge, and the dissemination of scientific discoveries?

Conclusions

As indicated at the outset, the purpose of this chapter has been to state issues and not to settle them. The statement of the issues does more, however, than merely pose problems for someone else to solve. It suggests several important conclusions: (1) that the problem of identifying and formulating the social responsibilities of businessmen is a complex matter which goes to the very root of our basic social and economic philosophy; (2) that, although it is easy to assert that businessmen should assume certain responsibilities, deeper analysis often shows that there are severe limits to the range and extent of responsibilities which they can reasonably be expected to assume; (3) that much careful study, research, and ethical analysis will be required before we shall be able to formulate the

[30] Leon Henderson, "Vital Issues Facing American Business Today," *Commercial and Financial Chronicle*, August 1, 1946, pp. 606, 634; Bernard De Voto, "Why Professors Are Suspicious of Business," *Fortune*, April, 1951.

[31] R. M. Mac Iver, *The More Perfect Union*, New York, The Macmillan Company, 1948, pp. 113-44.

[32] "Bread, Freedom, and Businessmen," *Fortune*, September, 1951, p. 174.

social responsibilities of business in a form which will be concrete, and which will receive wide acceptance; (4) that in such study, various points of view and various kinds of technical competencies must be effectively represented; (5) that the economic problems of our society—problems such as instability, insecurity, injustice, and lack of work satisfaction—cannot be solved merely by turning the responsibility over to business. Businessmen, and other groups as well, can contribute by assuming those responsibilities which they can reasonably bear. Part of the job rests with other groups, and part of it must be undertaken by government. One of the great needs of our society, therefore, is to achieve cooperative and mutual relationships among groups, and between government and groups, such that urgent social purposes can be effectively defined and carried out. In this, businessmen have an important constructive role to play—a role that includes both leadership and cooperation.

PART II

18

Commentary on the Ethical Implications of the Study

By F. Ernest Johnson

The task assigned to me is to write an "ethical critique" of the analysis that has been presented in this volume. Such a critique should obviously have two foci: the author's analysis itself, and the complex of businessmen's ideas and attitudes that the author discloses. I may say at once, then, that I find few points to argue about in Mr. Bowen's treatment of his subject. The comprehensiveness and balance that characterize his analysis are matched by that ethical sensitivity which one expects from a socially minded scholar. There are, to be sure, certain points at which I am disposed to counter the author's position, but in the main it will be my aim to set the entire discussion more definitely and specifically within a Christian ethical perspective, and to point up the relevance of the Christian ethic to the businessman's world.

Inevitably, this chapter will be in the nature of a running commentary on selected portions of the author's text, rather than a formal essay. I hope the lack of systematic organization will not obscure the ideas selected for discussion. In any case my own presuppositions should be set down at the outset.

First, there is in the Christian ethic a "frame of reference," a scheme of values that exalts persons in their own right and maximizes both integrity and fellowship. Overarching this value system is an absolute imperative in every situation and every relationship to do what one believes to be the will of God, which expresses itself in a universal law of love. Quite as clear and unmistakable as this ultimate imperative is the recognition that man in his finiteness, enmeshed in the incongruities and relativities of existence—nowhere more conspicuous than in business—cannot wholly fulfill this law of love which he nevertheless feels to be ultimately authoritative. This deep moral involvement is what theologians call the "human predicament."

In this situation man is confronted by two grievous temptations. On the one hand, he has an urge to rationalize his way out of his moral involvement and to content himself with not-too-costly virtues, reflecting that, after all, he was not endowed with wings. On the other hand, he is lured by the serenity of a life lived in isolation from the moral tumult of the secular world. On the one hand, self-deception; on the other hand, withdrawal. The Christian way, it is here taken for granted, is to reject both of these too easy alternatives and to accept the world of moral tension, in which a person must "toil terribly" toward a goal that forever eludes him. He must maintain a realistic view of human frailty, but he must avoid ethical negativism by sensing that even a choice between a greater and a lesser evil is a positive moral achievement. And he learns by experience and through the lessons of history that in a world full of imperfections and moral contradictions there are nevertheless indeterminate spiritual possibilities which it is his duty to actualize in fullest possible measure. He looks out on life without romantic illusion; he knows it is tough business, but he is "saved by hope." He is persuaded that his striving will make a difference, and this assurance encourages him to do his best.

It is in this context that I am disposed to interpret what the author calls the "optimistic doctrine of social responsibility." Indeed, the very word "responsibility" connotes both realism and hope. The concept derives from an austere appraisal of the realities; its vitality rests on a genuine anticipation of a worthy outcome.

CONFLICTING MOTIVES

The heart of the problem with which this book is concerned is, of course, the tension between self-interest and social obligation. Now, to begin with, it seems to me highly significant and encouraging that this tension in the realm of personal motive is recognized by "hardheaded" men who are reluctant to make it explicit. Again and again I have observed the tendency among businessmen to compensate the severities of competitive enterprise by a half-apologetic indulgence in ordinary human generosity, while palming it off as "good business," lest they may appear to be sentimental or even hypocritical. This tendency, which has been noted in these pages, points up the tension between the claims of elemental generous impulses and the rugged rules of business enterprise. Indeed, the effective pressure of community opinion as a restraint on undesirable business practices—a force which the author so rightly emphasizes—is the ultimate refutation of the laissez-faire philosophy, which gave to business an autonomy of its own, independent of the conscious corporate sanctions of the community itself.

The fallacy in this conception of a distinct "economic man" becomes evident when it is realized that even the man most dedicated to business has human impulses and urges which on occasion take precedence over his economic drives in the conduct of his work. It is a curious fact that this artificial concept of man for over a century furnished the capitalist system with its rationale—a brand of economic determinism quite as crude as that which has been attributed to Karl Marx. Mr. Bowen's "doctrine of social responsibility"[1] is pregnant with the liberating conviction that intelligence and good will can in considerable measure overcome the crudities and angularities of economic life.

A THEORY THAT NEVER WORKED

It is worth noting that the laissez-faire theory, as the writings of Adam Smith clearly show,[2] had something in common with religious faith, and, we may add, was very piously held. The complexities of production and distribution did not have to be worried about, because they were ultimately administered by "the invisible hand." The rationale of laissez faire made economic relations so deterministic in character as to enable the businessman to unload a considerable part of his ethical responsibility. This, be it noted, was as much a fault of the religious leadership that sanctioned the doctrine as of the business leadership that exploited it. As has been repeatedly pointed out, the end result was a divorce of the economic mechanism from its supposed moral motor power, making the economic sphere autonomous and amoral. Ethical man was permitted to abdicate to a hypothetical economic man.

[1] Chapter 10.
[2] See note on page 16.

As Mr. Bowen has shown, the laissez-faire theory was never fully actualized.[3] Fortunately, men never become so "utterly utter" in any respect as some of their theoretical formulations suggest. Also, in its earlier stages capitalism was kept to a degree within ethical bounds by a strong sense of Christian vocation. But the long struggle of the pulpit to win recognition of the relevance of Christian ethics to the economic sphere bears testimony to the extent to which a pernicious economic determinism had come to dominate the business mentality. Within my memory the sanctions of religion have won back much lost territory in the thinking of business leaders. Sharp controversies still occur over the implications of Christian ethics for economic life, but probably few persons are today ready to contend that "business is business," in the traditional connotation of that phrase.

Even the crude efforts currently made to read classical economic theories into the New Testament are perhaps preferable to the erstwhile habitual inclination of businessmen to deny that Christian ethics has a normative relation to economic affairs. I will recall the profane surprise of an industrial executive to whom I relayed, many years ago, an inquiry from a Christian gentleman about the company's labor policy. The latter had seen in the morning paper an advertisement of a new bond issue the company was floating, and he thought of investing—if he approved the labor policy. I got little information, and no encouragement to call again.

Self-Interest and Social Duty

Now, let us look more closely at the self-interest problem. A major concern of this book has been the vindication of self-interest to the extent that seems necessary in order to keep the nation's industrial plant operating. The author is apprehensive of anything that may "put too great a strain on altruism."[4] He finds satisfaction in discovering areas of coincidence between private interest and social concern, for he sees in this overlapping of motive the salvation of social responsibility, which is thus "reinforced by private interest." He quotes an eminent business leader as saying, "We may still be selfish, but let us be selfish in the long-range view."[5]

[3] P. 14 ff.
[4] P. 115.
[5] P. 106.

As an objective account of economic motivation, the author's discussion seems to me sound. He is careful to point out that we know all too little about effective incentives.[6] To be sure, I suspect that men are capable of active response to a vastly wider range of incentives than we ordinarily take for granted. One of the anomalies of the business scene is the preoccupation with public affairs and social-welfare projects on the part of men who are continually sounding the tocsin against some threat to private enterprise.

Yet this is not the real point. For even the most benevolent capitalist may quite legitimately feel concern about how great a load social motive by itself will carry. Self-interest is deeply embedded in human nature. The objective evaluation of incentives from a utilitarian point of view is as necessary in the economic sphere as it is in the matter of national defense. Moreover, self-interest has an authentic ethical aspect as a basis of self-improvement. But when full account has been taken of the practical importance of self-interest and of its ethical value, the Church must still insist on a Christian appraisal of the drives that govern economic behavior. The conditions of business success have to be discovered through experience as interpreted by economists and psychologists, but Christian ethics must still pronounce upon them in qualitative terms.

This is not to suggest, however, that "selfishness" is to be replaced by "altruism." That would surely be an oversimplification. I never hear that word altruism without being reminded of the lad who came home from church with a puzzled look and asked his mother, "What are we here for, anyhow?" To which his mother replied conventionally, "To help others." With a frown he asked, "Well, what are the *others* here for?" He was not the first person, nor the last, to find himself going round in circles about this question. I should like to see the idea of altruism as a supposed ethical norm permanently relegated and to have substituted for it a concept of mutuality, of involvement in fellowship with other human beings. As a matter of fact, so-called "private" interests often turn out on examination to be anything but private. Barring a miser here and there, and an occasional recluse, we are all members of a community, and most of us are members of the most exacting type of community, the family.

If I correctly understand the Christian ethic, no "selfish" motive can find sanction within it, for the very attribution of selfishness

[6] P. 87.

to one's behavior means that something potentially inclusive has been arbitrarily restricted. The real question is, what kind of "self" a person has—or is. To be selfish means to have a conspicuously and undesirably narrow self. Personality is a social achievement and is measured in terms of a widening capacity for human relationships.

SELF-INTEREST IS NOT STATIC

The ethical norm, then, is a growing, expanding self. Family life demonstrates this. The most elemental of human satisfactions, those of hunger and sex, may become degraded to the extent that they are without an aspect of mutuality. And the wider the range of social consequences that flow from an activity, the more important it is that "private" interest be transcended. I suggest that our highly competitive economic system would become intolerably cruel were it not mitigated by the moral discipline and voluntary restraint exercised by some of the businessmen who are most insistent that self-interest is paramount in business. It is of the nature of expanding business that it becomes more and more "impressed with a public interest," as has been pointed out in this book. And the health of business is largely determined by the extent to which the men in charge of it recognize this fact without waiting for government to remind them—as government must always be ready to do. It is important to remember also that government has a noncoercive function of facilitating voluntary group autonomy.

The link between self and other in the process of moral development is the steadily increasing mutual involvement. Mr. Bowen has seen this very clearly,[7] but it needs emphasis. "No man is an island." Life makes him "part of the mainland." When one accepts a new public sanction he does not merely "bow" to it; if it represents a genuine affirmative moral consensus, one enters into a new and satisfying experience when he accepts it. I heard a successful businessman say, "I have no doubt one can be a Christian and succeed in business, but I doubt if he can make as much money." Right or wrong, he was giving an authentic Christian testimony: he put the Christian ethic *first*. Such limitation as this entails is compensated by participation in a common effort toward a better life.

[7] P. 160 f.

Indeed, if this voluntary element is smothered by legal coercion, the spiritual quality of the process of social development is diluted. Then "social responsibility" is not enhanced; there is only a forced and precarious *modus vivendi*.

All good education is directed toward expanding and refining the sphere of self-interest. The people we admire most are those who have sought to reduce to the vanishing point the realm of the *purely* private—the exclusive—in their lives. Christian ethics emphasizes the social, or shared, aspect of experience. That is why we say that the Christian ethic is built on the family pattern. Let us be as realistic as we will about human nature as we find it. The theologians give ample support to the judgment that man has his ornery aspects and that we must, in the eyes of the Lord, be problem children indeed. But the most important thing about man from the Christian point of view is that he is indefinitely redeemable. There is no private preserve in man's heart that we may assume to be beyond redemption. And a Christian sociology, if the term is permissible, cannot set limits to the spiritual capacities of men on the ground that "human nature is like that." Cultural anthropology abounds in evidence that what are commonly taken to be fixed and given characteristics of human nature are, after all, cultural fixations. However valid an insight the doctrine of "original sin" may embody, it is a grievous error to assume that established patterns of behavior express the full moral potentialities of human nature.

A REGENERATING DISCIPLINE

Christian ethics has no significant contribution to make to the solution of social problems apart from the regenerating discipline which it involves. This book was written primarily for people who are willing to accept certain ethical presuppositions. And this chapter is written with a strong conviction that the salvation of our economic system depends heavily on the readiness of business-men who profess allegiance to Christianity to seek genuine Christian vocation in their daily work. I use the word vocation here in the sense of its current use in Christian ethics: the performance of daily work in full awareness of the relevance of Christian faith and teaching to every act and every decision incident to the pursuit of one's regular occupation. This realization can come about only when men are ready to add to all the secular "know-how," in which they now take pride, a discipline of life that subordinates all material rewards to fulfillment of the ethical requirements of a high calling. To say this does not call in question the analysis so painstakingly presented in this book. But it does imply that at the point where the secular analysis discovers the "given" elements of human nature, with all its wants and aversions, a Christian critique is impelled further. When elemental human nature is disclosed and we conclude, "That is the way we were born," Christianity intrudes the admonition, "You must be born again."

When William James was still living, Harold Begbie's *Twice-Born Men* appeared, with a dedication to the great psychologist and philosopher, and a modest description of it by the author as a "footnote" to James's classic, *Varieties of Religious Experience*. In a gracious acknowledgment James said concerning Begbie, "I would prefer to call my book a footnote to his." This was not intended, I think, merely as a gesture of respect. It was a great psychologist's testimony to his belief that nothing in the moral constitution of man is irrevocably "given" and irredeemable. This is authentic Christian doctrine. Man is not condemned to be dominated by his desire either for possessions or for power. But the question arises whether without a greater discipline of natural self-interest than business has thus far developed, men can be permanently entrusted with the power and privilege that under our system come into the hands of individuals. If Christianity has one specific counsel to give to American business, I think this is it. In the current lament over the present state of our national morals, it is no accident that the most grievous offenses complained of result from perverted economic motives for individual behavior.

THE QUESTION OF PROFITS

The major application of this discussion is, of course, to the question of profit and profit motive. I wish to make here what seems to me an all-important distinction between the profit *system* as an economic device for disposition of the social surplus and the profit *motive* (the profit *incentive* would be a more accurate term) as a central driving force in individual economic endeavor.

An outstanding merit of the analysis presented in this book is the clear statement of the meaning of profits. Much of the contemporary discussion of this subject obscures its nature and aggravates the problem. Let us recall the author's statement: "I shall assume that we mean by *profits* the total share of the national income paid to the equity owners of business after allowance for return at the market rate to all land and capital. This definition conforms to the economist's (but not the accountant's) concept of profit."[8] This interpretation is welcome in view of the many loose statements that have been made in which interest and profit, and even gross income, are confused. Under this definition, pure profit is the return over and above the following items: operating costs, interest on borrowed funds, rents, and a return (interest) on equity capital (common stock) computed at the "going rate." In practice, it is difficult to separate pure profit from interest on equity capital. Yet, conceptually, the distinction can be made, as the classical economists have always done, and as must be done if the ethical aspects of profits are to be considered adequately.

Failure to make this distinction is one reason for the interminable arguments about the size of profits. Apart from the bad habit, on both sides, of manipulating figures to make a case, it remains true that the sustained solvency of businesses often requires what appear like unconscionable profits in a prosperous period in order to be able to weather a depression. The swing of the business cycle, bringing recurrent booms and depressions, is a grievous fault of our economic system which its wiser defenders do not try to conceal. Our author is one of these. And a feature of the cycle not sufficiently recognized is the fact that it throws the question of profits in relation to wages and prices completely out of focus and often makes it impossible to effect adjustments that have any appearance of equity. This is one of the businessman's severest hardships.

In a money economy, profit, in the technical sense, is a source of capital formation and an important measure of efficiency. The crucial question does not concern the validity of profit, but its disposition. In Soviet Russia profits are, it is safe to say, as carefully computed as anywhere in the world, and as closely watched, though they do not accrue to private enterprises. And when the

[8] P. 147. This is not meant, of course, to obliterate the distinction between book profit and what is actually disbursed as dividends.

chips are finally down, the verdict of history on the Soviet economic experiment will be on the possibility of operating an industrial economy without using profit as an individual incentive—*and without depending on coercion to get the work done.* In this country there is general agreement that what is called a private-profit system, one which makes individual owners—now a large part of our population—the custodians of the social surplus, is vastly preferable to a system that entrusts it to government, or to government-controlled collectives. This conviction has been immeasurably strengthened by the current spectacle in the Soviet Union.

It is quite possible to maintain this position, while at the same time taking a critical attitude toward the profit *motive.* Criticism does not imply rejection, but rather the conscientious use of intelligence. When we go through a political campaign we take it for granted that the rewards of office in terms of influence and "kudos" constitute a big incentive to candidates for election. Yet we reserve a particularly high place in our esteem for those whom the office has to seek. We accept the system of primary and election campaigns, but we exalt those who can rise above the appeal of personal glory. And we are always apprehensive over the effects of the acquisition of political power. Similarly, we may fully support the profit system as the most salutary way of conserving the social surplus, and at the same time be concerned over the moral effect of seeking profit for its own sake.

In other words, we may agree with the late Professor Taussig of Harvard, who once wrote: "It is much to be wished that other and nobler motives could be substituted, and that the same courage, judgment, and strenuous work could be brought to bear for rewards of a different sort, and with less unwelcome consequences in the inequalities of worldly possessions."[9] This wishful reflection on the part of one of the greatest economists of his time did not for a moment lessen his conviction that the profit motive had to be employed. In such a situation Christian realism may accept imperfection as fact, but is never content to let it go at that.

I anticipate the objection that the foregoing and part of the following discussion is concentrated too much on business profits— that a person who works for a salary, a wage, or a commission, or who receives interest on bonds, is involved in the same ethical con-

[9] F. W. Taussig, *Principles of Economics*, The Macmillan Co., Vol. II, 1920, p. 169.

siderations that I have tried to point out. This is partly true. The reasons for the emphasis on profit are two: first, that this is a book about businessmen in their capacity as the principal managers of our economy, of which profit is generally held to be the nerve center; and second, that we must make a qualitative distinction between income that is determinate with reference to work done, services rendered, or capital invested and income which is theoretically unrelated quantitatively to any of these considerations, but is determined largely by fortuitous factors.

It should be said, however, that the receipt of a large income, from whatever source derived, *always* carries with it a measure of moral hazard. This is as true today as it was when Jesus pointed out the danger inherent in riches. And the more essential high salaries are held to be, as a stimulus to and reward for superior economic functioning, the more urgent is the need for a disciplined stewardship of possessions.

FACING THE MORAL HAZARD

Again, the question is not as to the propriety or wisdom of the system of private profit; it is rather as to the personal ethical consequences of such accumulations. We have noted that it is of the essence of business profit that it is indeterminate. Wages and salaries are assumed to compensate people for the work they do. Capital is assumed to be entitled to return at the "going" rate. (The early Church denied this, but it is generally accepted today.) But profit is over and above these returns; it may be 5 per cent or 500 per cent. It should go without saying that highly speculative ventures put a strain upon personal character. It seems to me that it is possible to justify profit only on a social basis, not as something to which an individual is morally entitled, or as something that is likely to advantage him as a person. Attempts to justify it on the basis of "abstinence from use" are not very convincing in view of the fact that investment is so largely of surplus funds, which there is little temptation, or even occasion, to use for increased consumption. "Risk" is economically important, but it finds moral justification in terms of what the whole economy has at stake. And as for the rewards of enterprise—"entrepreneurial reward"—the average investor is so remote from actual management as to have no chance to contribute more than a proxy vote in the conduct of the business. This means that the more free enterprise relies, as by definition it does, on the profit motive, the more must that motive be disciplined by voluntary restraint both for the sake of the individual and for the sake of society.

The author's thoughtful discussion (Chapter 16) of the ethical problem of distributing profits, and the current interest in profit sharing—which Mr. Bowen does not advocate—are evidences of a departure from traditional thinking about profit. For the very suggestion that labor, for example, "ought to" have a share in profit seems to involve an ethical limitation on the profit *motive*, on the part of owners. Moreover, if what is shared is still *profit*, rather than an increment to earned income, then obviously the wage worker too is involved in the ethical problem of the profit motive.

To write these words is perhaps to incur the risk of criticism for an immature or gratuitous judgment on the economic system. As a matter of fact I am passing no adverse judgment on it at all, but merely pointing out the hazards implicit in it. If the economic system is to be safeguarded against assault from without or from within, more must be done than anyone is now doing to stem the tide of discontent that is sweeping over the world. It is strange that references to discipline of the profit motive should be confused with attacks on the profit system. For the more determined Americans are to preserve their system of enterprise, the more urgent it is, just as a practical matter, to develop a sense of stewardship over wealth that will lessen preoccupation with the pursuit of gain.

Incidentally, the Christian doctrine of stewardship is the most radical of all doctrines concerning property. It maintains that a man owns *nothing*; what he has he holds in stewardship under God. It is the primary purpose of Christian ethical discipline to direct and empower a person to bring his life by voluntary commitment under the dominion of God, as understood in the Christian community. Those areas of life which offer the sharpest challenge to the Christian law of love—where deep-seated human drives and long-persisting patterns of conduct offer stubborn resistance to the Golden Rule—these are the areas where the Christian Church has the clearest duty to scrutinize human motives and to foster a vigorous voluntary discipline.

Does anyone question that the person who acquires and holds

his wealth in conscious stewardship can be more safely entrusted with it than one who is absorbed in the acquisition of wealth for the sake of acquiring it? The protest that arises from businessmen whenever a Christian preacher or a church pronouncement warns against the danger inherent in the profit motive is, it seems to me, as mistaken as one would be who objected to a warning to an athlete not to allow his body to lord it over his mind. The surest way to corrupt the moral base of our economic system is to impede the process of religious and moral education by which the human spirit is disciplined for the difficult task of acquiring, holding, and administering possessions that accrue not from labor, whose rewards are separately computed, but through a fortunate location on the receiving end of our enormously productive profit-making system.

It has been suggested to me during the preparation of this chapter that the meaning of voluntary discipline is easily lost in abstract discussion. I agree. Voluntary restraint often takes the form of willing acceptance of social factors such as the imposition of taxes or compliance with the procedures of collective bargaining.

Our author is, of course, right in pointing out that if one "attacks" the profit motive, he should, to be consistent, "attack also the rent motive, the interest motive, the wage motive, and the consumer motive."[10] What Christianity assails is selfishness, egocentrism; and it assails this everywhere, in personal as well as economic relationships. Christianity holds that man is a sinner, and it condemns sin everywhere. This is not to suggest the abolition of man! Neither does Christianity propose the abolition of the whole economic mechanism whereby we live. What it does insist upon is that no man-made device can be invested with ethical finality, and that all man's concerns and activities must be kept under constant scrutiny, looking toward their continual correction. As already suggested, the reason why the profit motive is especially singled out is that it is ethically a peculiarly subtle hazard; it is the one feature of the distribution of the product of industry that bears no direct relation to service performed and at the same time is not limited to a "going rate." A single investment may yield a phenomenal return—or a staggering loss. Here, as nowhere else in the economic system, does the acquisitive motive need disciplined restraint. By the same token the unwillingness of vast numbers of people to

[10] P. 143.

accept moral responsibility makes government intervention a necessary potential alternative—which also has to be ethically appraised.

THE CHRISTIAN CRITICISM OF LIFE

As I have already intimated, there is an impressive correspondence
between the current theological appraisal of man—as a grievous
sinner—and the traditional capitalist account of man as incurably
dominated by acquisitive motives. But there is an important difference between these conceptions. The theologian recognizes the ego-
centricity of man and seeks constantly to bring it under restraint,
while many of the defenders of the "American way" in business
have praised acquisitiveness as if it were God's great gift to man.
Unfortunately, this type of uncritical defense is given support from
some pulpits and from some avowedly religious publications which
have abandoned the task of a Christian criticism of life and become
merely spokesmen for business enterprise. In the long run I think
they are likely to be a frail support for our economy, which needs
from religion not an "assist" in public relations, but a steadying
moral and spiritual discipline which alone can give stability to an
economic order that inevitably fosters acquisitiveness if moral defenses are not built up against it.

What has just been said may seem to many unclear, and to
some objectionable. Why this should be so I am at a loss to know.
Acquisitiveness I take to mean a propensity for acquiring things
for their own sake. It is a besetting sin of humans—an aspect of
unregenerate human nature. Those whose social responsibility entails ownership on a large scale are in constant danger of this
corruption of motive. Nothing in the New Testament is clearer
than this. It is what the doctrine of stewardship is about.

Much adverse comment has been occasioned in this country by
the widely quoted statement on the economic order promulgated
by the Amsterdam Assembly of the World Council of Churches in
1948. Mr. Bowen reproduces it, and I wish to draw attention to it
in the context of the present discussion.[11] The Assembly said in
part:

> The Church should make clear that there are conflicts between
> Christianity and capitalism. The developments of capitalism vary from

[11] P. 38 f.

country to country and often the exploitation of the workers that was characteristic of early capitalism has been corrected in considerable measure by the influence of trade unions, social legislation and responsible management. But (1) capitalism tends to subordinate what should be the primary task of any economy—the meeting of human needs—to the economic advantages of those who have most power over its institutions. (2) It tends to produce serious inequalities. (3) It has developed a practical form of materialism in western nations in spite of their Christian background, for it has placed the greatest emphasis upon success in making money. (4) It has also kept the people of capitalist countries subject to a kind of fate which has taken the form of such social catastrophes as mass unemployment.

We are not concerned here with the substance of this statement, which, it will be remembered, is preceded by a categorical denunciation of communism. The specific propositions may be debated. The point is that this is precisely the *kind* of critical appraisal which all secular institutions need—when given in humility—from organized religion. That is to say, it raises genuine ethical questions. A pulpit, a religious assembly, or a religious journal which becomes an undiscriminating apologist for any existing secular institution is defaulting in its duty and forfeiting its right to be regarded as a spiritual guide.

On many occasions I have contended that pronouncements on social issues from the pulpit or by church assemblies often leave much to be desired in terms of authentic Christian testimony. In the past there have been too many ill-considered pronouncements, and I do not wonder that businessmen are often irked by them. Our Protestant churches are in theory lay-controlled, and corporate pronouncements should embody only convictions recognized as valid by the main body of the constituency. (This, of course, does not apply to the findings and judgments of special groups of churchmen that do not claim the authority of the *Church*.) Nor has the Church any particular expertness in economic or political matters; it is in no position to prescribe economic procedures. But the Church is concerned with the ethical aspects of all human behavior. Far from resenting ethical criticism from the Church, business should expect, welcome, and even demand it. Wherever the Church has been a vital force, the people have expected from it spiritual and moral discipline. The Church does not exist to make people comfortable, except as satisfaction results from being kept spiritually alert and sensitive and repentant for the sinfulness of which all men are guilty.

RELATIONS WITH ORGANIZED LABOR

An illustration is in order here, and one is at hand that bears on the present discussion in an important way. I refer to the attitude of employers toward labor unions. The long battle over the principle of collective bargaining between management and labor is familiar history. Now, however, it is customary for business spokesmen to affirm this principle, though often with reservations as to the geographical scope of contracts. One must not generalize, of course, but I have been impressed recently that many employers, when not speaking for the press, seem to have "accepted" labor unions only with reluctance, and to be making the best of what they consider a bad situation. No one knows, by the way, how much this attitude is responsible for the annoyingly belligerent tactics of many labor unions.

One must avoid a superficial judgment on this matter. I happen to think that the encouragement long given by churches and civic organizations to labor in its efforts to organize has been wholly justified, but often supported by rather naïve assumptions. In a sense the "underdog" is always right: he is justified—if there is such a concept in the canine universe—in wanting to get out from under. But he has no special right to be on top. It is one of our maturer ethical insights that a power struggle can never be analyzed in purely moral terms. There is no basis for thinking that the mere fact of inferiority with respect to strength creates a presumption of greater rectitude with respect to the matter at issue. Many labor leaders and churchmen have fallen into a way of thinking that tends to identify the labor cause *per se* with the cause of Christianity. This is as wrong in principle as is the corresponding disposition, not lacking in some quarters, to seek Christian sanction for the cause of business management, as such.

But the acceptance of bargaining between freely chosen official representatives of labor and of management, as a matter of principle, may cut across the issues of equity in a particular case. It is a truism in a democratic society that no person or group of persons is either wise enough or good enough to control others, except as specifically delegated to do so. A wise and competent administrator of any going concern will be better content to have those of whom he has oversight make their own mistakes, even when he shares the cost of them, than to prevent mistakes by restraining the exercise of initiative. In the long run the welfare of the enterprise itself is at stake in the preservation of mutual liberty.

The author's analysis points up the significance of "participation" by labor in the conduct of business.[12] Labor's claim to a "share in management" has occasioned some resentment on the part of the managerial group, but I strongly suspect that a commitment on the part of management to a sharing of decisions with those who are directly affected by them would usually result in voluntary acceptance by labor of a practical delimitation of responsibility. There are many things—perhaps too many—that labor is not keen on sharing with management. In any case, to pronounce arbitrarily that "management shall manage" seems to me wholly unrealistic and ethically objectionable. It is unrealistic because every contract signed with a union is an effective limitation of management's right to unilateral action. It is ethically objectionable because a democratic philosophy of management calls for sharing in proportion to proved capacity to take responsibility, and to stand the gaff. This is something that only experience can determine. The question of sharing of managerial decisions is involved and difficult. My point here is that an attempt to make an absolute separation of functions is unrealistic and unhelpful.

One contention that used to be put forward is now largely outmoded, but it doubtless lurks in the background of much discussion of labor-management relations. This is the proposition that the "interests of capital and labor are identical." On that theory management might well decide everything, since it is in position to command the superior intelligence and skill necessary to determine what these identical interests are. But the interests of labor and management are never fully identical. Both have much at stake in the survival of the enterprise, but they are definitely in competition and contending for advantage—labor on its own behalf, and management on behalf of the stockholders, with whom management is closely identified. From an ethical standpoint neither side

[12] P. 41 f., 102.

is in position to press a claim until it has been reconsidered in the light of the claim put forward across the table. Broadly speaking, "unilateral" is an unethical word.

WHAT DOES "FREEDOM" MEAN?

It may seem an intrusion to bring in at this point some reflections on the meaning of freedom, concerning which businessmen evidence so much concern. Yet I think an ethical discussion of this kind would be lacking without it. How seldom we think of the difference between freedom in the ordinary secular use of the term and freedom as the New Testament defines it. In ordinary parlance freedom is synonymous with liberty—absence of restraint. This is, to be sure, a priceless possession in all areas where unhampered choice is essential to human dignity. But such liberty exists only prior to the political organization of society. Democratic liberty is defined in terms of rights bounded by equivalent rights of others, which it is the business of the community as a whole to maximize. Individual liberty, in business enterprise as elsewhere, is a threat to moral freedom unless kept within bounds. Now, what induces men to accept such bounds? Only force, or sublimation of the demand for complete liberty of action. It is of the essence of Christian ethics that liberty in the sense of absence of restraint can be transformed into spiritual freedom only through willing acceptance of the laws of life—through obedience to what one feels to be the will of God. "In His will is our peace." Saint Paul gave the world a classic formula when he declared that the free man is the "bond-servant of Christ." And George Matheson put it into classic verse when he wrote:

> My will is not my own
> Till Thou hast made it Thine.

One of the most suggestive features of the author's analysis is the recurrent reference to the "long view." In my youth I was impressed by the remark of one of my professors in philosophy that morality begins with the substitution of a remote for a proximate goal. This means that imagination is an important part of our ethical equipment. It is indispensable for an understanding of social responsibility, exercised in a context of rapid social change.

But to say this is not merely to counsel prudence—to suggest that business should beat the government to it! It is one thing to look at a situation philosophically, as Carlyle suggested, in his often-quoted comment on Margaret Fuller's avowed readiness to "accept" the Universe: "Gad, she'd better!" There is, no doubt, a certain worldly wisdom in anticipating "controls" and forestalling them, just for the sake of not being "pushed around" by government. But it is quite another thing to see in the inevitable approach of heavy social responsibilities a new and richer satisfaction, a better way of life. This is the higher freedom.

BUSINESS COMPETITION

It is when the realities of competition are faced that the most stubborn ethical problem is encountered; here the prevailing business ethic and the Christian ethic seem to be in flat contradiction. To put it as baldly as possible at the outset, business says competition is the life of trade, while Christianity says the strong must bear the burdens of the weak. Manifestly, there is something wrong with this picture.

The fact is, of course, that the very same passage in the New Testament (Gal. 6:2-5) which commands the sharing of burdens declares that every man must carry his own burden. Each of these utterances is ethically authentic. If, standing together, they are paradoxical, that is because the Christian interpretation of life is paradoxical. In the effort to resolve the paradox we arrive at something like this: Everyone must be ready to help his neighbor with his burden *when it is evident that he cannot carry it himself*; that is to say, when he falls out of the ranks. This is charity in the original, rich sense of that word. It means that brotherhood is prior to economic function. Indeed, it may be in large measure definitive of that function. But since human beings have a tendency to shirk their obligations, there must be devices for insuring that they put forth their best efforts and do not exploit their fellows.

I take it competition is such a device. It is part of the regulatory mechanism whereby society tries to keep every man on his toes. Without it, presumably, prices would tend to be too high, products would tend to deteriorate, and the economic system would in all probability suffer demoralization all along the line. I have said that this would "presumably" happen; as has already been observed, no one knows the strength of the cooperative impulse, but there is a mass of evidence that, taking humanity collectively, all the higher incentives there are must be supplemented by some pressure of necessity to get the world's work decently done.

Yet there is something very unlovely about the competitive struggle. It has compelled many people to work beyond their powers, sapping their health and depressing their spirit. It forces innumerable men out of business and gives ulcers to countless others. It leads to all manner of shady trade practices, especially in advertising. The files of the Federal Trade Commission constitute a veritable arsenal for anyone disposed to attack business practices in America on ethical grounds.

What are we to make of this contradictory situation? How shall a businessman with sensitive conscience determine his social responsibility in the face of all these facts? Theologically speaking, this situation is one phase of the perennial problem of evil. It seems impossible to eradicate evil from the world. The enthusiastic perfectionist is miscast for life on this earth. This brings us back to reliance upon a discipline of life.

THE ETHICS OF ADVERTISING

Let us look particularly at the advertising scene. At incalculable cost to consumers, who ultimately pay the bill—and to the government in the form of tax deductions—a continual barrage of advertising is maintained in promotion of competing products. Mr. Bowen has given us the picture: ballyhoo, chances, prizes, hawking, "high-pressure" methods of persuasion, making prospective customers dissatisfied with the goods they already have regardless of what they can afford, artificial creation of obsolescence by rushing new models and styles to the market. To be sure, these practices are not characteristic of the whole economy. Yet judged by its own avowed standards business advertising presents a rather sorry picture.

The Royal Bank of Canada, in a recent *Monthly Letter,* described an incident recorded in the Alexander Hamilton Institute's textbook, *Salesmanship and Sales Management.* A mild-mannered salesman, in pursuit of a large machinery order, approached a company president in this fashion: "I'm not much of a salesman; you see, I have been on the buying end nearly all my life, and I find myself constantly taking the buyer's point of view." The *Monthly Letter* comments: "It was not until he had walked out with the order in his pocket, after making the little speech which sums up admirably the principles of constructive selling, that those who had heard him realized just how good a salesman he really was." Would anyone contend that this language characterizes advertising practice as we know it today in the United States?

It should go without saying that any adequate appraisal of advertising must assess its social value, actual and potential, as a stimulus to economic activity. Advertising may be broadly educative as well as competitive. We are here chiefly concerned with the latter aspect.

Granted, there has been substantial improvement in advertising standards during recent decades, improvements which Mr. Bowen rightly points out. No reasonable person can be unappreciative of what business has done toward putting its house in order. But what I was asked to do was to write a Christian critique, and the contrast between what is and what Christian businessmen agree ought to be is shockingly great. Moreover, if the matter is looked at from a merely prudential point of view, the public mood of criticism which businessmen so commonly complain of—unfair and misinformed though it may often be—reflects a new situation that business needs to face.

The "doctrine of social responsibility" as it applies to business has so far taken possession of the public mind that the old answers are not good enough, the improvements in standards not rapid enough. From a practical viewpoint there is not only the question whether the public is fair to business, but the question what the public is going to insist on. The American outlook and habit of thought are so favorable to the enterprise economy that if business as a whole should undertake vigorously to implement *its own highest standards,* the public response would, I believe, be overwhelming. This last observation may be more in the nature of *ad hominem* argument than of Christian critique, but I will let it stand.

CONSCIENCE AND CORPORATIONS

A major problem is, of course, the achieving of a transition from individual to corporate responsibility. Private enterprise inevitably maximizes centralization of authority in the interest of efficiency. The increasing importance of technical know-how accentuates this tendency—ownership becomes less and less articulate, and management assumes command. Stockholders gladly turn over their proxies —what else is there to do? Not only so, but the directors, who are theoretically in authority, often have no "live option" other than to follow management's lead. This is not said in disparagement of managerial leadership, but in order to point up the relative impotence of directors and stockholders in a typical situation where crucial decisions must be made.

I remember vividly what a labor-relations expert holding a very important position said to me some years ago about this separation between theoretical and actual responsibility, in relation to labor policy. He had seen a manager, he said, pound the table in a board meeting and declare, "Gentlemen, I am delivering to you on a lot of business essentials. Don't rock the boat about labor policy."

While an individual employer is in position to assume total responsibility for management policy, a corporation executive is the agent of invisible and mostly inaudible owners. The legal representatives of the owners—the directors—are mostly men of undoubted probity, but ill-equipped for forming independent judgments. The executive, burdened with a sense of trusteeship, required to think first of dividends, is in a position where real social responsibility tends to dissolve away. That it does not more often dissolve away is a credit to those managers who are giving to their work the character of a profession. I think there is something less than fully ethical in a situation in which management is called on to wield, in effect, a power of ownership which it does not possess —to exercise a sort of artificial authority. Such action cannot be fully responsible in Mr. Bowen's sense of the term, because real power is separated from the ultimate legal authority for its exercise. Is it not possible to devise instruments for the exercise of a more authentic corporate responsibility?

THE MORAL CLIMATE

It is in this context that I wish to consider Mr. Bowen's significant suggestions concerning codes of practice, the composition of boards of directors, industrial councils, and that enlightened concept of a "social audit."[13] Background for such consideration is furnished by the author's insightful discussion of the changing social-moral climate in America. He points to the creation of a "social environment and a set of public attitudes which constantly threaten to produce more governmental and social controls over business." But since the businessman is "a person sharing with all other members of the society a common social environment and common influences," he has "come to assent in his own way to the newer social ideals and has participated in the struggle to realize them."[14] Obviously, this does not refer to the type of businessman who sees socialism around every corner and thinks that every act of government must, in the nature of the case, be mischievous. Rather, it indicates a core of business integrity, striving to become the conscience of the business community.

The essential point here is that the dynamics of ethical progress are furnished by the interpenetration of the business community and the community as a whole. In a sense the ethical tension to which I have repeatedly referred is a tension between men's concerns as businessmen and their concerns as citizens and participants in community life. The fact that these conflicting concerns are encountered in the consciences of the same persons makes the tension supportable, and orderly progress possible.

CODES OF BUSINESS ETHICS

The making of codes of business practice illustrates admirably this twofold functioning. When business executives meet for the purpose of appraising their own behavior they are turning the searchlight of a general moral consensus upon their own particular segment of the economy. Mr. Bowen shrewdly comments that the businessman is "more inclined to respect and follow ethical rules which are formulated and supported by groups of his own peers

[13] P. 155 f.
[14] P. 75.

than he is to follow rules laid down by moralists, economists, or politicians."[15] Quite so. And let it be noted that there is wisdom as well as pride behind that attitude. The manager can easily inform himself about what outsiders are thinking and saying, but only insiders can make workable rules. Incidentally, the soundest objection to government intervention in business is not that the matter is none of the government's affair, for it is everybody's affair; the essential point is that controls imposed from without are always less authentic in a dynamic sense than those evolved from within.

But some of the code-writing that has been done seems to me singularly inept. In some cases the people who wrote the codes seem to have been so inhibited as to confine their attention to reprehensible practices that no good citizen would be guilty of, code or no code. To be significant and useful a code must seek to raise the level of marginal and tolerated practice and to raise a standard of excellence which is supported as ideal and practicable by a genuine consensus. More important than putting a formal ban on practices already definitely disapproved by the community is a pushing upward of the "central tendency," a strengthening of ethical consensus, that will keep a functional group abreast of the developing public conscience.

RESPONSIBILITIES OF DIRECTORS

I approach with some hesitancy the question of placing representatives of groups other than stockholders on the boards of directors of business corporations.[16] Beardsley Ruml's proposal that boards include members chosen to represent such groups, but elected in the regular manner, is an arresting one. It seems to me distinctly wiser than the idea of having members of that board chosen *by* consumers, employees, "vendors," or that vague entity known as the general public. Any device which suggests that members of the board *not* so designated have responsibility only to the stockholders seems to me reactionary. But a director who, in addition to sharing the common social responsibility of his fellow directors, has a special assignment to study, understand, and faithfully present the interests of one of the groups concerned might

[15] P. 98.
[16] P. 152 f.

make an important contribution in terms of equity to the management of a business. He would not be isolated as the consumers' man, or labor's man, any more than a lawyer appointed by the court to represent a defendant becomes personally indentified with the defendant's cause. Such a plan, adopted as Mr. Ruml has suggested, gradually and experimentally, might prove to be an effective way of keeping management continually aware of nonfinancial equities which are basic considerations in the exercise of social responsibility.

INDUSTRIAL COUNCILS

The "industrial council" proposal is also aimed at achieving for business enterprise responsibility on an inclusive scale. As the author has shown, it is variously elaborated and very complex in any of its forms.[17] I would like to add to what he has said only a word concerning the role of government. Readers with long memories may recall the theory developed in England many years ago under the name of guild socialism. The industrial council plan is reminiscent of it, in that functional economic interests would be integrated with political interests—the former related to production, the latter to consumption and to citizenship. This does not mean that the industrial council plan is "socialism." The fact that the Catholic Church advocates a form of the plan is sufficient evidence against that assumption. But all such proposals look in the direction of a functional organization of society, in which government plays its indispensable role in implementation, while every legitimate and genuine interest is represented in planning and design. This is wholesome, for a pressing economic need at the present time is a rationale that will provide for the exercise of legitimate state power in a way that will make government a servant of society, and not its master.

As in all other matters in which government has a conspicuous part, it is important that its role in relation to industrial councils be closely defined and definitely limited. It is one of the great political paradoxes that the locus of power which is theoretically the least corruptible—that is, the people as a whole—may become the most corrupt of all when society and state become synonymous. That is totalitarianism. But one cause of swollen and diseased state

[17] P. 171 f.

power is the failure of a government to perform efficiently the necessary functions of economic coordination.

The Social Audit

The "social audit" is to my mind a climactic concept in the development of the theme of social responsibility. It is a happy phrase, signifying a wholesome extension of the principle of appraisal and certification. Why should not businesses "subject themselves to periodic examination by independent outside experts, who would evaluate the performance of the business, from the *social* point of view?"[18] This would mark the emergence of business management as a profession. But it will not be easy to perfect the process. I doubt very much whether, in the absence of well-defined standards and established procedures such as business audits involve, "Smith and Brown, Social Auditors," could make a go of it. Much the better approach, I think, is an alternative suggestion by Mr. Bowen: "an independent cooperative organization, created by a group of business corporations each of which would agree to underwrite a share of the expense for a specified number of years, and each of which would agree to subject itself to audit at specified intervals."[19] This seems to me the normal way for a big but novel idea to get itself implemented in the rough-and-tumble of modern competitive business. It has enough evident utility to make it "good business," while its aim is ethical in the broadest sense.

In Conclusion

In sum, I have tried to make clear the necessity for a sustained Christian criticism of business practices because of the constant tension between Christian standards of life and the secular rules of the game which reflect human imperfections and perversities. The most effective corrective influence is self-criticism, not that which comes from without. There is gratifying evidence that more and more Christian businessmen are engaged in this wholesome activity. The current emphasis on Christian vocation gives promise

[18] P. 155.
[19] P. 156.

of a continually growing recognition of the relevance of Christian ethics to the conduct of business.

But the increased tempo of social change in America and throughout the world makes the present study timely and should increase the concern of businessmen for a fuller recognition and acceptance by business of its social responsibilities. Too many of the public-relations experts of American business seem unaware of the necessity, in this age of revolutionary change, to build up the moral defenses of the American economy.

As major objectives I suggest a concerted attempt to eliminate the excessive display and conspicuous waste that result from large incomes; an all-out effort to establish codes of practice for business that will mitigate the harshness of the competitive struggle—in other words, to eliminate unfair practices instead of depending on the government to do it; a resolute undertaking to outlaw the exploitive aspects of advertising and make it in reality a form of service to consumers; encouragement, in all sectors of the economy, of the nonfinancial human incentives which temper acquisitiveness and make for social harmony; and a bold attempt, in cooperation with labor, the community, and government, to tame that most dangerous enemy of our economy—the business cycle of boom and depression.

These evils violate our national moral standards, and constitute serious threats to our national stability. Safeguards against subversive activities, however important and useful, are less urgent than the removal of the faults and weakness that make us vulnerable to criticism. The central imperative of Christian vocation for the American businessman would seem self-evident: to make business and industry in America a consistent expression not merely of our inventiveness, our energy, and our shrewdness, but of a resolute purpose to bring all our economic life increasingly under the discipline of the Christian conscience.

Appendix A

Bibliography of Protestant Views on the Social Responsibilities of Businessmen[1]

The following are some of the sources on which the text of Chapter 5 was based. This list does not include the many reports and statements by denominational bodies and excludes minor fugitive items. It is in no sense intended to be a complete bibliography of the subject. A complete bibliography would run to literally thousands of items.

1. *Official or Semiofficial Statements by Interdenominational and Ecumenical Bodies*

OLDHAM, J. H., *The Oxford Conference* (Official Report), Chicago, Willett, Clark & Co., 1937.

VISSER 'T HOOFT, WILLEM A., AND OLDHAM, J. H., *The Church and Its Function in Society* (Oxford Conference Books), New York, 1937.

ARCHBISHOP OF YORK'S CONFERENCE, *Malvern, 1941: The Life of the Church and the Order of Society*, being the proceedings of the Archbishop of York's Conference, London and New York, Longmans, Green and Co., 1942.

WORLD COUNCIL OF CHURCHES, "The Church and the Disorder of Society," Vol. III of *Man's Disorder and God's Design*, The Amsterdam Assembly Series (5 vols.), New York, Harper & Brothers, 1949.

FEDERAL COUNCIL OF CHURCHES, *Social Ideals of the Churches*, 1932.

——, *The Church and Economic Life: Basic Christian Principles and Assumptions*, September, 1948.

—— *Equality of Sacrifice: A Christian Approach to Mounting Economic Pressures*, 1950.

—— *Report of the National Study Conference on the Church and Economic Life* (Pittsburgh), 1947.

—— *National Study Conference on the Church and Economic Life: General Statement and Topic Reports* (Detroit), New York, 1950.

NATIONAL COUNCIL OF CHURCHES, *North American Lay Conference on the Christian and His Daily Work* (Buffalo), 1952.

[1] See Chapter 5.

2. *Summaries of Pronouncements by Religious Bodies and Leaders or Unofficial Expositions of the Protestant Position*

FEDERAL COUNCIL OF CHURCHES, *Pronouncements on Religion and Economic Life: Excerpts from Statements by Religious Bodies and Leaders,* 1947.

——— "Christianity and the Economic Order," a series of 12 "white papers," published at intervals in the weekly *Information Service,* from February 23, 1946, to December 30, 1950. Many other issues of this valuable *Information Service* contain reports of Protestant statements on economic life.

MACHELL, JOHN VINCENT, JR., "The Christian Churches' Critique of Contemporary Capitalism: An Analysis in the Light of Economic Theory," unpublished doctoral dissertation, Urbana, University of Illinois, 1950.

MAYER, OTTO, and DONOHUE, WIEBE E., *Social Pronouncements by Religious Bodies Affiliated with and Related to the International Council of Religious Education, 1930-1939,* Research Bulletin No. 16, Chicago, International Council of Religious Education, 1939.

TROTT, N. L., and SANDERSON, R. W. *What Church People Think About Social and Economic Issues,* New York, Association Press, 1938.

LANDIS, BENSON Y., *The Social Ideals of the Churches for Agriculture and Rural Life,* New York, Christian Rural Fellowship, 1942.

3. *Writings of Protestant Leaders and Scholars*

BEACH, WALDO, "The Protestant Church and the Middle Class," *Social Action,* March, 1949.

BENNETT, JOHN C., *Social Salvation,* New York, Charles Scribner's Sons, 1935.

——— *Christian Ethics and Social Policy,* New York, Charles Scribner's Sons, 1946.

BRUNNER, H. E., *Christianity and Civilization,* Parts I and II, New York, Charles Scribner's Sons, 1948 and 1949.

DUN, ANGUS, *The Church Has Responsibility in Economic Life,* Federal Council of Churches, 1947.

ELIOT, T. S., *The Idea of a Christian Society,* New York, Harcourt, Brace & Company, 1940.

HALL, CAMERON P., *What Churches Can Do About Economic Life: Programs and Resources,* Federal Council of Churches, 1948.

INGE, W. R., *Christian Ethics and Modern Problems*, London, G. P. Putnam's Sons, 1930.

JOHNSON, F. ERNEST, *Social Work of the Churches*, Federal Council of Churches, New York, 1930.

—— *Economics and the Good Life*, New York, Association Press, 1934.

—— *The Church and Society*, New York, The Abingdon Press, 1935.

—— and HOLT, ARTHUR E., *Christian Ideals in Industry*, New York, The Methodist Book Concern, 1924.

KNIGHT, F. H., and MERRIAM, T. W., *The Economic Order and Religion*, New York, Harper & Brothers, 1945.

LANDIS, BENSON Y., *Manual on the Church and Cooperatives* (Revised), Federal Council of Churches, 1948.

—— (ed.), *Religion and the Good Society*, National Conference of Christians and Jews, 1943.

—— and MYERS, JAMES, *Christianity and Work*, Federal Council of Churches, 1946.

LINDSAY, A. D., *Christianity and Economics*, London, 1934.

MACKAY, JOHN A., *Christianity on the Frontier*, New York, The Macmillan Company, 1950.

MATHEWS, SHAILER, *Jesus on Social Institutions*, New York, The Macmillan Company, 1928.

MAY, HENRY F., *Protestant Churches and Industrial America*, New York, Harper & Brothers, 1949.

NIEBUHR, REINHOLD, *An Interpretation of Christian Ethics*, New York, Harper & Brothers, 1935.

—— *Moral Man and Immoral Society*, New York, Charles Scribner's Sons, 1932.

—— *The Irony of American History*, New York, Charles Scribner's Sons, 1952.

NIEBUHR, H. RICHARD, *The Social Sources of Denominationalism*, New York, Henry Holt & Company, 1929.

—— *Kingdom of God in America*, Chicago, Willett, Clark & Company, 1937.

PATTEN, SIMON N., *The Social Basis of Religion*, New York, The Macmillan Company, 1911.

POPE, LISTON, *Millhands and Preachers*, New Haven, Yale University Press, 1942.

RAUSHENBUSCH, WALTER, *Christianizing the Social Order*, New York, The Macmillan Company, 1914.

SCARLETT, WILLIAM (ed.), *Christianity Takes a Stand*, New York, The New American Library, 1946.

—— (ed.), *The Christian Demand for Social Justice*, New York, The New American Library, 1949.

STAMP, JOSIAH C., *The Christian Ethic as an Economic Factor*, London, The Epworth Press, 1926.

——*Motive and Method in a Christian Order*, London, The Epworth Press, 1936.

TEMPLE, WILLIAM, *The Hope of a New World*, London, Student Christian Movement Press, 1940.

—— *Christianity and the Social Order*, New York, Penguin Books, 1942.

TROELTSCH, ERNST, *The Social Teaching of the Christian Churches*, New York, The Macmillan Company, 1931.

VAN DUSEN, H. P., (ed.), *The Christian Answer*, New York, Charles Scribner's Sons, 1945.

WARD, HARRY F., *Our Economic Morality and the Ethic of Jesus*, New York, The Macmillan Company, 1929.

Appendix B

1. *Partial List of Businessmen Whose Published Statements Pertaining to the Social Responsibilities of Business Have Been Consulted*

Frank W. Abrams, Chairman, Standard Oil Company (New Jersey)

S. C. Allyn, President, National Cash Register Company

Chester I. Barnard, (formerly) President, New Jersey Bell Telephone Company

Adam S. Bennion, Vice-President, Utah Power and Light Company

John D. Biggers, President, Libbey-Owens-Ford Glass Company

S. Bruce Black, President, Liberty Mutual Insurance Company

L. R. Boulware, Vice-President, General Electric Company

E. R. Breech, Vice-President, Ford Motor Company

Lewis H. Brown, (formerly) President, Johns-Manville Corporation

Harry A. Bullis, Chairman, General Mills, Inc.

Curtis E. Calder, Chairman, Electric Bond and Share Company

W. Gibson Carey, Jr., (formerly) President, The Yale and Towne Manufacturing Co.

Erle Cocke, President, Fulton National Bank (Atlanta)

John L. Collyer, President, B. F. Goodrich Company

Carl H. Cotter, President, Merrit-Chapman and Scott Corp.

Frederick C. Crawford, President, Thompson Products, Inc.

Henry S. Dennison, President, Dennison Manufacturing Company

Richard R. Deupree, Chairman, Proctor and Gamble Company

George S. Dively, President, Harris-Seybold Company

J. M. Dodge, President, The Detroit Bank

Benjamin F. Fairless, President, United States Steel Corporation

Edward A. Filene, (formerly) Chairman, William Filene's Sons Company

Lincoln Filene, President, William Filene's Sons Company

Sen. Ralph E. Flanders, (formerly) President, Jones & Lamson Machine Company

Frank M. Folsom, President, Radio Corporation of America

Marion B. Folsom, Treasurer, Eastman Kodak Company

[1] See Chapters 6 and 7.

Henry Ford, (formerly) President, Ford Motor Company

Henry Ford II, President, Ford Motor Company

William C. Foster, (formerly) President, Pressed and Welded Steel Products Co., Inc.

Clarence A. Francis, Chairman, General Foods Corporation

Samuel C. Gale, Vice-President, General Mills, Inc.

R. W. Gallagher, (formerly) Chairman, Standard Oil Company (New Jersey)

Walter Geist, (formerly) President, Allis-Chalmers Manufacturing Company

William T. Gossett, Vice-President and General Counsel, Ford Motor Company

Joseph B. Hall, President, The Kroger Company

Eldridge Haynes, Publisher, Modern Industry

Eugene Holman, President, Standard Oil Company (New Jersey)

Charles R. Hook, Chairman, Armco Steel Corporation

Walter Hoving, President, Hoving Corporation

B. E. Hutchinson, Vice-President, The Chrysler Corporation

Austin S. Igleheart, President, General Foods Corporation

Gen. Robert W. Johnson, Chairman, Johnson & Johnson, Inc.

Eric A. Johnston, (formerly) President, Chamber of Commerce of the United States

T. R. Jones, President, ATF, Inc.

K. T. Keller, Chairman, The Chrysler Corporation

William J. Kelly, President, William Kelly & Co.

Fred Lazarus, Jr., President, Federated Department Stores, Inc.

James F. Lincoln, President, Lincoln Electric Company.

M. Albert Linton, President, Provident Mutual Life Insurance Company

Leverett S. Lyon, Chief Executive Officer, Chicago Association of Commerce

Charles Luckman, (formerly) President, Lever Brothers Company

Franklin J. Lunding, President, Jewel Tea Company; Chairman, Executive Committee, Lever Brothers Company

Thomas B. McCabe, President, Scott Paper Company

John L. McCaffrey, Chairman, International Harvester Company

Arthur W. McCain, (formerly) President, The Chase National Bank

Charles P. McCormick, Chairman, McCormick and Company

Don G. Mitchell, President, Sylvania Electric Products, Inc.

J. D. Mooney, (formerly) Chairman, Willys Overland Motors Company

Ben Moreell, Chairman and President, Jones and Laughlin Steel Corporation

J. C. Penney, Chairman, J. C. Penney Company, Inc.

Leslie N. Perrin, President, General Mills, Inc.

J. Howard Pew, (formerly) President, Sun Oil Company

Frank W. Pierce, Director, Standard Oil Company (New Jersey)

Henry Pope, Jr., President, Bear Brand Hosiery Company

H. W. Prentis, Jr., President, Armstrong Cork Company

Gwilym A. Price, President, Westinghouse Electric Corporation

Edgar M. Queeny, Chairman, Monsanto Chemical Company

Clarence B. Randall, President, Inland Steel Company

Philip D. Reed, Chairman, General Electric Company

Richard H. Rich, President, Rich's, Inc., Atlanta

A. W. Robertson, Chairman, Westinghouse Electric Corporation

Raymond Rubicam, (formerly) Chairman, Young and Rubicam

Beardsley Ruml, Chairman, Macy's, Inc.

Morris Sayre, President, Corn Products Refining Company

Lansing P. Shield, President, Grand Union Company

E. O. Shreve, (formerly) Vice-President, General Electric Company

Alfred P. Sloan, Chairman, General Motors Corporation

H. E. Smith, Chairman, U. S. Rubber Company

Donald B. Snyder, Publisher, The Atlantic Monthly

Thomas G. Spates, Vice-President, General Foods Corporation

Herman W. Steinkraus, Chairman, Bridgeport Brass Company

Jack I. Straus, President, R. H. Macy & Co.

Gerard Swope, (formerly) President, General Electric Company

Henry P. Taylor, President, Taylor and Caldwell, Inc.

W. C. Teagle, (formerly) Chairman, Standard Oil Company (New Jersey)

Enders M. Voorhees, Chairman, Finance Committee, United States Steel Corporation

J. B. Walker, Goldman-Sachs Company

Walter H. Wheeler, Jr., President, Pitney-Bowes, Inc.

Charles E. Wilson, (formerly) President, General Electric Company

Robert E. Wilson, Chairman, Standard Oil Company (Indiana)

Robert E. Wood, Chairman, Sears Roebuck & Co.

James C. Worthy, Director of Personnel, Sears Roebuck & Co.

Owen D. Young, (formerly) Chairman, General Electric Co.

William Zeckendorf, President, Webb and Knapp

2. *Some General Statements by Business Groups on the Social Responsibilities of Business*

The Boston Declaration of Fifty Businessmen "Given this eighteenth day of May, 1950, in Faneuil Hall, Boston, Massachusetts." Reprinted by Massachusetts Investors Trust, Boston, Mass.

NATIONAL ASSOCIATION OF MANUFACTURERS, *Constructive Industrial Practices: The Report of the N.A.M. Committee on Industrial Practices,* New York, 1939.
—— *Industry's Program for a Better America,* New York, 1943.
—— *Present Economic Conditions,* A Report by the Economic Stability Committee, New York, 1946.
ROTARY INTERNATIONAL, *Service Is My Business,* Chicago, 1948.

3. Books, Monographs, and Official Documents (Other Than Those Cited in the Text)

BAKKE, E. WIGHT, *Mutual Survival, The Goals of Unions and Management,* New York, Harper & Brothers, 1946.
BARNARD, CHESTER I., *The Functions of the Executive,* Cambridge, Harvard University Press, 1938.
—— *Organization and Management,* Cambridge, Harvard University Press, 1948.
—— and others, *Basic Elements of a Free Dynamic Society,* New York, The Macmillan Company, 1950.
BATCHELOR, BRONSON, *New Outlook in Business,* New York, Harper & Brothers, 1940.
BAUM, MAURICE, *Readings in Business Ethics,* Dubuque, W. C. Brown Co., 1950.
BLAISDELL, D. C., and GREVERUS, JANE, *Economic Power and Political Pressures,* Washington, Temporary National Economic Committee, Monograph No. 26, 1941.
BURSK, EDWARD C., *Thinking Ahead for Business,* Cambridge, Harvard University Press, 1952.
CENTERS, RICHARD, *The Psychology of Social Classes,* Princeton, Princeton University Press, 1949.
CHASE, STUART, RUTTENBERG, STANLEY H., NOURSE, EDWIN G., and GIVEN, WILLIAM B., JR., *The Social Responsibility of Management,* Edward L. Bernays Foundation Lectures of 1950, New York, New York University, 1950.
COPELAND, MELVIN T., *The Executive at Work,* Cambridge, Harvard University Press, 1951.
Current Price Developments and the Problem of Economic Stabilization, Hearings before the Joint Committee on the Economic Report, 80th Congress, 1st Session, 1947.
Establishment of a Commission on Ethics in Government, Hearings before a Subcommittee of the Senate Committee on Labor and Public Welfare, 82nd Congress, 1st Session, 1951.

HOLDEN, P. E., FISH, L. S., and SMITH, H. L., *Top-Management Organization and Control*, California, Stanford University Press, 1948.

HURFF, GEORGE B., *Social Aspects of Enterprise in the Large Corporation*, Philadelphia, University of Pennsylvania Press, 1950.

KAPLAN, A. D. H., *Small Business: Its Place and Problems*, New York, McGraw-Hill Book Co., 1948.

KNAUTH, OSWALD, *Managerial Enterprise; Its Growth and Methods of Operation*, New York, W. W. Norton & Company, 1948.

LEARNED, E. P., ULRICH, D. N., and BOOZ, D. R., *Executive Action*, Cambridge, Harvard University, Division of Research, 1951.

McCLOSKEY, ROBERT G., *American Conservatism and the Age of Enprise*, Cambridge, Harvard University Press, 1951.

MARDEN, CHARLES F., *Rotary and Its Brothers, An Analysis and Interpretation of the Men's Service Clubs*, Princeton, Princeton University Press, 1935.

MILLER, WILLIAM (ed.), *Men in Business*, Cambridge, Harvard University Press, 1952.

SIMON, HERBERT A., *Administrative Behavior*, New York, The Macmillan Company, 1947.

SOCIAL SCIENCE SURVEY COMMITTEE FROM THE UNIVERSITY OF CHICAGO, *Rotary? A University Group Looks at the Rotary Club of Chicago*, Chicago, University of Chicago Press, 1934.

STALEY, EUGENE (ed.), *Creating an Industrial Civilization*, A Report on the Corning Conference, New York, Harper & Brothers, 1952.

STERN, F. M., *Capitalism in America*, New York, Rinehart & Company, 1951.

SURVEY RESEARCH CENTER, UNIVERSITY OF MICHIGAN, *Big Business from the Viewpoint of the Public*, Ann Arbor, University of Michigan, 1951.

THOMPSON, KENNETH M., *Profit Sharing*, New York, Harper & Brothers, 1949.

WATKINS, RALPH J., *Toward Enlarging the Sphere of Freedom*, Berkeley, University of California, 1951.

4. Articles (Other Than Those Cited in the Text)

BURNHAM, JAMES, "The Suicidal Mania of American Business," *Partisan Review*, January 1950, pp. 47-63.

"Business in Search of a Soul," *Christian Century*, Sept. 29, 1948, pp. 998-99.

CANHAM, ERWIN D., "American Business and the World Crisis," University of Washington, School of Business, 1951.

COLE, A. H., "Evolving Perspective of Businessmen," *Harvard Business Review*, June, 1949, pp. 123-28.

CULLITON, JAMES W., "Business and Religion," *Harvard Business Review*, May, 1949, pp. 265-71.

DAVID, DONALD K., "Business Responsibilities in an Uncertain World," *Harvard Business Review* (supplement), May, 1949.

———— "Danger of Drifting," *Harvard Business Review*, January, 1950, pp. 25-32.

DRUCKER, PETER F., "Look What's Happened to Us," *Saturday Evening Post*, January 19, 1952, pp. 30, 83-86.

GRAS, N. S. B., "Leadership Past and Present," *Harvard Business Review*, July, 1949, pp. 419-37.

"Business Is Still in Trouble," *Fortune*, May, 1949, pp. 67-71, 196-200.

"The Language of Business," *Fortune*, November, 1950, pp. 113-17, 134-40.

"U.S.A., The Permanent Revolution," *Fortune*, February, 1951.

"How Good Is 'Economic Education,'" *Fortune*, July 1951, pp. 84-86, 122-28.

"Molasses and Public Taste," *Fortune*, January, 1952, p. 57.

ORTON, WM. A., "Business and Ethics," *Fortune*, October, 1948, pp. 118-24.

ROPER, ELMO, "The Changing Face of Business," *Saturday Review of Literature*, January, 19, 1952, pp. 12, 40-41.

SLICHTER, SUMNER H., "The Businessman in a Laboristic Economy," *Fortune*, September, 1949, pp. 108-18.

Index of Subjects

Accounting, 194-8
Advertising, 41, 214-6, 219, 252-3, 259
Advisory councils, 185-6
Altruism, see Self-interest, Social responsibility
Attitudes and values, 75, 135-9
Audit, social, 155-6, 255

Bargaining, collective, 41, 248-50. See also Labor
Boards of directors, 152-3, 255, 256-257
Business, defined, 6; improvement in practices, 69-71, 111-2, 236, 238; influence on cultural life, 227; as a profession, 50, 79, 93-9
Business education, 78-80, 94-5
Businessman, defined, 6-7; conception of social responsibilities, 44-68, 234, 235, 236; economic views, 46-8; education for free enterprise, 47; and government, 77-8, 105, 158-9, 223-5, 235; and power, 34-5, 118-21, 246, 247, 248

Capitalism, 7, 25-8, 235, 236, 246-247; popular education for, 54; Christian criticism of, 247. See also Laissez faire
Catholic economic ideas, 164-5, 257
Charitable contributions of business, 125-7
Churches and education for social responsibility, 188-9
Civil liberties and business, 228
Codes of business ethics, 98, 161, 255, 256, 259
Codetermination, Germany, 179-80
Communications, mass, 214-6
Community, 11; and business, 63, 235, 237
Competition, 18, 47-8, 66, 234, 251, 259; ethics of, 226; as factor preventing assumption of social responsibility, 107-12
Conservation of natural resources, 23, 39, 66-7, 227

Consumer choice, 48
Cooperative movement, 35, 43
Corporation, 80-9; economic philosophy, 82; goals, 88; maturity of, 80-3, 104-5; as person, 87-8; planning in, 82; selection of managers, 86-7; separation of ownership and control, 84-5, 254; trusteeship of management, 88-9
Costs of production, 195-8
Costs of social responsibility, 112-5, 115, 149
Costs, social, 213
Council of Economic Advisers, 186
Cycle, business, see Stability

Decisions of businessmen, 3-4
Democracy in business, 121, 138-40, 160-1
Depression, Great, 75. See also Stability
Dignity of man, 40
Discrimination, personal, 40
Distribution of income, see Income distribution
Doctrine of social responsibility, 2-7, 107 24
Dodge vs. Ford Motor Co., 128-30

Earnings of management, 91
Economics, classical, 16. See also Laissez faire
Economists in business, 154
Economy, mixed, See Mixed economy
Education, of businessmen, 56, 157-158; of American public, 53-9; for social responsibility, 188-9, 239. See also Business education
Education, moral, 245
Employment Act of 1946, 187-8
England, joint industrial councils, 178; working parties, 179
Ethic, Christian, 233 f., 236, 237, 238, 239, 240 ff., 244, 245, 246 ff., 259. See also Freedom, Profit, Self-interest
Ethical conduct and self-interest, 14, 235
Executive class, 211-13

Family life, 40, 237, 239
Financial structure of business, 217
Fischer plan, 181-3
Freedom, 10, 19, 27, 250-1; and social responsibility, 5-6, 251

Germany, codetermination in, 179-180
Goals of economic life, 8-13, 250
Gospel of wealth, 118
Government and business, 22-4, 63-64, 77-8, 105, 158-9, 223-5, 238, 239, 242, 256-7
Goyder plan, 180-1

Health and safety of workers, 23, 37-8, 40, 208-11
Honesty in business, 207
Human dignity, 61-3
Human relations in industry, 40, 60-3, 226

Incentives, economic, 46-7, 64, 236 ff., 242, 245, 259. See also Profit
Income distribution, 23, 37, 47, 91, 193-206, 240 ff., 244
Industry Council plan, 164-76, C. I. O. proposal, 169-70; evaluation, 170-6, 257 f.; and Fascism, 167
Integrity, personal, 12, 41
Inventory policies, 219-20

Justice, 9, 30, 61

Labor, benefits, 208-11; organizations, 35, 41, 76, 248 ff.; relations, 23, 60-3, 226, 236, 248 ff. See also Bargaining, collective
Laissez faire, 193-4, 236; in theory, 13-20; social responsibilities and, 20; decline of, 21, 235; efforts to preserve, 24-7; Protestant view of, 32; neo-laissez faire, 224-5
Law and social responsibility, 125-134
Law observance, 207

Management, education of, 157-8; as mediators among interest groups, 49-50; as profession, 50, 93-9; proposed changes, 153-5, 249; as trusteeship, 49
Managers of corporations, earnings

of, 91; motives, 87-93; participation in government, 158-9; prestige, 92; selection of, 86-7
Mass communications, 214-6
Maturity of large corporations, 80-83, 104-5
Mixed economy, 21, 25
Monopoly, 23, 81, 83
Morality, and laissez faire, 17-9; as basis for law, 13
Motives, economic, 35, 237, 240, 242, 245, 259. See also Profit motive, Service motive
Motives of managers, 87-93, 115-7

National Labor Management Conference, 184-5
New Deal, 73-4
N. R. A., 168

Opportunity, personal, 40, 61-3
Order as social goal, 9
Organized groups, 25, 38, 76, 106, 224-5

Participation in business decisions, 41-3, 61-3, 99-102, 164-77, 224-225; Detroit Conference, 183-4; England, 178; Sweden, 179
Paternalism, 42, 63, 120-1
Personal development, 10
Planning in large corporation, 82
Power of businessmen, 34-5, 118-21, 240, 247; decline of, 120
Price policies of business, 220; low prices as goal, 64-5, 198-201; and profits, 198-201, 241
Private property, 33-5
Private vs. social interests, 29
Productivity as a goal, 48, 64-5
Profit motive, 36, 39-40, 46, 89-91, 115-7, 143-50, 240 ff.
Profits, 41, 48, 113, 143-50, 193-206; costs and, 195-8; definition of, 147-8, 194-5, 241; distribution to workers, 201-2; and payments to suppliers, 202-3; and prices, 198-201; principles to determine, 205-6; residual claimants, 203-4
Professional aspects of management, 50, 79, 93-9, 258

Profit sharing, 203-4

Progress, economic, 9, 111

Protestant economic doctrine, 32-41; on blueprints, 32; capitalism, 32-33, 247; cooperative movement, 35; income distribution, 37; organized groups, 38; power, 34-5; private property, 33-5; profit motive, 36, 39-40; vocation, 36-7. *See also* Ethic, Christian

Psychology, 240

Public opinion, as control over business, 52-9, 67-8, 75, 83, 103, 120-1, 137-9, 159-61, 235, 238, 253, 255, 256; and corporation law, 130; toward business, 44-5; as sanction, 13

Public relations, 54-9, 154, 246; legal aspects, 127-8

Publicity of business operations, 159-61

Religion, 235, 236, 245. *See also* Ethic, Christian

Research, 228; in business, 161-3; and social responsibility, 188-9

Residual claimant in income distribution, 203-4

Resources, natural, 39, 66-7, 227

Responsibility, social, *see* Social responsibility

Responsibility to workers, 19

Restraint, 244 ff. *See also* Freedom, Self-interest

Secrecy in business, 159-61

Security of large corporation, 81-2

Security, national, 11

Security, personal, 9, 23, 40, 61-3

Self-interest, 16, 20; long-run, 14, 68, 103; as motive, 35, 234, 236 ff., 240, 244 ff. *See also* Ethic, Christian, and Freedom

Selling activities, 41, 214-6, 219

Separation of ownership and control, 84-5, 104, 254

Service motive, 144-5

Shifting of costs of social responsibility, 115

Social audit, 155-6, 255

Social ideals, evolution of, 71-6

Social legislation, 22-4

Social reforms, 71

Social research, by business, 161-3; and social change, 72

Social responsibility of the businessman, 234, 235, 236 ff., 239, 242, 245, 251, 253 ff.; and altruism, 53; as alternative to social control, 28, 51; businessman's view of, 5; and business attitudes, 135-7; definition, 4-5, 6, 13, 29-30; education for, 188-9; a department of, 155; and future generations, 227; and the law, 125-34; and long-run self-interest, 53, 250; and prejudice, 228; toward greater effectiveness of, 135-50; and technical knowledge, 141-2; research on, 188-9; remote vs. immediate, 122

Social responsibility of non-business groups, 29

Stability, economic, 9, 23, 29, 65-6, 75, 216-23, 241, 247, 259

Standard of living, 8, 46, 110-15

Standards, socially accepted for business conduct, 120-1, 138-40

Steinway case, 126

Stewardship, 36, 39-40, 44, 243 ff.

Suppliers, and profits, 202-3

Swedish enterprise councils, 179

Technical knowledge and social responsibility, 141-2

Trade associations, 98

Trusteeship of corporate management, 48-9, 88

Unemployment, 38, 247

Utopian thinking, 33

Values and attitudes, 24, 233 ff.

Values, social, 213, 234

Vocation, Christian, 33, 36-7, 40, 60-3; defined, 239 f.; and businessmen, 135, 236, 258, 259

Wages, 41, 210; wage policies, 220; and productivity, 47; and profits, 201-2, 241

Welfare capitalism, 21

White-collar class, 211-13

Working conditions, 208-11; as part of standard of living, 110-15

Index of Names

(See also Appendix A and B)

Abbe, Ernst, 181
Abramovitz, Moses, 90
Abrams, Frank W., 50, 58
Agee, James, 122
Alexander Hamilton Institute, 252
American Association of Collegiate Schools of Business, 78, 80
Andrews, F. E., 127

Baker, R. J., 130
Barnard, Chester I., 96
Batchelor, Bronson, 49
Beard, C. A., 11
Begbie, Harold, 240
Bell, Daniel, 170
Berle, A. A., Jr., 84, 131, 133
Bernays, Edward L., 158
Bjornberg, Arne, 217
Bossard, H. S., 80
Boulding, K. E., 24, 25, 143
Bowen, H. R., 15, 93, 145, 199, 233, 235, 236, 238, 246, 252, 253, 254, 255, 258
Bowen, Lois S., xii
Brady, R. A., 118-9
Brandeis, Louis D., 96-7, 131, 161
Brown, D. V., 117
Brown, Lewis, 49
Brown, William Adams, Jr., xii
Buchanan, N. S., 85
Burnham, James, 85
Bursk, E. C., 95

Cabot, Richard C., 207
Calder, John, 178
Calkins, Robert D., 80
Carey, Irene, xii
Carlyle, Thomas, cited, 251
Carr-Saunders, A. H., 95-6
Catholic Church, 257
Chamber of Commerce of the United States, 155, 211
Chamberlain, John, 73
Chamberlain, Neil, 178
Chernick, Jack, 216
Clark, D. T., 95
Clark, J. M., 8, 10, 29, 83, 96, 117, 121, 178, 186, 190, 205

Cleveland, Alfred S., 55, 68
Clinard, M. B., 207
Coit, Stanton, 116
Collins, G. Rowland, 219
Commission on Freedom of the Press, 215
Committee for Economic Development, 55, 58-9, 64
Congregational and Christian Churches, 43
Congress of Industrial Organizations, 169-70
Cooke, Morris L., 178
Cooley, C. H., 11
Copeland, Morris A., 216
Council of Economic Advisers, 175, 182, 187
Courtauld, Samuel, 226
Cronin, J. F., 165, 180
Cruikshank, Nelson, 224

Davenport, Russell W., 178, 190
David, Donald K., 80
Davies, George R., xii
Day, E. E., 80
Dean, Joel, 219
Dempsey, B. W., 165
Dennison, Henry S., 96, 161
De Voto, Bernard, 228
Dewhurst, J. Frederick, 79, 80
Dimock, M. E., 137, 152, 161
Dodd, E. M., Jr., 130, 132
Donham, Wallace B., 98
Douglas, W. O., 152
Drucker, Peter F., 82, 143, 178, 196, 205
Drury, Horace B., 198
Duddy, E. A., 152, 193
Dulles, Allen W., 183
Dunlop, John T., 205

Eliot, Charles W., 28, 161
England, 257
Evangelical Church, 43

Federal Council of Churches, vii, viii, 32, 36, 43, 184
Federal Trade Commission, 252

274

Feiker, F. M., 96
Feldman, Herman, 216
Fischer, John, 161, 181
Flanders, Ralph E., 51, 106, 220
Flexner, Jean A., 179
Flubacher, J. F., 165
Flynn, John T., 161
Fortune Magazine, 44, 59, 71, 88, 93, 95, 182, 186, 196, 213
Fox, P. G., 207
Francis, Clarence, 49
Fuller, Margaret, 251

Galbraith, J. K., 161, 224
Gale, Samuel C., 57
Garrett, Ray, 126
Gass, Oscar, 141
Geiger, Theodore, 127
God, 233, 239, 244, 246, 250
Golden, Clinton S., 178
Gordon, R. A., 85, 90, 95, 102
Goyder, George, 152, 178, 180, 205, 206
Griffin, Clare E., 82, 106

Haas, Francis J., 168
Hadley, Arthur T., 28, 207
Hall, Cameron P., ix, xii
Hamilton, Walton, 131
Hapgood, Norman, 207
Hart, Albert G., 226
Hayek, F. A. von, 27
Heermance, E. L., 161
Heilman, Ralph H., 96
Heller, Walter W., 218, 222
Henderson, Leon, 228
Hickman, C. Addison, xii
Hobson, J. A., 93, 116
Hoffman, Paul G., 56
Holt, Arthur E., 211
Hook, Sidney, 215, 228
Husslein, Joseph C., 165
Hutt, W. H., 83, 161
Hyde, H. K., 137

Ince, Sir Godfrey, 178

Jackson, J. Hugh, 78
James, William, 240
Javits, B. A., 178
Johnson, Alvin S., 20
Johnson, F. Ernest, xii, 211

Johnson, Robert W., 60
Joslyn, C. J., 95

Kapp, K. W., 213
Katona, George, 83, 85, 90, 91
Keynes, J. M., 100, 101, 147, 161, 178
Kheel, T. W., 77
King, W. L. Mackenzie, 178

Lange, Oscar, 147
Lasswell, Harold D., 161
Lee, James M., 207
Lerner, A. P., 147
Lerner, Max, 73
Lewis, J. Spedan, 178
Leys, W. A. R., 194
Lilienthal, D. E., 188
Lippincott, B. E., 147
Lippmann, Walter, 23, 53, 85, 99
Lord, Everett W., 207

MacIver, R. M., 228
Marquand, John P., 213
Marshall, Alfred, 91
Marshall, L. C., 80
Marx, Karl, 235
Mason, A. T., 117, 119
Mason, Edward S., 82, 117
Matheson, George, 250
Mays, Elton, 209
McCormick, Charles P., 178
McLemore, E. W., 213
McPherson, W. H., 180
Mead, Shepherd, 213
Meadows, Paul, 95-6
Means, G. C., 84, 133
Merrell, H. F., 65, 106, 183
Metcalf, H., 177
Methodist Church, 43
Miller, Arthur, 212
Miller, William, 95, 173
Moulton, H. G., 8, 216
Müller, Eberhard, 180
Munier, J. D., 170
Murray, Philip, 169, 178

Nathan, Robert R., 141
National Bureau of Economic Research, 216
National Council of Churches, vii, ix, 31

National Industrial Conference
Board, 127, 152
National Planning Association, 174
Nell-Breuning, Oswald von, 165
New Testament, 236, 250; cited,
251
Niebuhr, Reinhold, 121, 189
Nourse, Edwin G., 27, 94, 198

Odets, Clifford, 213
Opinion Research Corporation, 57
Oxenfeldt, A. R., 90

Page, Edward D., 207
Parsons, Talcott, 95, 117
Paul, Saint, 250; cited, 251
Pepper, Stephen C., 27
Pesch, Heinrich, 165
Pierce, Frank W., 51
Pigou, A. C., 147, 213
Pius XII, 168
Polanyi, Karl, 22
Protestant churches, 247

Radin, Max, 207
Reed, H. B., 207
Riesman, David, 212
Robinson, H. M., 188
Rockefeller Foundation, viii
Roethlisberger, F. J., 209
Roper, Elmo, 57, 75, 127
Royal Bank of Canada, 252
Ruml, Beardsley, 49, 127, 152, 256,
257
Ruttenberg, Harold J., 178
Ryan, John A., 165

Samuelson, P. A., 74
Sanders, Thomas H., 92
Saveth, Edward N., 71
Sayre, Morris, 52
Schnepp, G. J., 169
Schumpeter, J. A., 108
Sears, John H., 49, 85
Seaver, Charles H., ix, xii
Sharp, F. C., 207
Simons, Henry C., 26, 116
Slichter, S. H., 178, 205
Sloan, Alfred P., Jr., 127

Smart, William, 91
Smith, Adam, 16, 18, 235
Smithies, Arthur, 221
Snider, Joseph L., 216
Sorokin, P., 117
Soviet Russia, 241-2
Spengler, J. J., 17
Steinkraus, Herman W., 54
Stocking, G. W., 117
Straus, Jack I., 65
Survey Research Center, 75
Sutherland, E. H., 208

Taeusch, Carl F., 207
Taft, Charles P., vii, xii
Taussig, F. W., 93, 95, 159, 242
Taylor, F. M., 147
Taylor, Frederick W., 93
Taylor, G. R., 188
Tawney, R. H., 95, 152, 161, 180
Tead, Ordway, 177
Thompson, Kenneth M., 203

Upjohn Institute for Community
Research, 217

Vandenberg, Arthur H., 184
Veblen, Thorstein, 84, 115
Vickrey, William, xii
Voorhees, E. M., 83

Ward, A. Dudley, ix, xii
Warren, W. C., 131
Watkins, M. W., 117
Wheeler, W. H., Jr., 203
Whitehead, T. N., 209
Whyte, William H., Jr., 59, 212,
225
Williams, Francis, 212
Wilson, F. A., 95-6
Wootton, Barbara, 27
World Council of Churches, 38,
188, 246-7
Worthy, James C., 61

Young, Owen D., 49

Zeiss Foundation, 181